Theology
and
Revolution
in the Scottish
Reformation

THEOLOGY
AND
REVOLUTION
IN THE SCOTTISH
REFORMATION

Studies in the Thought of John Knox

by
Richard L. Greaves

CHRISTIAN UNIVERSITY PRESS
*A Subsidiary of Christian College Consortium
and Wm. B. Eerdmans Publishing Company
Grand Rapids, Michigan*

Copyright © 1980 by Christian College Consortium
1776 Massachusetts Ave., N.W., Washington, D.C. 20036

Available from Wm. B. Eerdmans Publishing Company
255 Jefferson Ave., S.E., Grand Rapids, Mich. 49503

Library of Congress Cataloging in Publication Data

Greaves, Richard L.
Theology and revolution in the Scottish reformation.

Bibliography: p. 262
1. Knox, John, 1505-1572.   I. Title.
BX9223.G73   230'.52   80-15338
ISBN 0-8028-1847-1

CONTENTS

PREFACE

Although he is indisputably the most prominent figure in the Scottish Reformation, John Knox has attracted little scholarly attention with respect to his thought. Fine biographies have appeared in recent years by W. Stanford Reid and Jasper Ridley, and Gordon Donaldson's work on the Scottish Reformation has added to our knowledge of Knox. It is hoped that the studies presented in this volume will contribute further to a serious understanding of this extraordinarily influential Scot by focusing on critical aspects of his thought. There are no pretensions here to present a systematic study of all his theological and political concepts, but rather, the aim is to gather together in a more convenient format a number of previously published studies, most of which are not readily accessible, and to add to this corpus several fresh studies dealing with the predestinarian controversy, the church, the ministry, and the sacrament of baptism.

The study of Knox's concept of authority first appeared in *Fides et Historia*, 10 (Spring 1978), while that on the Lord's Supper was published in the *Archiv für Reformationsgeschichte*, 66 (1975). *The Journal of Ecclesiastical History*, 24 (January 1973), a publication of Cambridge University Press, included the study of Knox and the covenant tradition, and the essay on Knox's political thought and the democratic tradition appeared in the *Occasional Papers of the American Society for Reformation Research*, 1 (1978). An abbreviated version of the study of Knox's views on resistance was published by the *Journal of Modern History* in September 1976 as a demand article, while the analysis of Knox's views of female sovereigns appeared in a new periodical, *The Red River Valley Historical Journal*, 2 (Spring 1977). *Renaissance and Reformation* published the study of Knox's views on poor relief and educational reform (Spring 1976). The article on ecumenism and nationalism in Knox's thought appeared in the *Records of the Scottish Church History Society*, 19 (1973). Although this essay summarizes some of the arguments developed at length in the preceding studies, it remains substantially in the form in which it was read to the Scottish Church History Society on the historic occasion of the fourth centenary of Knox's death. Those studies have been modestly edited for this volume.

I have incurred many debts to scholars in the course of preparing these essays, a task which has extended over the past decade. For their generous assistance I am especially indebted to Professor Maurice Lee, Jr. of Rutgers University for reading an early version; to Professor Robert Hannen, recently retired from the Central Baptist Theological Seminary, and Professor Walter Moore of Florida State University, for incisive comments on the various essays; to Professor C. W. Dugmore of King's College, University of London, for his suggestions on covenant thought; to Professor Lewis Spitz of Stanford University for his comments on the section on the Lord's Supper; to Professor Robert Linder of Kansas State University and Professor Keith Sprunger of Bethel College for their criticism of the study of authority; and to Professor Egil Grislis of the University of Manitoba, Professor Leo Solt of Indiana University, and Dr. Geoffrey F. Nuttall, recently retired from the University of London, for their comments on the essay on ecumenism and nationalism. I have received valuable assistance and encouragement from other Scottish specialists, notably the dean of Knox studies, Professor W. Stanford Reid of Guelph University; Professor Charles Haws of Old Dominion University, Professor Sidney Burrell of Boston University, Professor Richard Kyle of Tabor College, Professor R. Glen Eaves of Auburn University, and Miss Jane Dawson of Durham University. We have not always agreed on the interpretation of the enigmatic Mr. Knox, but I have never failed to benefit from their knowledge, and to them goes the credit for any merit which these studies possess. I am also thankful to Mr. John Novotney, Mr. John R. Dellenback, and the Christian University Press for making possible the publication of this book, and to Miss Sandra Nowlin of Eerdmans Publishing Company for her editorial expertise. As always, my wife and daughters, Sherry Elizabeth and Stephany Lynn, have provided crucial reassurance and have been more than generous in sharing me with John Knox. This book is dedicated to my brother Gary, whose unflagging support has been a source of encouragement and inspiration through the years. In his own way he reflects the tenacity and talent of John Knox.

R. L. G.

St. Bartholomew's Day, 1979

SECTION
§ ONE §

THEOLOGICAL
FOUNDATIONS

John Knox has been portrayed by his contemporaries and most modern scholars as a prophet. Although he may not have thought of himself as "that maist notable profet and apostle of our nation," as James Melville described him after his arrival in St. Andrews in July 1571,[1] he was a man of assurance with respect to his relationship to God. His opposition to Mary Stewart prompted the English diplomat Thomas Randolph to write to Sir William Cecil in December 1562, that Knox acted "as thoughe he wer eyther of God's privie consell . . . or that he knewe the secretes of her harte so well, that nether she dyd or culde have for ever one good thought of God or of his trewe religion."[2] Knox rejected such accusations, asserting in 1571 that if those making such charges "understoude how fearfull my conscience is, and ever hes bene, to exceid the bowndis of my vocatioune, they wold nocht so boldlie have accused me. I am not ignorant, that the secreitis of God aperteine to him self alone: but thingis revealed in his law aperteinis to us and to our children for ever." Emphasizing that he did not speak as one privy to God's secret wisdom, he insisted that he was called to preach about "the sentence of Godis law" on those who violated it. In his eyes he was a proclaimer of divine intentions with regard to both saints and sinners.[3]

Basic to Knox's sense of prophetic vocation was his firm conviction of biblical authority and his personal sense of divine election. Like the Hebrew prophets, he viewed history in terms

1

of the will of God and issued apocalyptic warnings for the future. In his letter to Cecil of October 6, 1563, he was very much the prophet in warning of "the multitude of calamities coming upon the isle through the inordinate affections of her that is born to be a plague to the realm. . . ."[4] This prophetic consciousness is the basis for his assurance in dealing so firmly with monarchs and those in high positions. As he wrote in 1568, "the justice of God is my assurance, for it cannot spaire to punishe all realmes and nations that is or sall be like to Jerusalem, against whose iniquitie God long cried be his servants the prophets, but found no repentance."[5]

The effect of Knox's assurance had an immense impact on his followers. In a letter to Heinrich Bullinger and Lewis Lavater written in February 1566, John Jewel, Bishop of Salisbury, reported that Knox was "declaiming with his accustomed boldness, before a crowded congregation, against the mad idolatries, and the whole pontifical dominion."[6] Likewise, the testimony of James Melville was probably not unusual: when Knox preached on Daniel at St. Andrews in 1571–72, very likely dealing with questions of judgment and proper Christian behavior, Melville wrote: "In the opening up of his text he was moderate the space of an half hour; but when he entered to application [i.e., began applying the text], he made me so . . . [shudder] and tremble that I could not hold a pen to write."[7]

Knox's forte was prophetic sermons on Old Testament texts, preached with clearly visible assurance. He was comfortable with the Old Testament as with the New, perhaps even more so. When, as a prisoner on a French galley in 1548, he summarized and prefaced the compendium of theology by Henry Balnaves, he omitted many of Balnaves' New Testament references but did not similarly slight the Old Testament.[8] This was an indication of what was to come. His language thereafter must have evoked memories of the Hebrew prophets to his readers and listeners, even when the Old Testament allusions and references were not obvious. In his 1554 tract to England, *An Admonition or Warning*, he played openly with the parallels between Hebrew prophecy and his own sermons. Just as Jeremiah (chapters 7 and 26) had prophesied the destruction of the temple, so Knox proclaimed that the doctrine propounded by the Bishop of Winchester and his colleagues would provoke divine vengeance. Similarly, as Jeremiah (21) prophesied the destruction of Jerusalem, so Knox prophesied the ruination of London if the authority of Mary Tudor was maintained.[9] Four years later, in his *Appellation* to the nobility and estates of Scotland, he echoed Ezekiel (8—9) in reminding his readers that God had punished entire cities for the sins of their rulers (Deut. 7), and he closed his tract by likening himself to the new Ezekiel. If his readers did not attack tyrants, then "as it was commaunded to Ezechiel boldly to proclaime, so must I crie to you, 'that you shall perishe in your iniquitie.' . . ."[10] The prophetic message continued well after the work of reform was underway. In the context of his sermon on Isaiah 26 at St. Giles' on August 19, 1565, he thundered, "O ye troublers of God's people, howsoever it appeareth to you in this your bloudy rage, that God regardeth not your crueltie, nor considereth not what violence ye doe to his pore afflicted, yet shal ye be visited. . . ."[11] He was still thinking in these apocalyptic terms on his deathbed. Against the background of Psalm 9, he talked of the divine justice which would "neuer be satisfiet against the schedderis of innocent bloud, vntill the bloude of the schedder be sched againe, be order of justice, to satisfie the same; or els, that God vtherwayis move his heart vnto vnfained repentance. . . ."[12] The Old Testament tone of such declamations is unmistakable, and they were uttered with a confidence attributable to the faith he had in biblical authority.

Knox's assurance of his responsibility stemmed from his interpretation of Scripture, where he found both a sense of personal election and a divine calling for his prophetic task. Personally convinced of the validity of the biblical record, he made it the basis on which his reforming work was founded. It was a crucial decision, for essentially on that record alone he rested his case against a Catholic church that for centuries had held sway as an authoritative institution in the Western world. It was also by appeal to Scripture that he defended the doctrine of predestination when it was under attack by religious radicals who threatened the work of reform to which he and his colleagues in the Reformed tradition were committed. Because Knox was moved above all by religious conviction, it is essential that the theological basis of that conviction be clearly understood.

3

CHAPTER
‡ ONE ‡

THE NATURE OF AUTHORITY

As the principal theologian of the Scottish Reformation, John Knox played a major role in charting the future course of that movement in his enunciation of the principle of religious authority. Perhaps the most crucial doctrine of the Reformation, the question of authority and the place assigned to Scripture determined the nature of the theology, polity, and worship of the Reformed church. For the reformers authority involved the fundamental question of the basis of belief and practice, that is, the standard by which all things must be judged. In rejecting the broad Catholic doctrine of authority, the Protestants gave varying degrees of consideration to the authority of the church, councils, and even civil government, but ultimately the final standard was Scripture. Few of Knox's beliefs had as much impact on the future of Scottish Protestantism as did his concept of the standard or authority by which faith, morals, and polity were to be determined.

In the main, Knox sought to make Scripture the sole basis for his authority, though at times he allowed some scope to apostolic tradition. Shortly after his first sermon at St. Andrews in 1547, Knox and John Rough were summoned to a meeting with the Subprior of St. Andrews, John Winram, and some friars. One of the articles Knox and Rough were accused of teaching was that "man is bound to observe and keep the religion that from

From the Spring 1978 volume of *Fides et Historia*, journal of the Conference on Faith and History. Copyright by the Conference on Faith and History, and reprinted by permission of the editor.

God is received, without chopping or changing thereof."[1] A debate ensued with Winram and Friar Arbuckle. In the course of it Knox based his argument on Deuteronomy 4, which he cited as "Not that thing which appears good in thy eyes, shalt thou do to the Lord thy God, but what the Lord thy God has commanded thee, that do thou: add nothing to it; diminish nothing from it."[2] Knox maintained the same doctrine when he resumed his preaching in Edwardian England. In the spring of 1550, he was preaching in Berwick that the mass is idolatry and he was refusing to use vestments or to have the people kneel in the communion service. Summoned to appear before the Council of the North at Newcastle in April, his defense rested on the proposition that ecclesiastical ceremonies could not be justified without express biblical sanction "in all poyntis."[3]

It was on the basis of this belief that Knox opposed the rubric on kneeling at communion in the *Second Book of Common Prayer*. He took related action when he was one of six divines who received copies of the *Forty-five Articles* drafted by Thomas Cranmer, Archbishop of Canterbury. Knox objected to the thirty-eighth article, which stated that all the ceremonies prescribed in the *Second Book of Common Prayer* had scriptural sanction. Because kneeling at communion did not, he insisted that the article be modified.[4]

During the Marian exile Knox's insistence on explicit biblical precedent was the major reason for the bitter controversy at Frankfurt, where the opposing faction was led by Richard Cox, former Chancellor of Oxford and future Bishop of Ely. Cox was convinced that the *Second Book of Common Prayer* should continue to be used because it had been authoritatively established in Edward's reign and hallowed by usage. It was Knox's judgment that "by God's book they must seek our warrant for Religion, and without that, we must thrust nothing into any Christian congregation. . . ."[5] Although Knox failed to prevail at Frankfurt, he clung to his position through the exile. In a letter to some Protestant women in Edinburgh he asserted that in matters of religion anything lacking "the express Word of God" was service to devils.[6] In a 1558 expansion of a letter written to the Regent Mary of Lorraine, he firmly stated that in religious matters the Bible alone and not human authority was to be respected. His *Appellation* to the nobility, estates, and commonalty of Scotland of the same year defined vain religion and idolatry as anything done to serve and honor God without the express commandment of his Word.[7] The following year the exiles at Geneva urged suppressing the old disputes over superfluous ceremonies, but the Frankfurt congregation reaffirmed its willingness to follow forms of worship established by ecclesiastical and civil authority so long as the forms were not wicked. The dispute continued in Elizabethan England between the Puritans and the Anglicans.[8]

North of the Tweed the Scottish reformers generally followed Knox. The *Book of Discipline*, which Knox coauthored, echoes his concept of idolatry in defining it as "all honouring of God not contained in his holy Word."[9] Nothing in the *Book of Discipline* was to be binding unless it could be supported by Scripture. The *Scots Confession* likewise affirms the sufficiency of Scripture. The authors, of whom Knox was one, requested that they be notified if anyone found something in the *Confession* contrary to the Bible.[10]

An excellent illustration of the application of this principle occurred with respect to a request to the Kirk of Scotland in 1566 to approve the *Second Helvetic Confession*. The *Confession* had been written by Heinrich Bullinger in 1561, and subsequently was widely received by Reformed churches. Chapter xxiv of the *Confession* dealt, among other things, with the festivals of Christ and the saints. It specifically approved religious celebrations of Jesus' nativity, circumcision, passion, resurrection, and ascension into heaven, and of the sending of the Holy Spirit to his disciples, though feasts for saints were rejected. On September 4, 1566, the Kirk of Scotland replied to Theodore Beza's letter requesting approval of the *Confession*. Using Knox's scriptural principle, the *Confession* was commended with the exception of the provision calling for the remembrance of the festivals associated with Jesus. Such festivals, the Scots (including Knox) wrote, "obtain no place among us; for we dare not religiously celebrate any other feast-day than what the divine oracles have prescribed."[11]

Knox cited his belief in Scripture as the sole authority to justify his conduct in his debates with Mary Stewart. Defending himself from charges that he had unjustly attacked Mary, he said:

> When thai sall teiche me, be Godis plaine written word, that the repruife of vice is a civile and prophane thing, and that it is a thing that perteaneth not to the ministrie, I sall do as Godis word

commandis me: Bot vnot'that tyme . . . I mon hold that sentence and power pronunced and gevin be God to his prophetis, be Jeremie and Ezechiell, to stand for a perpetuall law and rewle to all true ministers. . . . [12]

Knox's most significant departure from reliance on biblical authority had to do with the formulation of the sections on polity in the *Book of Discipline*. The problem of authorship, however, must be taken into account. In April 1560 the Great Council of Scotland appointed Knox and five colleagues — John Spottiswoode, John Douglas, John Willock, John Winram, and John Row — to draft the *Book of Discipline*. It has generally been agreed that the guiding hand was that of Knox, and this is undoubtedly correct to the extent that Knox's views dominated those of the reform movement in Scotland by this date. Spottiswoode's own son regarded Knox as the framer of the *Book of Discipline*. Nevertheless, with respect to the actual authorship, the various parts probably came from different hands and may have been put together somewhat hastily. The sections on polity in the *Book of Discipline* refer principally to expediency, not Scripture, for their rationale, and the preface itself requests that the Great Council not "reject such ordinances as *equity*, *justice*, and God's word do specify."[13]

The *Scots Confession*, presented to the Scottish Parliament in August 1560 by Knox and his fellow ministers, recognizes the practical problems involved in establishing broad policies for the Kirk, openly admitting that "one policy and one order in ceremonies can [not] be appointed for all ages, times, and places. . . ."[14] Changes must be made when ceremonies foster superstition rather than edify the church.

Knox may not have written the sections of the *Book of Discipline* and the *Scots Confession* which allow recourse on specified matters to things other than Scripture, but there is no evidence that he disapproved of them, despite his usual position on needing express scriptural warrant. Calvin was well aware of Knox's strictness, for less than a year after the *Book of Discipline* was drafted, Calvin wrote to Knox (April 1561) pleading that the latter temper his strictness by discretion, and that he tolerate certain ceremonial things even though they had no positive warrant in Scripture.[15] It is an enlightening letter with respect to Knox's usual strict adherence to biblical precepts.

The role of conscience as an authority in religious matters was raised by the Protestant reformers. Like Luther, who had refused to violate his conscience at the Diet of Worms, Knox appealed to his conscience when confronted by Mary Stewart, concluding his conference with her (following his sermon on her marriage) by asserting that "I must sustain (albeit unwillingly) your Majesty's tears rather than I dare hurt my conscience, or betray my Commonwealth through my silence."[16] Later in 1563, Knox, having been called before the Queen and her Council, was reminded as he sermonized that he was not in the pulpit. He retorted with the remark: "I am in the place . . . where I am demanded of conscience to speak the truth; and therefore I speak."[17] Yet Knox did not believe that an appeal to conscience *alone* was enough. He manifested no patience when Mary appealed to her conscience at their first meeting in September 1561. Conscience, he told her, required knowledge, and she had no "right knowledge."[18] Although Mary retorted that she had both heard and read the Scriptures, Knox accused her of having learned false interpretations, which were contrary to the plain teaching recorded in the Bible. Thus conscience in itself meant nothing unless it was based on knowledge obtained from Scripture, the ultimate authority.[19]

Knox was also forced to deal with the vexed enigma of the relationship between scriptural and ecclesiastical authority. The question was raised in the course of a debate with Quintin Kennedy, Abbot of Crossraguel. Preaching in Ayrshire in August 1562, Knox had attacked a sermon preached by Kennedy and was challenged to a disputation. Held the following month, it revolved chiefly around matters pertaining to the mass. In Knox's account of the debate he took issue with Kennedy's reliance on the authority of the church, general councils, and the doctors of the church, while firmly maintaining biblical supremacy. If a body calling itself the church put forth essential doctrines not expressly sanctioned in Scripture, it was clearly not the church of God.[20]

The same issue was raised in the controversy with Ninian Winzet, who ignored Knox's occasional remarks about *essential* doctrines and attacked him for his usual statements about the unacceptability of religious observances lacking express scriptural sanction. Where, Winzet asked, did Scripture explicitly set aside

Sunday for a day of worship? If the Protestants could rely on ecclesiastical authority to fix Sunday as the sabbath, the Catholics could use similar authority to support their practices. Winzet insisted that the traditions of the primitive church were not to be lightly regarded.[21] Knox, interestingly enough, allowed the practices of his own tradition to bear some authority when he wrote: "We build our doctrine upon evident testimonies of the Scriptures, and upon the chief principalles of our religion and faith."[22] The fundamental difference between Knox and his Catholic opponents on the issue of Scripture and church was the belief of Knox and his colleagues that the church derived its authority from Scripture, not Scripture from the church.

Hugh Watt has attempted to demonstrate that Winzet and Knox were closer than they believed on the authority of Scripture and the traditions of the primitive church. Knox, Watt argued, had respect for tradition as long as it was not abused and did not become obligatory, contravene Scripture, or lead to superstition. Knox, according to Watt, never taught that things not expressly commanded in Scripture could not be used in religion.[23] Yet, as already observed, this was precisely what Knox normally taught throughout his career as a reformer. Principal exceptions occur in certain sections of the *Book of Discipline* and the *Scots Confession*, which Knox may not have written, though he did approve them. Exceptions also occur in his acceptance of early conciliar dogma regarding the Trinity and Christology. Watt calls attention to two important passages in the 1556 preface to *The Forme of Prayers and Ministration of the Sacraments &c. Used in the English Churche at Geneva*. One approves singing: "Seingè therfore God's Woorde dothe approve it, antiquitie beareth witenes therof, and [the] best reformed Churches have receyved the same, no man can reprove it. . . ."[24] Knox's position would have been content with biblical support alone. Even more explicit is the statement that religious ceremonies devised by man ought to be abolished "*if* they be once abused," but as long as they are not, their use is obviously permissible.[25] Knox is not traditionally supposed to have been the author of this document, although he approved it as he did the *Book of Discipline* and the *Scots Confession*. The probable author was William Whittingham, a supporter of Knox at Frankfurt and an elder of the English congregation at Geneva. Although Whittingham had departed from the use of the *Second Book of Common Prayer* before Knox arrived in Frankfurt, Whittingham was less rigid than Knox on the subject of religious ceremonies which lacked scriptural sanction. One can therefore conclude that the usually intractable Knox was willing to undertake some compromise with Whittingham in Geneva and subsequently with his fellow authors of the *Book of Discipline* and the *Scots Confession*.

The authority of general councils was much discussed in the sixteenth century, especially as various Continental Protestants called for a general council to settle the religious issues of the Reformation. Knox, in his 1558 *Appellation* addressed to the nobility and estates of Scotland, likewise called for a general council. Having been condemned *in absentia* as a heretic by the Scottish clergy and burned in effigy, he angrily demanded that a general council be convened. Even in the heat of controversy, however, Knox did not lose sight of the supremacy of Scripture over councils. If his enemies thought councils would be advantageous to their cause, he warned them that he would accept no conciliar decision that contradicted "the plaine veritie of Goddes Word" or, significantly, the first four councils of the church, thus allowing some scope for apostolic tradition.[26] In effect this meant that he would accept no conciliar decision unless it supported his beliefs. In his letter to the Scottish regent, Mary of Lorraine, he insisted that the proclamation of one man founded on biblical truth was of more authority than an extrabiblical judgment reached by a council of the entire church.[27] In his debate with Quintin Kennedy, Knox stated that he respected the decisions of the general councils "gathered duelie and in the name of God" to deal with heresy, but only to the extent that their decisions could be verified by Scripture.[28] The coauthored *Scots Confession* made it clear that Knox and his colleagues reserved the right to examine the doctrinal pronouncements of the general councils with a view to rejecting erroneous beliefs. Because councils were composed of men, they are not infallible, and in fact some councils "manifestly erred" in doctrinal matters of the greatest significance.[29] The *Confession* pointed out that general councils had justly been held for two reasons: to confute heresy and publicly confess the true faith, and to promote good policy and order in the church. General councils did not have the power to make new and binding laws for the church, to formulate new articles of belief, to give authority to Scripture, or to develop new and authoritative interpretations of Scripture contrary to what was manifestly revealed therein.[30]

Knox's position with respect to the authority of the church fathers was stated in his controversies with Castellio's disciple (concerning predestination), Quintin Kennedy, and the Jesuit James Tyrie. The essence of Knox's position appears in his treatise on predestination, where he informs Castellio's disciple:

> Wonder it is, that amongest the ancient Doctors ye will seke patrocinie or defense in this mater, seing it is a statute amongest you, that ye will beleve nor admit the wordes nor authoritie of no writer in any mater of controversie, but all things you will have decided by the plaine Scripture. And truly I am not contrary to your mynd in that case, so that you can understand that ye will not admitt the authoritie of man against God's plaine trueth; neither yet that you will beleve man any further, then that he proveth his sentence by God's evident Scriptures. If you had produced any Doctor who had confirmed his interpretation by the plaine Worde of God, of reason I oght to have answered, either by the same, or by some other Doctor of equall authoritie, or els to have improved his interpretation by the plaine Scriptures. But seing that ye produce none, ye leave me at greater libertie; and yet I will shewe you the mynd of one Doctor, comparable to any that ever wrote before him, either in the Latin or in the Greke Churche, I meane of Augustine. . . .[31]

The appeal to Augustine also appears in the controversy with Tyrie. The Jesuit had written from France to his brother in Scotland, a Protestant laird, who in turn had asked Knox to reply to the letter. Knox's response, written in 1566 or 1567 (though not published until 1572), repudiated any patristic doctrines which did not have the express warrant of Scripture.[32] Knox had earlier expressed the same position to Kennedy, citing Augustine and Jerome to substantiate his argument:

> With Augustine I consent, that whatsoever the Doctors propone, and plainly confirme the same by the evident testimonie of the Scriptures, I am hartlie content to receave the same; but els, that it be laughful to me with Jerome to say, whatsoever is affirmed without the authoritie of God's Scriptures, with the same facilitie it may be rejected as it is affirmed.[33]

Knox respected the church fathers and cited them when his thesis seemed to call for added testimony, though not to the extent, for example, of Calvin. The highly controversial *First Blast of the Trumpet*, as one might expect, made use of patristic citations as well as citations from classical literature and Roman and canon law. As in the case of patristic references, however, the classical citations in Knox's writings are relatively meager in comparison with the writings of most other reformers. Knox's favorite church fathers, judging by his citations, were Augustine and Chrysostom, followed by Tertullian and Ambrose, though on the matter of authority he was closer to Tertullian than Augustine. Various others are mentioned, including Athanasius, Basil the Great, and Jerome.[34]

Knox recognized the authority of civil government, but only to the extent that higher powers did not command things contrary to Scripture, the ultimate authority. The advice he gave to his Berwick congregation in 1552 was to obey civil magistrates, however wicked, unless their commands contravened a principal point of religion as determined by the Bible. In the ensuing years he formulated a doctrine of resistance that relied heavily on the concept of a covenant, an idea rooted in Scripture and the ancient Scottish custom of banding. By 1558 he was calling for the overthrow of idolatrous sovereigns, using the biblical precedent of Jehoiada's campaign against Athaliah as a key precedent. So far was civil authority subordinate to biblical authority that tyrannicide itself became not just a viable option but a Christian responsibility; it was actually the sin of rebellion not to slay an idolatrous ruler if the occasion permitted. The ultimate appeal to the people which Knox made in his summer tracts of 1558, firmly grounded on Deuteronomy 13 with its covenant motif, underscored the extent to which Knox was willing to use scriptural authority in his challenge to the civil powers.[35]

One of the sources for Knox's concept of authority, as he expressly says, was the writings of the church fathers. Most of his references to church fathers appear during the Marian exile, but he would certainly have been introduced to the fathers in the course of his theological education. His basic principle of accepting nothing without biblical warrant was a position adopted at one point by Tertullian. Knox's acceptance of the sufficiency of Scripture is an old doctrine, enunciated, for example, by Athanasius: "Divine Scripture is sufficient above all things. . . ."[36] Knox's willingness to relinquish any belief demonstrated to be unscriptural is akin to that of Augustine, though the latter went farther than Knox would have allowed with respect to tradition. Augustine accepts an authoritative extrascriptural oral tradition.[37] This belief, coupled with the similar position of Basil the Great, was the foundation for one of the two general later medieval positions on tradition. The second of these later medieval positions, which adheres to the sole authority of Scripture as the standard of revealed truth, owes more to Irenaeus and Tertullian. The former position was defended in the later medieval era by such men as William of Ockham, Jean Gerson, Pierre d'Ailly, and Gabriel Biel, whereas the latter position was asserted by such men as Thomas Bradwardine, John Wyclif, Wessel Gansfort, and John Hus.[38] One can only speculate about the possible extent of Knox's knowledge of this debate, in which his own position was more in accord with the latter than the former.

Knox likely also learned from George Wishart on the matter of authority. In reply to the Catholics' charge that Wishart rejected belief in purgatory, he retorted that "without express witness and testimony of Scripture I dare affirm nothing."[39] With regard to general councils, he expressed a willingness to agree with them insofar as they agreed with Scripture,[40] which was precisely Knox's position. The *First Helvetic Confession*, which Wishart took to Scotland, was somewhat more liberal. Religious practices lacking scriptural precedent are prohibited *if* they keep believers from the Bible. *Adiaphora* are allowable if they edify and are used judiciously with love. In theory Knox closely followed Wishart, but in practice he found it necessary to adopt the more liberal *Helvetic Confession*.[41]

Henry Balnaves too may have influenced Knox in the development of his concept of authority. Two passages in Balnaves' theological compendium are akin to the views of Wishart. The first passage urges the destruction of all worship and superstition contrary to the Word of God and not commanded therein. The second passage asserts that nothing is as displeasing to God "as to invent any maner of worshipping of him which he hath not commanded."[42] Both passages are contrary to the general tenor of

Luther's views on the subject, yet in his commentary on Galatians (5:19– 20) he wrote: "All the highest religions, the holiness and most fervent devotions of those which . . . worship God without his Word and commandment, are idolatry. . . . He commandeth us to believe his Word, and to be baptised, &c., and not to devise any new worshipping or service of God."[43]

Further impetus to Knox's doctrine of authority may have occurred during the course of his work in Edwardian England. There the views of Zürich were being expounded by the ex-Cistercian monk John Hooper, who was Knox's senior by some nineteen years. He had imbibed Zwinglian views in the early 1540s, and had thereafter gone to Strasbourg and Zürich, where he lived with Bullinger for a while. In 1549 he returned to England and was made Bishop of Gloucester the following year, but refused to wear episcopal vestments for his consecration on the grounds that they lacked biblical sanction. Thomas Cranmer, Nicholas Ridley, Martin Bucer, and Peter Martyr, Regius Professor of Divinity at Oxford, opposed his stand, but Hooper was supported by John à Lasco, superintendent of the churches of foreigners in London. Hooper was forced to yield, though in 1552 he was one of those, like Knox, who fought for more radical changes in the *Prayer Book*. Knox would certainly have been aware of Hooper's conviction that nothing was to be tolerated in religion unless it was prescribed in Scripture,[44] a conviction likely to have reinforced Knox's own strict theory of biblical authority.

The Swiss influence on Knox through Wishart and possibly Hooper also appears in the coauthored *Scots Confession* and *Book of Discipline*. The *First Confession of Basle* (1534) concludes with the statement: "We desire to submit this our confession to the judgment of the divine Biblical Scriptures. And should we be informed from the same Holy Scriptures of a better one, we have thereby expressed our readiness to be willing at any time to obey God and His holy Word. . . ."[45] This is echoed in the prefaces to the *Scots Confession* and the *Book of Discipline*,[46] and can be traced back to the outbreak of the Swiss Reformation in Zürich in 1523.

The Zwinglian concept of biblical authority must be understood in an hermeneutical context. Zwingli tended to read the Bible as a guide for the reform of ecclesiastical abuses. Like Erasmus, who influenced him, he tended to look upon even the New Testament as a book of precedents, with special emphasis on patterns of worship. Zwingli sounds very much like Knox when, in 1523, he wrote: "Everything which is added to the true institutions of Christ is an abuse. But if they are not all done away with at once, then it will be necessary to preach the Word of God firmly and steadfastly against them."[47]

The basic Lutheran concept of the Bible is different, despite the passage in Luther's commentary on Galatians (5:19) paralleling this statement by Zwingli. For Luther the Zwinglian approach to Scripture entailed the danger of a new legalism. Instead of the Bible being fundamentally a book of precedents, it contained the gospel of *sola gratia*.[48] In it were the articles of belief necessary for salvation, hence it was not looked upon primarily as a collection of authoritative precedents for worship and ecclesiastical polity. Things not expressly prohibited by Scripture could therefore be used in the church, though Luther appears to have denied this in his commentary on Galatians.

Calvin adopted what was basically a mediatory approach between Luther and Zwingli. His strong emphasis on Christology made the use of the Bible as a set of authoritative precedents subordinate to his stress on it as a revelation of the gospel of grace to the elect. The Christological centricity is apparent, for example, in his explanation that divinely prescribed ceremonies are intended to manifest Christ. Moreover, while Calvin did lean toward the rigid Zwinglian position in theory, his practice was more lenient.[49]

Knox thus appears to have learned his doctrine of authority from the *First Helvetic Confession*, Wishart, Balnaves, the church fathers, and perhaps John Hooper. Yet some theologians in Edwardian England, such as Thomas Cranmer, were developing a line of thought akin to that taught by Calvin. On several occasions Knox moves in this direction. In his letter to the congregation at Berwick he refers to his administration of the sacraments in accordance with the "preceptes and practice of Christ," but counsels them to kneel at communion in order to continue in fellowship with those who on all important points agree with Christ and his doctrine.[50] This is Calvin's attitude toward Knox in 1561 when he urges moderation in matters of religious ceremony. Indeed

Knox may have already compromised by then with the men who helped him draft the *Book of Discipline*.

Certainly Knox reiterated the substance of his advice to the Berwick congregation when he was questioned later in Scotland about the propriety of separating from a Church of England which lacked expressed scriptural warrant for all of its beliefs and practices. In effect Knox was sufficiently pragmatic to temper his strict position on *adiaphora* in order to avert a damaging schism, but this pragmatism created a visible tension in his attitude toward authority. His recommendations to the Berwick church and the English Separatists were not based on an appeal to the authority of the Church of England but rather to a scriptural principle of Christian unity akin to that which one finds in Paul's epistles to the church at Corinth. Ecclesiastical or civil authority did not make the "unreformed" elements of the Church of England acceptable, but neither was there biblical authority to allow the latter to disrupt the unity of Christian fellowship as long as "the substance of doctrine and salvation in Christ Jesus" was maintained.[51] Yet in fairness to the totality of Knox's writings, he must be viewed as a major source of influence on those who, in the late sixteenth and seventeenth centuries, "barricaded themselves behind the divine walls of a new scholastic legalism based largely on the use of the Bible as a precedent."[52]

To argue that Knox's doctrine of authority was derived in part from Wishart, the *First Helvetic Confession*, and possibly Hooper, and was thus closer to Zwingli than to Calvin, is certainly not to suggest that Knox was a thorough-going Zwinglian. Nor is it a novel argument, for Calvin himself clearly recognized that Knox's doctrine of authority was more rigid than his own. From the time of his conversion to Protestantism Knox would have had to wrestle with the question of authority, for he was flying in the face of much of what Rome claimed to be true. There is no evidence that he read Calvin this early, but it is known that he was personally acquainted with Wishart and almost certainly read the *First Helvetic Confession*. While he never cites the latter, as he does Calvin later in his career, Knox was clearly influenced by it, as has been demonstrated elsewhere with regard to his doctrine of the Lord's Supper.[53] Knox's sympathy with what was essentially a Zwinglian doctrine of authority was hardly enough reason to persuade him to go to Zürich during the Marian exile, especially when he was not sympathetic to the Zwinglian doctrine of the Lord's Supper. Instead he went, as W. Stanford Reid remarks, with "the more radical English reformers . . . to Frankfurt where . . . they found what they believed to be a more thoroughly reformed church."[54] In any case, the fact remains that in his crucial, formative period following his conversion to Protestantism, his views are known to have been subjected to the influence of Wishart and Balnaves, and probably the *First Helvetic Confession*, not (to the best of our knowledge) to Calvin, despite his later associations with Calvin and his reading of Calvin's works.

The crucial role of Scripture for Knox's concept of authority necessitates an examination of his understanding of the Bible. He believed that Scripture proclaimed the Word of God to man. With Luther and Calvin he agreed that the Word could not, however, be equated with Scripture, though the terms are sometimes used synonymously. In his *Faithful Admonition* of 1554 the Word of God is depicted as the means through which heaven and earth were created. The Word of God cannot possibly be equated with the Bible in such a context. In the same tract the Word of God is also referred to as the divine power which brings salvation to believers (following Paul) and a lantern to guide one's path in a world characterized by darkness (following a Psalmist). Although both of these references have been used to refer to Scripture, there is no indication that Knox meant them to be. Instead, the remainder of the relevant passage in the *Faithful Admonition* makes it clear that here Knox did not make an identification of the Word of God with Scripture. The Word for him had the power to comfort those experiencing hardships, to provide wisdom and happiness for those who sought it, to purge sin, to vanquish death, to suppress tyranny, and to overthrow Satan.[55] Knox felt a spiritual power which worked through persons as no mere written record could do.

Knox's conception of the Word of God is thoroughly compatible with his prophetic role. In 1554, early in Mary Tudor's reign, and in 1558, on the eve of its conclusion, Knox wrote two pamphlets in which he discussed, among other things, God's use of his messengers to deliver his Word. The historical context was, for Knox, not unlike that in which the Hebrew prophets had been commanded to speak the divine Word. In the *Faithful Admonition*, written from Dieppe in May or June 1554, the devout in England were reminded that God spoke through messengers, and that the spoken Word drew the elect after it. The power of the Word was such that it took precedence over material gains, personal relationships, and even civil laws.[56]

Knox returned to this thesis in 1558, in *An Answer to a Great Number of Cavillations* (published in 1560). There he indicated how the Word of God, conveyed through God's messengers, either led a man to salvation or burdened and destroyed him. The Word both illumined and blinded, as did the historical ministry of Jesus. For those who had embraced Christianity the Word of God was the divine instrument used to sustain the Christian life. The Word was the foundation of faith, the means of strengthening those weak in piety and comforting the afflicted, and the instrument to bring the careless to repentance and preserve the souls of believers. In short, the Word of God was a vibrant, living power, not simply a written body of religious prescriptions.[57] Knox's conviction that he was a special vehicle for the transmission of this Word increased the vehemency of his message and the fervency of his effort.

Knox believed that the Word of God was normally communicated to persons through Scripture.[58] In the discussions resulting from the presentation of the *Book of Discipline* to the nobility in January 1561, Knox and his colleagues asserted that their faith was "grounded upon God's word, and fully expressed within his holy Scriptures. . . ."[59] It is on this basis that the framers of the *Book of Discipline* invited correction; it is the Word of God as written in Scripture which is to be the ultimate judge.[60] One is reminded of Calvin's *Catechism*: "Where shall we seeke for . . . his word? It is conteined in the holy Scripture."[61] Yet Knox did not have to derive such a general conception from Calvin, for among the many possible sources was the *First Helvetic Confession*, whose opening sentence defines Scripture as the Word of God.[62] Wishart, in fact, seems to have understood the Word of God only in this narrow sense.[63] Balnaves, on the other hand, conceived of the Word in a much broader context, identifying it not only with Scripture, but also with the Son of God. It could be "printed" in the hearts of believers and spoken directly to Noah and his sons "by the mouth of God."[64] Knox's broad understanding of the Word of God may therefore be due to Balnaves.

Knox regarded the Word of God, including its revelation in Scripture, as infallible. Thus in his 1554 letter to the Protestants of London, Newcastle, and Berwick, he wrote of the "verie simplicitie and playne infallible trewthe of Godis Word. . . ."[65] His attack against the doctrine of the mass was based on "the infallibill Word of God" revealed in "the haill bodie of Godis Scriptures. . . ."[66] While it is true that Knox did not oppose the infallibility of Scripture to the infallibility of pope or church, he did oppose the infallibility of Scripture to Catholicism. His use of the Bible and his belief in scriptural infallibility point to a doctrine of verbal inspiration, but he was not unique in this regard. Augustine, for example, believed Scripture was free from error.[67] Calvin may never have developed a doctrine of verbal inerrancy, but he was very close when he described the apostles as "sure and genuine scribes of the Holy Spirit" and their writings as "oracles of God."[68] Moreover, he used the Bible "in such a way as to emphasize its literal inerrancy."[69] Luther accepted the divine origin and inspiration of Scripture, though he was critical of certain elements in it.[70]

Knox and his Scottish colleagues apparently gave little thought to the canon. Like the Church of England, Knox gave no canonical recognition to the Apocrypha, though the teachings contained in it were acceptable for purposes of edification if they were not contrary to the canonical Scriptures. In his treatise on predestination he wrote:

> To your Scriptures, which ye alledge from the book of Wisdom, and frome Esdras (his fourth booke), I will shortly answere, That albeit ye will ten thousand tymes deck and decore them with the title of the Holie Ghost, I wil not the more creditt them. Not that I deny but that in them there be thinges conteined profitable to edification, but if that therefor ye will, upon any place written within them, conclude a doctrine contrarie to the rest of the canonicall Scriptures, I will answer the Ancient writers, that they were not written that upon them should our faith be established.[71]

They are useful for exhortation but not doctrine, which had to be based on canonical Scripture alone. Knox believed the Bible was sealed and confirmed in the apostolic period, and to alter it in any way was extreme impiety.[72]

Knox believed Scripture was basically understandable to all persons who sincerely sought it and in whom the Spirit dwelt. Like the other Protestant reformers, he was convinced that the Bible was intelligible to the ordinary person. He stressed this to Mary Stewart in the course of their first meeting in September 1561. When Knox's citations of scriptural examples as proof of his position prompted Mary to inquire whose interpretation of Scripture was correct, Knox replied that God spoke plainly in the Bible. If any passage appeared obscure, it was to be understood in the light of other scriptural passages, since the Holy Spirit never contradicted himself. With complete assurance Knox informed Mary "that there can remain no doubt [in the interpretation of Scripture] but unto such as obstinately remain ignorant."[73] Like Augustine, Knox was convinced of the essential plainness of biblical language. His doctrine of *perspicuitas* is reflected in article xviii of the *Scots Confession*, an article which may have come from his own pen.[74]

Failure to grasp this principle of Knox (and of the Protestant reformers in general) can lead to a serious misunderstanding of his position. Michael Walzer has argued that Knox based his political views on knowledge which was not available to magistrates and lords by appealing to special truth, that is, to knowledge restrictively identified with religious illumination or dedication.[75] On the single occasion when Knox did appeal to secret revelations from God, he was clearly guilty of basing his political views (in this case the condemnation of Mary Stewart) on knowledge unavailable to civil authorities. Yet normally Knox appealed only to the Word of God revealed in Scripture, where it could potentially be understood by any man. Knowledge of the divine Word was intelligible to magistrate, lord, laird, burgess, or artisan if they diligently sought it with the Spirit's help. If Scripture could not be understood by the ordinary mind (guided by the Spirit) Knox would not have encouraged Bible reading by families or weekly assemblies to read and discuss Scripture. He did not plead special knowledge, but opposed those, including magistrates, who refused to avail themselves of the knowledge of the divine Word contained in Scripture.[76]

The intelligibility of Scripture was aided by Knox's practice of interpreting it, as Calvin tended to do,[77] literally. His view of the Bible is thus quite removed from the medieval conception with regard to general exegesis. The literal interpretation of Hebrew prophecies and divine judgments gave his message a sense of awesome terror. God had commanded death to idolaters in the Old Testament, and Knox, with a terrifying adherence to the literal Word, preached death to idolaters in the sixteenth century.[78] There is no reason to believe that he meant his exhortations to be taken as hyperbole.[79] Catholic idolaters in a Protestant land had to be rooted out and their influence abolished, he insisted, hence his relentless attacks on Mary Stewart long after she was a serious threat to his cause were no charade, and his approval of the murder of Mary's secretary Riccio was very real.[80] Yet Knox was not a persecutor by nature, for in practice he normally shrank from persecution. He could not actually bring himself to engage in the war of extermination against idolaters commanded in Deuteronomy.

Unlike Luther, Knox conceived of the unity of Scripture in such fashion that the rigor of Old Testament precepts was not ordinarily mitigated by the subjugation of the Old Testament to the New. Knox did not stress discontinuity or supersedure in the Scriptures, but like Calvin, freely employed passages from various parts of the Bible, whether Old or New, to confirm one another. Like Augustine, he believed the Old Testament foreshadowed the things revealed in the New, but this did not mean the New superseded the Old.[81] The coauthored *Scots Confession* plainly affirms that "the Holy Ghost uniformly speaks within the body of the Scriptures. . . ."[82] The applicability of the Old Testament to contemporary concerns is particularly evident in Knox's views on political matters, notably gynecocracy. *The First Blast of the Trumpet* makes sustained use of Old Testament material to justify his attack on all female magistrates except those who, like Deborah, were the recipients of a divine dispensation.[83]

The role of the Holy Spirit in understanding Scripture is accepted but not stressed in Knox's theology.[84] Calvin makes the *testimonium internum Spiritus Sancti* of fundamental importance to the believer's recognition of Scripture as God's divinely inspired message. "Those whom the Holy Spirit has inwardly taught truly rest upon Scripture, and . . . Scripture indeed is self-authenti-cated; hence, it is not right to subject it to proof and reasoning. And the certainty it deserves with us, it attains by the testimony of the Spirit."[85] The authors of the *Scots Confession* may reflect something of this concept in their affirmation that the interpre-tation of Scripture "appertaineth to the Spirit of God," who wrote the Bible and speaks uniformly in it.[86] Knox himself gives more emphasis to the recorded words of Scripture than to an inner spiritual testimony of their validity and meaning. Doctrine is built upon the evident testimony of Scripture ("and upon the chief principalles of our religion and faith");[87] its words — the words of the Spirit — are not to be wrested to deviate from the evident meaning.

Knox was in full accord with the *First Helvetic Confession*'s statement that "the interpretacion, or exposicion of this holy wrytte, ought and shuld be sought out of it selfe, so that it shulde be the owne interpretour. . . ."[88] The emphasis is literal and external: it is "the plain Scripture [that] convicteth you."[89] The external emphasis is very obvious in Knox's discussion with Mary Stewart in 1561 about the correct interpretation of the Bible. Knox con-tended that if any Scriptural passage was obscure, its meaning was to be ascertained by other passages, in accord with the mode of the Spirit's operation.[90] Yet when it served his purpose Knox was willing to discuss an experiential affirmation of Scripture. In one of his numerous letters to Mrs. Elizabeth Bowes, the inveterate spiritual hypochondriac, Knox counseled her to examine her heart for testimony that the Word of God is true.[91] Yet he could hardly give such counsel to Mary Stewart, for it would have made it virtually impossible for him to defend his position. Mary was clearly intelligent enough to make the most of an *ad hominem* argument. Certainly the Spirit could have confirmed the correct-ness of *her* understanding of Scripture, which would have forced Knox to advance the dubious counterassertion that she was being misled by evil spirits. As it was, Knox's position left him open to the charge that he prized impeccable dogma above moral integrity.[92]

Knox's advice for reading Scripture was patterned after his preaching. He followed the tradition of the Reformed churches, dating back to Zwingli, of preaching continuously through the Bible, pairing books of the Old and New Testaments.[93] He agreed with the *Catechism's* admonition that "every man is bound to haunt dulie all Sermons made in the Congregation of Christ, where this word is expounded."[94] Those who attended his sermons heard one of the masters of the craft, who could preach well in either French or English. "He had a real gift of eloquence, coarse, crude, and vulgar sometimes beyond belief, but shrewd, racily vernacular, and hypnotically voluble. . . ."[95] He was a popular preacher not only in Edinburgh but also at the Edwardian court earlier in his career. He did not hesitate to apply Scripture to contemporary events and personages, though many of his sermons were probably devoid of personal references.[96] On his deathbed Knox assessed his preaching, asserting that he had taught only sound doctrine:

> beating doun, be the threatnings of Godis judgments, the proud and stubborne, and raising vp and comforting the trubled con- sciences be the promises of Godis mercies; and that howsoeuer that he had bene against only man, it was neuer for hatreat of the persons, but only to beat doun in thame thair vice, and that quhilk was in them that rebelled against God, quhilk he wald nocht leive unpunishit, and for discharge of his conscience afoir God; and that he made not merchandise of the word. . . .[97]

The conviction revealed in these words is expressed many times throughout Knox's writings, and is ultimately grounded in large measure on his concept of biblical authority.

Although Knox's understanding and use of Scripture was in fundamental accord with the views of Calvin, this study has sought to underscore the differences between the two men on the subject of authority. As Calvin himself recognized, Knox adhered to a more rigid insistence on express biblical sanction than did the Geneva reformer. Nevertheless, Knox was pragmatic enough to take a less severe approach, as in the case of his advice to the Berwick church and the English Separatists, when the alternative was a schism among those who agreed on the fundamentals of Christian doctrine. In the later 1550s the two men also differed on the nature of resistance to civil authority when Knox found in the pages of the Bible support for his extension of the right of rebellion against idolatrous monarchs to the commonalty. All of this is not, of course, to deny the closeness of the two men on many issues, but it is to recognize that Knox was less of a Calvinist than he is often made out to be, and that he freely drew on the richness of the Reformed heritage in formulating the theology on which the reformed Kirk of Scotland was founded.

THE PREDESTINARIAN QUESTION

I. THE BACKGROUND OF THE PREDESTINARIAN TREATISE

Knox's longest theological treatise, which was devoted to the doctrine of predestination, reflects and explicitly defends Calvin's doctrine. Various works of Calvin are specifically cited: *The Institutes*, *Concerning the Eternal Predestination of God*, and the commentary on Isaiah, as well as Beza's *Ad Sebastiani Castellionis calumnias, quibus unicum salutis nostrae fundamentum, id est Aeternam Dei Predestinationem, evertere nititur, responsio*. Following the quotation of twenty-nine propositions from the latter work, Knox pointedly wrote: "Thus have you briefly the summe of our doctrin in this mater. . . ."[1] The treatise was no mere tract dashed off by a hurried writer, for Knox devoted considerable effort to it, producing a text that runs to some 170,000 words, exclusive of lengthy quotations from the work he was refuting. Yet there is sufficient evidence to indicate that there was a special reason for the composition of the work, and that it probably does not reflect Knox's normal theological expression.

The atypicality of the treatise has been noted by several writers. The perceptive Lord Percy observed that the principles set forth in the treatise had little effect on Knox's mind, and that when Knox returned to Scotland "he took little of these elaborations home with him."[2] James McEwen similarly was hesitant in assuming that Knox's treatise represented either his inmost convictions or the teaching he expressed to his congregations.[3] There is evidence to support these views.

The ostensible occasion for the work was a request from Protestants in England to refute an anonymous work entitled *The Confutation of the Errors of the Careless by Necessity*. The author was allegedly an Anabaptist, but the name was probably used to describe him because it was one of opprobrium, which he deserved (in the eyes of most Protestants) for rejecting the doctrine of predestination. Heretical doctrines were spreading in England in the late 1550s, causing the English government to act in 1560 with "A Proclamation for the Banishment of Anabaptists that Refuse to Be Reconciled, 22 Septembris."[4] In the flurry of anti-Anabaptist writings, the epithet was loosely applied to those who held unorthodox views.

The writing of Knox's treatise must be viewed in the context of contemporary theological controversy on the Continent. In October 1553 Michael Servetus was burned at the stake for rejecting paedobaptism and the doctrine of the Trinity. Knox subsequently supported this punishment.[5] A protest against Servetus' treatment soon appeared in *De Haereticis*, composed by Sebastian Castellio, Professor of Greek at Basle. Calvin and Castellio had tangled earlier, in 1543, when the latter sought appointment as a preacher in Geneva but was rejected because he repudiated the canonical status of the Song of Songs and denied Calvin's interpretation of the credal affirmation that Christ descended into hell. *De Haereticis* was primarily concerned with religious toleration, but it also took note of predestination. As the book spread, Calvin became worried. He wrote to the Reformed church at Poitiers in February 1555, complaining that the book asserted that "the beliefs of all Christians in the Trinity, predestination, and free justification are non-essentials to be debated at pleasure."[6]

The doctrine of predestination was the main subject at issue in Calvin's debate with Jerome Bôlsec, an ex-Carmelite and a physician who was arrested in 1551 for attacking Calvin's doctrine of predestination. When the magistrates of Geneva asked for the advice of other Swiss churches, the replies from Basle, Zürich, and Berne counseled moderation. Only the unrequested reply from Neuchâtel, where Calvin's friend William Farel was influential, was sufficiently denunciatory to satisfy Calvin. Bôlsec was banished from Geneva for life, though he kept up his attacks on Calvin into the late 1570s.[7]

In Geneva Knox presumably heard much about the alleged errors of Bôlsec and Castellio and the writings about the doctrine of predestination that were sparked by Calvin's concern over the spread of antipredestinarian views. Theodore Beza, who would succeed Calvin as leader of the Genevan church at Calvin's death, published a summation of Calvin's doctrine of predestination in 1555, entitled *Summa totius Christianismi sive descriptio causarum salutis electorum et extii reproborum, ex sacris literis collecta et explicata*. A year later it was translated into English as *A Briefe Declaration of the Chiefe Points of the Christian Religion Set Forth in an Index of Predestination*. The translator was William Whittingham, who had opposed the use of the *Second Prayer Book* at Frankfurt before Knox's arrival, and had been one of Knox's supporters in the ensuing controversy with the party of Richard Cox. Knox and Whittingham were friends — the latter was godfather to Knox's eldest son in May 1557 — and Knox must have known of Whittingham's work. In 1556 another work on predestination appeared at Geneva: Anthony Gilby's *A Briefe Treatise of Election and Reprobation*.[8] Gilby, like Whittingham, had supported Knox at Frankfurt. All three men had collaborated (with John Foxe and Thomas Cole) in drawing up the *Order of Service* that, in 1560, was adopted as the *Book of Common Order* in the Kirk of Scotland. Gilby and Whittingham were also elders of the English church at Geneva, the pastors of which were Knox and Christopher Goodman. Knox would thus have known of the work of both Gilby and Whittingham on predestination.

There is still a basic question to be answered: Why would a busy pastor with a strong interest in the fate of Protestantism in England and Scotland take the time to perform the arduous task of refuting a minor theological work in a wearisome text of some 170,000 words, especially when his previous writings give only limited attention to the doctrine of predestination? Was he suddenly overwhelmed with the importance of this doctrine? If so, the new awareness presumably should have been manifested in his writings after he returned to Scotland, but it is not. His post-Continental writings do not reflect a marked interest in the doctrine of predestination. The reason for the composition of the predestinarian treatise must therefore be found elsewhere.

Probably late in 1557, at Dieppe, Knox wrote his notorious

challenge of female sovereigns, *The First Blast of the Trumpet against the Monstrvovs Regiment of Women*, which was printed at the press of the Genevan printer, John Crespin, the following year. In the resultant furor, Calvin was incensed at the rashness of Knox. In a letter to Sir William Cecil, composed sometime after January 29, 1559, he wrote:

> I had no suspicion of the book, and for a whole year was ignorant of its publication. When I was informed of it by certain parties, I sufficiently shewed my displeasure that such paradoxes should be published; but as the remedy was too late, I thought that the evil which could not now be corrected, should rather be buried in oblivion than made a matter of agitation. . . . If my easiness has occasioned any offence, I think there would have been just reason to fear, lest if the subject had been brought under consideration, by reason of the thoughtless arrogance of one individual, the wretched crowd of exiles would have been driven away not only from this city, but even from almost the whole world. . . .[9]

The First Blast was published in 1558, and Calvin claims he did not know of its existence for a full year after publication — a claim that is suspect. Knox left Geneva for England on January 28, 1559, but was denied passage and had to remain in Dieppe. The predestinarian treatise was written either during the sojourn in Dieppe or prior to the departure from Geneva. If Calvin was, in fact, aware of *The First Blast* sooner than a year after publication, Knox may have written the predestinarian treatise in Geneva to atone for the rashness of his ways. Yet during this period his time was occupied in part with the writing of two works to English Protestants: the *Epistle vnto the Inhabitants of Newcastle & Barwike*, written in November 1558, and *A Brief Exhortation to England for the Spedie Imbrasing of Christs Gospel*, written in January 1559. More likely Knox wrote the predestinarian treatise in the late winter of 1559 at Dieppe,[10] primarily to soothe the ire of Calvin and to preserve Geneva as a base of operations if his return to England or Scotland should not materialize.

Regardless of where the treatise was written, it was undertaken in the aftermath of the publication of *The First Blast*, which had not only displeased Calvin but also "blowne from me all my friends in England."[11] In order to restore himself to some degree of acceptability, if not open favor, Knox therefore determined to enter the lists in support of Calvin's doctrine of predestination against Castellio and his followers.[12] Some motivation may also have been provided by remembrance of the affairs at Frankfurt, when he was forced to leave the city for using intemperate language against the Holy Roman Emperor. Thus the predestinarian treatise was largely a pedantic exercise to maintain Knox's working relationship with Calvin and his disciples, as well as a message to English Protestants to remain loyal to Reformed doctrine.

II. THE CONTENTS OF THE PREDESTINARIAN TREATISE

An Answer to a Great Nomber of Blasphemous Cauillations Written by an Anabaptist, and Aduersarie to Gods Eternal Predestination does not give systematic and logical treatment to the doctrine of predestination. Knox followed the accepted method of quoting the adversary paragraph by paragraph and answering each in turn. The method is no more appealing to the modern reader than it probably was to most Christian readers in the sixteenth century, which may account for the fact that the book apparently did not cross the Channel until after Knox's death.[13] It certainly was not one of Knox's more inspired writings. He was first of all a proclaimer of the prophetic message, but he did also debate, as his interviews with Mary Stewart and this treatise demonstrate. Nevertheless, Knox's debating ability was inferior to his ability in prophetic declamation, perhaps because the two tasks do not mesh well together. Prophets do not argue; they proclaim.

James McEwen has asserted that Knox's *Answer* discusses predestination in a context akin to that of Luther rather than Calvin. Luther treated predestination in the context of the sinner's salvation, whereas Calvin launched his discussion of predestination in the context of creation and then moved to the salvation of the sinner. (In fact, however, Calvin deals with predestination in the context of the benefits of Christ, not the doctrine of creation, in the 1559 *Institutes*.) Knox, McEwen contended, followed Luther's method, beginning with predestination in the context of salvation and then moving to the eternal decrees of God on which predestination is founded.[14] Although there is some truth to this argument with respect to Knox, his discussion of predestination was influenced mostly by the work he was attempting to refute. It is also doubtful, despite *The Bondage of the Will*, if Luther would have been willing to deal with the subject at such length. If Knox had set out to develop his doctrine of predestination systematically, comparisons of this nature would have been more meaningful. As it is, the nature of his work is a strong cautionary element to such a pursuit. Knox's own testimony was that he did not dissent from Calvin on the subject.[15] He could hardly afford to say otherwise, having provoked Calvin's ire for having published *The First Blast*.

Early in his *Answer* Knox presented reasons for the importance of the doctrine of predestination. Without that doctrine, he claimed, faith cannot be truly taught or surely established. Man can never become genuinely humble and possess true knowledge of himself, nor can he praise God as he ought. Faith is properly established only when, through the aid of the Holy Spirit, man recognizes that his election is based on God's eternal and immutable good will. Man must know that he was elected to salvation and hence to his present faith before the creation. God, because of his nature, remains faithful to this election, so that once made it can never be revoked.[16] Theologically, the doctrine of election is thus a psychological comfort as well as a doctrinal necessity, but in practice, as Knox knew, the doctrine of predestination was as apt to cause psychological turmoil as comfort. To Knox personally it apparently brought assurance, but to his close friend, Mrs. Elizabeth Bowes, it brought agony.

Knox's theological training made him conscious of the importance of carefully defined terms, which he provided in his *Answer*. By "prescience" Knox meant that God sees all things as if they were present in the exact way in which they had occurred or would occur. He defined God's "providence" as his sovereign dominion over all things in the universe, including man. "God's PROVIDENCE we call that soverane empire and supreme dominion, which God alwayes kepeth in the governement of all thinges in heaven and earth conteined."[17] Calvin likewise defined "providence" as "His rule of the world which He made; for He is not the creator of a moment, but the perpetual governor. . . . He is said to rule the world in His providence, not only because He watches the order of nature imposed by Himself, but because He has and exercises a particular care of each one of His creatures."[18] Men's actions, according to Knox, are directed by divine providence so that they, with everything else in the universe, move to the divinely determined end. "He so worketh, that willingly they tend and incline to the end to which they are appointed by him."[19] God's omniscience and omnipotent providence provide the foundation for the doctrine of predestination.

By "predestination" Knox meant the eternal and immutable decree by which God determined what to do with each man, not each class of men (believers and unbelievers). To refute the libertine objection that the doctrine of predestination enables men to live as they wish because their eternal fate has been determined, Knox broadened his definition of predestination to include vocation (or calling), justification, and sanctification. Thus before the creation of the universe God decreed to call some men to saving knowledge and to assure them of their adoption as sons of God through their justification by faith and subsequent good works. No man who lives a wicked life can have the assurance of predestination to salvation, for his conscience torments him until he lives a godly life, as has been ordained.[20]

For Knox, predestination has two aspects. Whereas God has decreed the salvation of some men, he has also decreed the eternal damnation of others. The former were elected because of divine love and mercy, not because of their actions, and conversely the reprobate were damned in spite of anything they might do. "To those whom he hath decreed to leave in perdition, is . . . shut up the entrie of life. . . ."[21] Some reprobate were left in their natural blindness; others had grace offered to them (so that not all offers of grace are irresistible) but refused, as God ordained. Others accepted the offer of grace for a limited time, but ultimately returned to their original infidelity, as God ordained, and must perish. Knox's language often gives the impression that he taught only single predestination (God *chose* the elect and *left* the rest to damnation), but in fact he adhered, rather hesitantly, to double predestination. God, he argues, appointed the damnation of the reprobate as a conscious, active decision. "Man's fall . . . was no less determined in the eternall counsell of God then was his creation."[22]

The most difficult question relating to the doctrine of predestination was why a God of infinite love and mercy condemned some men before they were born to an eternity of damnation. Knox dealt with the enigma unflinchingly. It was a matter, as Calvin had asserted, of God manifesting divine glory. For that glory to be properly declared, both just judgments and super-abundant mercy had to be demonstrated, and this could only be done through reprobation and election. Even though God created man after his own image, he determined that all men must fall and be condemned in Adam. "And albeit he created man after his own image, yet did God never determine that mankind should stand in Adam; but his just counsell and purpose was, that all men should fall in Adam. . . ."[23] Knox was a supralapsarian because the decree for the fall followed the decrees of predestination as an instrument to actualize them. "He, in his eternal counsel, appointed the end to every creature, to the which they shall once atteine, by such meanes as he most justly hath appointed."[24] Only by falling would the elect realize the price of their salvation. The Scripture, concluded Knox, offers only one reason for God's unchangeable determination of each person's fate: the will of God. Why that will acts as it does is incomprehensible and secret, but because it is the will of God it must be just and holy, and therefore must be reverenced.[25]

Knox was torn between the inclination to rest on the notion of the incomprehensibility of the divine will in predestination and the desire to find meaning in God's actions. This accounts for his wavering between an explanation that rests on the manifestation of divine glory and no explanation at all, but a simple confession of faith. Knox did not want God to appear as a sadist, hence he urged that God did not will earthly destruction or the sinner's damnation in order to punish for the sake of gaining psychological satisfaction. Punishment is meted out because it reveals divine glory and demonstrates that in his punishment God is always stable and constant. "God will[s] neither the death of the sinner, neither yet the destruction of Jerusalem, nor of the house of Israell; but in respect of his glorie to be shewed in their just punishment, and of his veritie and sentence to be approved, alwaies stable and constant. . . ."[26] To Knox this conception was harmonious with Scripture.

Knox also sought to avoid the accusation that God is capricious and unjust in his dealings with men. Through the agency of the Holy Spirit, God effectually works in the elect to bring them to a life of salvation and godliness. Admittedly, the process of accomplishing this necessitates that they strive against their natural tendencies, for grace as it operates in the elect has to be irresistible. "In the heartes of his Elect, effectually and by the power of his Spirit, doeth he so worke in them the motions that be aggreable to his holie commandments, that they strive and contend against their natural corruption." The reprobate, however, are left "to themselves, and to Sathan their father," to follow their natural iniquitious tendencies.[27] No divine compulsion is needed for the reprobate, but Knox's theory of dominion would not tolerate letting the elect follow their natural inclinations without divine governance of their actions. Knox therefore approached paradox by contending that the elect will to be saved and the reprobate will to be iniquitous as God has determined they must. They cannot effectually will something contrary to the divine will, for to say that human will can prevail against God is blasphemy. Knox was forced to the conclusion that a holy God wills man to sin, and that man must obey. This raises many enigmas, the chief of which is God's will and human responsibility. Knox's position has the effect of making both virtue and vice the result of God's will, thus creating difficult problems for Christian ethics.

Knox was concerned not to dilute divine sovereignty by allowing man to act in a manner not divinely decreed, but simultaneously he determined to make man responsible for his endeavors. If people are nothing but puppets in the hands of God, the prophetic mission loses much of its meaning. Yet Knox's conception of his prophetic role and the doctrine of predestination are compatible. He did not conceive of himself as an evangelist to convert the masses to Christianity, but a prophet through whom the divine will effectually operates to summon the elect to faith and repentance. It was also his perceived task to warn the reprobate that the course of action they willingly followed would lead to their damnation. Knox did not consider himself as one who uttered curses upon people who were not responsible for their actions. Both his dealings with men and his theology make this evident, but not without driving him to paradoxical (some would say contradictory) convictions. All Calvinists are subject to the same enigma.

Knox insisted that Adam had free will and was created righteous, wise, and just, but that he willingly succumbed to the enticements of Satan and challenged the authority of God. There was no compulsion for him to obey Satan, nor was any compulsion used to get Satan to tempt man. Both acted as free agents. Nevertheless, Knox argued, Adam's fall was foreseen and decreed by God for the manifestation of his glory.

> Here we see how the creatures and their willes, without compulsion, do serve God's purpose and counsell. For Sathan was neither sent nor commanded of God to tempt man, but of malice and hatred did most willingly and gredely runne to the same: The will of man being free before, was not by God violently compelled to obey Sathan; but man of free will did consent to Sathan, and conspire against God. And yet was the fall of man not only foresene and foreknowen of God, but also before decreed, for the manifestation of his glorie.[28]

Looking logically at Knox's argument, Adam sinned by free choice and therefore deserved his punishment, yet because his sin was divinely decreed, he was never free *not* to sin. The fairness of the punishment is then open to question.

What was true for Knox of Adam was generally true of all men, though unlike Adam before the fall "all men are ready bent of naturall corruption." Nevertheless "the willes of men are neither violently moved nor enforced by God to committe iniquitie. . . ."[29] Although men are no longer righteous, wise, and just, they still have free will, which is used by God to bring about what he has already decreed will transpire. Man might not intend to do God's bidding, or he might be ignorant of the entire matter, but he does that bidding and in a voluntary manner. At no point does God compel man by either forcing his will to obey or temporarily suspending his will. "Neither was the purpose nor counsell of God any cause of sinne. . . . The cause whereof was the malice of the Devill, and that free consent of man to rebellion, whose will was neither inforced, neither yet by any violence of God's purpose compelled to consent. . . ."[30] Knox admitted that men are "compelled to serve to God's glory" in accord with what has been divinely determined for them, but their wills are never divinely forced to choose iniquitous actions, which they opt for naturally and freely because of their corrupt natures. God cannot be charged with the responsibility for their corrupt natures, for Adam's consent to the rebellious proposition of Satan was ultimately responsible. Man and Satan freely do those things which God has decreed, hence Knox was logically forced to the position that God wills man to sin. Knox was aware of the conclusion to which his premises were leading him, yet he was not willing to sacrifice God's moral purity in order to assert his total sovereignty in a manner that will satisfy logic. Both must be preserved in a manner that will not destroy human responsibility. In consequence, according to Knox, God does not will iniquity *directly*, nor does he simply permit or allow man to sin. "But yet that his eternal and almightie power shall be judged so ydle, that it doeth nothing in such actions but onely suffer, we can not admitte. . . ."[31] God controls the situation even when man sins, so that when a person wills an evil act he is only doing what God has previously willed he must do. An act of will in the sense of choosing freely between good and evil alternatives, both of which are possible courses of action, is an illusion. Natural man can only will what is evil, and when he chooses what is evil he is an agent of the divine will. This is either a paradox that defies logical explanation or a logical absurdity. Knox was driven at this point, perhaps consciously, to find refuge with Tertullian: *Credo quia absurdum est*.[32]

Knox believed that election was wholly a matter of grace. Although God has prescience, his knowledge of the faith man will have or the good works he will do played no role in the process of election. If Knox had taken any other position he would have violated the Protestant doctrine of salvation *sola gratia*. Faith and good works proceed from divine election, which is their cause, just as the basis of election is the goodness and mercy of God, who had the freedom to discriminate in selecting the recipients of saving grace. "Of free grace did God electe; . . . of mere mercie doeth he call; and of his onelie goodnes, without all respect had to our dignitie (as to be any cause first moving him) doeth he perfourme the worke of our salvation. . . ."[33] Because of the necessity of satisfying divine justice, election takes place only through the mediatory work of Christ and thus against the backdrop of the atonement.

Those who have been selected as recipients of saving grace

cannot refuse it when it is offered to them. Knox tried not to violate the freedom of their wills, though he would not admit that a member of the elect has the freedom to refuse permanently the offer of grace. Knox used an analogy to make his point: A man with normal faculties will not obstinantly refuse meat and drink if he is on the verge of starvation. In like manner the elect, feeling their spiritual hunger and thirst and seeking relief from the sinful burden they bear, cannot refuse the grace offered to them as a consequence of Christ's work. Knox also recognized, however, a more general offer of grace that can be refused, for he distinguished between a general vocation that calls all men to God and a "vocation of purpose" which applies to the elect alone. The irresistible offer of grace is associated only with the "vocation of purpose."[34] Knox's God does not treat all persons equally — nor did Knox.[35]

Knox's exposition of the divine act of reprobation is enigmatical. Man's fall and subsequent punishment (eternal damnation for all but the elect) were foreseen and determined by God before the creation of the world. It was God's counsel that man must fall and become subject to damnation in order that the elect might receive salvation through the work of Christ.[36] Knox's argument thus implies that the Father desired to sacrifice his Son in order to manifest his glory. He therefore created the world, had Adam freely sin in accordance with his decree, and then punished Adam and all his posterity. Essentially, God conceived of a remedy (Christ) and then a disease (rebellious man) which it could cure. Implicitly, Knox reversed the order usually perceived by theologians in Scripture.

Knox's concern with human responsibility and God's love and justice made him hesitant about asserting the full sovereignty of God in the act of reprobation. He would not accept the idea that a divine ordinance was the principal cause of reprobation, sin, or damnation. Why God rejected some persons and not others is a mystery, yet Knox was certain that the mysterious cause is a just cause. "Why the others were rejected, we affirme the cause to be most just, but yet secrete and hid from us, reserved in his eternall wisdome. . . ."[37] Likewise Calvin wrote that "in the sin of man God willed nothing but what was worthy of His justice."[38] Knox was convinced that the divine decree of reprobation was not the *cause* of reprobation, though he could not say what the cause was. "We say not that God's ordinance is the cause of Reprobation, but we affirme that the just causes of Reprobation are hid in the eternall counsell of God. . . ."[39] Sin, death, and damnation were caused by man's wilful consent to the rebellious schemes of Satan, but Knox would not make this consent the cause of reprobation, though he would go so far as to say that sin was "ordained" by God, but not "willed" or "created" by God. "Sinne, we confesse, was foresene, yea, and ordeined in the incomprehensible counsell of God, and that for the most just and the most righteous end and purpose. But that it was made or created by God, that are ye not able to prove by our doctrine."[40] Calvin had similarly asserted that "though . . . He ordained it so, I do not allow that He is properly the author of sin."[41] If the reprobate sought the reason for their reprobation, Knox would not admit that their present sins were either the chief or the only cause, but referred them to John 8:47, where Jesus asserted that those who do not hear the words of God "are not of God."[42] The clarity of Knox's argument was not aided by this reference. Interpreting it as Knox did, the Johannine passage simply states that the reprobate do not hear the Word of God because they are not elect. It does not explain the reason for their different status.

Knox was apparently troubled by his inability to find a just cause for reprobation, but he repeatedly made the point that the cause could not be unjust because of God's nature. Although he turned to Paul and the analogy of the potter and the clay, the incomprehensibility remained. Nor was Augustine any help because he too had been similarly baffled. "The cause may be secrete (as Augustine speaketh), but unjust can it not be, because it procedeth from God's will, which is the perfecte rule of all justice and equitie." In apparent frustration Knox accused his English adversary of being blind to the truth if he could not see what Knox could not explain — the manifestation of divine glory in the damnation of the reprobate.[43]

Knox condemned people for the hardness of their hearts, their blindness to the divine Word, and their stubborn malice, yet he also argued that these are the effects of their reprobation, just as faith and obedience are the results of election. Man is punished for what God decreed. It is understandable that Knox found this doctrine hard to defend. Blaming his opponent's blindness for failing to see what he himself could not perceive with any clarity, he could find only temporary comfort (if any at all) in observing that the reprobate refuse to accept the divine Word, for hearing the Word hardens and blinds them because of their incurable corruption. Indeed, the reprobate were blinded from the very beginning. Like men born physically blind, they never had a genuine opportunity to see. When Jesus was asked about physical blindness, he replied that a man was blind from birth in order to manifest God's glory (John 9). This passage was Knox's only port in the storm of doctrinal difficulties surrounding the problem. With rhetorical intent he asked: "If God's glorie be declared, and made manifest, even by the miseries which some creatures sustein, dare you therfor accuse God of creweltie?"[44] The implied negative reply, judging from Knox's concern about the problem, was more assuring to him theologically than psychologically.

III. PREDESTINATION IN KNOX'S OTHER WRITINGS

Knox first makes serious mention of the doctrine of election in his 1552 epistle to the congregation at Berwick. He frequently uses the word "elect," and in his summation of the gospel he cites Ephesians 1:4 about the adoption of believers before creation. He goes on to assert that there was no "other cause moving God to elect and choose us than his awin infinitt goodnesse and meare mercye."[45] This is essentially the doctrine of election taught by Hooper, who learned it from Bullinger while in Zürich. There is, however, no evidence to indicate the precise source of Knox's doctrine.[46]

Numerous references to the elect occur in Knox's 1554 exposition of Psalm 6, but there is nothing remotely like a systematic statement of a doctrine of election. It is interesting to note that this exposition also contains several specific references to the reprobate, indicating that Knox was apparently moving toward a doctrine of double predestination by May 1554, four months after meeting Calvin.[47] At this point he viewed Calvin as "that singular instrument of God," and was reading and citing his commentary on Jeremiah,[48] but he had at least a vague doctrine of reprobation before meeting Calvin. In a letter to Mrs. Bowes written on February 26, 1553, he explained the impossibility of the reprobate ever loving God.[49] Another letter of the same year noted that "the nature of the dampnit and reprobat is ever to flie fra Chryst."[50] Yet in his 1554 *Admonition or Warning* Knox failed to make advantageous use of the doctrine of predestination to buttress some of his arguments, which is also true of his epistle to England of May 10, 1554. His epistle of May 31, 1554, did no more than make several passing comments about the elect, but by July he was referring frequently to the elect and making scattered remarks about the reprobate in *A Faythfull Admonition*.[51] Yet there was still no concise or systematic statement of the doctrine of predestination.

The 1556 works of Knox begin to show increased interest in the doctrine. In the *Letter of Wholesome Counsel* Knox explained that the elect are called from their ignorance and given a feeling of God's mercy, which prompts them to exercise their faith by reading Scripture.[52] Nothing of consequence was said about a doctrine of reprobation. *The Ansueris to Sum Questionis concerning Baptisme* made several references to election. The league between God and the elect is so firm that the promises made to the elect cannot be frustrated, and Ephesians 1:4 was cited once again. Moreover, wrote Knox, God's "giftis and vocatioun ar suche, as of the whilk he can not repent him towardis his elect."[53] *The Forme of Prayers* (which includes Calvin's *Catechism*) mentions the elect and the reprobate in connection with baptism and the last judgment, and refers to the church as "onely knowen to God, who of the loste sonnes of Adam, hath ordeyned some, as vessels of wrathe, to damnation, and hathe chosen others, as vessels of his mercie, to be saved. . . ."[54] Yet these statements are made in the *Forme's* Confession of Faith, which was probably written by Whittingham, though Knox approved it.

By 1556 interest in predestination was very strong in Geneva. Whittingham had translated Beza's compendium and Gilby wrote his book on predestination. The interest of Knox's friends was manifested in his writings of 1556 and especially 1557. In December 1557 he wrote to the Scottish Protestants, attacking those who claimed that there was no certain election and reprobation because every man has free will. To deny predestination, Knox argued, was to deny the "hale Godheid" with its three essential "properties, to wit, wisdome, frie regement, and power. . . ."[55] Thus about a year before Knox wrote his predestinarian treatise he had arrived at a doctrine of double predestination. The development occurred primarily because of Genevan influence, including contact with the views of Beza, Whittingham, and Gilby. Yet Knox devoted very little time in these writings to predestination; one must look for it. At the same time enough is said about predestination in these earlier writings to indicate that the doctrinal views set forth in the predestinarian treatise were theologically acceptable to Knox. What was altogether unusual and out of keeping with the tenor of his writings before and after this treatise was the emphasis given to predestination.

The treatment accorded predestination by the editors of the Geneva Bible is worthy of passing comment here because of Knox's possible involvement in that endeavor. According to Strype the translators included Knox, Miles Coverdale, Whittingham, and Gilby. A contemporary life of Whittingham, however, indicates that Knox's friend was aided only by Coverdale, Gilby, Goodman, Thomas Sampson, and William Cole. According to a letter from Coverdale to Cole (February 22, 1560), William Kethe, John Baron, and William Williams were also involved. Apparently the translators varied from time to time, thus making it possible for Knox to have contributed. Whether or not he did, as a pastor of these men he would undoubtedly have discussed their work with them, and they would have been thoroughly familiar with his views through his sermons and conversations.[56]

The men responsibile for the Geneva Bible added numerous marginal notes, some of which were frankly anti-Catholic, and others Calvinist, but in the main the scholars avoided the temptation to make their version an open work of pamphleteering. Furthermore they were more concerned with the actual translation being factual, grammatical, and exact than with propagating their own theological views.[57] They did, however, include the doctrine of predestination in the marginal notes, as in this comment on Romans 9:15:

> As the onelie wil & purpose of God is the chief cause of election & reprobacion: so his fre mercie in Christ is an inferior cause of saluacion, & the hardening of the heart, an inferior cause of damnacion.

In Romans 11:2 the translation begins, "God hathe not cast away his people which he knewe," and the margin adds, "and elected before all beginning." The marginal note to Romans 11:29 reads:

> To whome God giueth his Spirit of adoption, and whome he calleth effectually, he can not perish: for Gods eternall counsel neuer changeth.

It is clear, therefore, that the leading figures of the English church at Geneva, including Knox, were adherents of Calvin's doctrine of predestination in the years 1556–59. Knox's predestinarian treatise, incidentally, was the first work to quote the Geneva Bible.[58]

The year following the authorization of the publication of Knox's treatise by the Little Council of Geneva, Knox and his colleagues drafted the *Scots Confession*. No article was devoted to the full doctrine of predestination. The chapter entitled "Election" opens with an affirmation of the election of believers in Christ before the creation, closely reflecting the words of Ephesians 1:4, but the remainder of the chapter deals with the redeeming work of Christ. There is no mention here of reprobation. The chapter on original sin affirms the utter defacement of the *imago Dei* in man and the consequent need for redemption. The Holy Spirit undertakes the task of regeneration, "working in the hearts of the elect of God an assured faith in the promise of God. . . ." The chapter on the church explains it as a company of men chosen by God, including the elect of the past and the future, and the ensuing chapter, which discusses the immortality of the soul, mentions not only the elect of past and present but also "the reprobate and unfaithful departed. . . ." In the chapter on the nature of the sacraments, notice is taken of their role in assuring the elect of union with Christ. The concluding chapter of the *Confession*, dealing with gifts given to the church, observes that reprobate as well as elect may belong to the visible church.[59]

The *Confession* thus includes periodic references to election, though making only token mention of reprobation. Generally the references to election are closely scriptural and experiential, not speculative or dogmatic.[60] The close relationship of election to the work of Christ has elicited much comment. It has been asserted that the "close identity of the doctrine of Christ and salvation with election, or decree, is found in all the early Reformed confessions . . . ,"[61] but one does not find this in Zwingli's *Sixty-seven Articles* of 1523, the *Ten Theses of Berne* of 1528, the *Tetrapolitan Confession* of 1530, the *First Confession of Basle* of 1534, the *First Helvetic Confession* of 1536,[62] the *Lausanne Articles* of 1536, or the *Geneva Confession* of 1536. Confessional interest in election really commences in Geneva in the aftermath of Calvin's controversies with Bôlsec and Castellio. The *Confession of Faith* written (probably) by Whittingham for the English church at Geneva mentions the elect and the reprobate in connection with Christ's second coming, the church, and baptism. Thereafter predestination is regularly included to some degree in the Reformed confessions. It is, however, given more prominence in the *French Confession* of 1559, the *Belgic Confession* of 1561, and the *Second Helvetic Confession* of 1566 than in the *Scots Confession*.[63]

Earlier examples of interest in predestination can be found, but not in confessions accorded ecclesiastical approval. Zwingli's *Fidei Ratio* of 1530, for example, discusses election but not reprobation. Not unlike the later doctrine of the *Scots Confession*, Zwingli stated that

> the election of God stands and remains firm; for those whom he elected before the foundation of the world he elected in such a way as to choose them for himself through his Son. . . . It was goodness to have elected whom he so willed; justice, to adopt the elect and unite them to himself through his Son, who was made the victim to satisfy the divine justice on our behalf.[64]

Despite statements of this nature, predestination does not receive a marked place in the Reformed confessions until after the 1552 *Consensus of Geneva Concerning the Eternal Predestination of God*.

Knox, then, was party to the formulation of the *Scots Confession* at a time when he had just been thoroughly exposed to the Calvinist doctrine of predestination. Yet the treatment of predestination in the *Confession* does not manifest Calvin's doctrine. Duncan Shaw has shown that the references to predestination in the *Confession* reflect the teaching of Bullinger, à Lasco, and the churches of Basle, Berne, and Zürich. Knox knew Bullinger, had read the writings of à Lasco, and had visited the leading Swiss churches, yet in 1560 his views on predestination were Calvinist. The influence of Bullinger and others on the idea of predestination in the *Scots Confession* likely came from John Willock.[65]

Willock, who had come into contact with Lutheran views at Ayr in the 1530s, fled to England around 1534–35. Approximately twelve years later he became a chaplain to the Marquis of Dorset, in which capacity he met Bullinger's disciple, John ab Ulmis. Through ab Ulmis, Willock asked Bullinger to dedicate the fifth book of his *Decades* to the Marquis, and Bullinger thereupon dedicated it to both the Marquis and Willock. In 1550 and 1551 Willock was aware of the attack made on the predestinarian views of John Hooper, a Bullinger disciple, by the Calvinist Bartholomew Traheron. When, in 1551, Willock went to the Scottish border areas to preach, he probably met Knox for the first time. In May 1552, he wrote to Bullinger on the subject of marriage. Following his attempts to overthrow Mary Tudor, he fled to Emden and became a preacher to the English congregation, which followed the Zwingli-Tyndale tradition. He briefly returned to Scotland in 1555, and met with Knox and others that fall. He returned to Scotland again in October 1558, became actively involved in the work of reformation, and was an obvious choice to be a coauthor of the *Confession*.[66]

The influence of Willock appears to be largely responsible for the treatment of predestination in the *Confession*. Knox was agreeable for two reasons. First, as James McEwen observed, the *Confession* closely reflects the teaching of John 17, a favorite passage of Knox's, and therefore was acceptable as a simple expression of his own faith.[67] McEwen's implication that Knox was the author of the passage cannot, however, be sustained, for Willock's influence is too discernible. Secondly, Knox's approval of a confessional statement lacking a specific chapter on predestination, coming in the same year that his 170,000-word treatise on predestination was published, indicates once again that Knox did not apparently accord a major role in his personal theology to the doctrine of predestination.

THE CHRISTIAN
COMMUNITY:
Ecclesiological Considerations

The challenge to the Catholic church posed by Knox and his fellow reformers entailed not only a repudiation of the broad authority on which that church was founded but also a rejection of its nature, polity, and sacramental system. With other early Protestant writers in the apocalyptic tradition Knox regarded Rome as the whore of Babylon described in the book of Revelation, an identification he made in the first sermon he preached.[1] Subsequently his career was marked by a sustained effort to put as much ground as possible between the Catholic church and what he conceived to be the true Christian church. Nowhere is this endeavor more pronounced than in the militant dichotomy he developed in his treatise on predestination, in which the two churches are likened to two armies, "whom God in his eternall counsell hath so devided, that betwixt them there continueth a battell, which never shalbe reconciled untill the Lord Jesus put a finall ende to the miseries of his Church. . . ."[2] In effect, Knox's views on the church, ministry, and sacraments were developed against this apocalyptic background, and his own sense of prophetic responsibility was understood in the context of this cosmic struggle.[3]

The campaign to establish a godly church and ministry had to be fought on two fronts, for in addition to the Catholics Knox faced a challenge from early English Separatists. Against the Catholics he trumpeted the charge that their institutions lacked the essential mark of holiness, but this was a double-edged sword which could be turned with effect against the new Protestant churches by Separatists. While Knox turned back the threat from the left by equating separation with a denial of the Protestant ministry, the threat did underscore the tremendous importance of discipline in the church in order to preserve its holiness. It is therefore natural that Knox insisted upon the exercise of discipline as one of the marks of the true church.

To establish discipline, effective preaching, and the proper administration of the sacraments necessitated a carefully structured, adequately trained, and suitably supported ministry. To this end Knox worked indefatigably. While his writings manifest the care with which he approached the problem of a ministry structured in accord with Scriptural precepts, the problems of training and financially supporting a Reformed clergy were enormous. The refusal of Parliament to enact the *Book of Discipline* and provide revenues for the reformed Kirk seriously weakened but never destroyed Knox's program for Scotland.

CHAPTER
‡ THREE ‡

THE CHURCH

I. THE NATURE OF THE CHURCH

One of Knox's most difficult problems was developing a church that corresponded to the relatively sketchy injunctions of the New Testament. Against the Catholics Knox had to develop a church whose oneness was fundamentally spiritual rather than visible in nature, that did not depend on the traditional doctrine of apostolic succession, and that had biblical sanction for its repudiation of the historical church of the preceding centuries. Simultaneously, Knox had to give considerable attention to the church as a visible institution because of New Testament precepts, the need to guard against a radicalizing movement that might end in Anabaptism, and the necessity of careful organization to survive as a revolutionary institution in sixteenth-century Scotland.

The revolutionary character of the early Protestant church in Scotland raised other enigmas. It needed the support of powerful lords and lairds to succeed — support which comprised their political acumen as well as their military strength and wealth. Such men had to be embraced within the church if Catholicism was to be routed, yet their lives were often far from holy, making it difficult for Knox to contrast the purity of his church with the general immorality of the Roman church. Morality in any case was at a fairly low level in sixteenth-century Scotland. Knox, to a greater degree than Calvin, faced nearly insuperable problems in imposing discipline on church members. Without the imposition of some discipline, he might have succeeded in justifying the Protestant movement on theological or even nationalistic grounds, but the former would have been insufficient for most uneducated laymen and the latter was no guarantee of Protestant success. Since the fifteenth century, Scottish Catholics had been introducing nationalistic elements into their church and fostering the growth of nationalistic feelings.[1] Moreover, Knox himself was not inclined toward Scottish nationalism except in a nominal way. For practical as well as theological reasons he had to organize a church whose ministry and laity reflected a higher level of morality than had been manifested under Catholicism. Finally, he had to adapt New Testament principles, formulated for small congregations in a pagan state, to the needs of a state church.

The importance of the church in Knox's thought is indicated at the outset of his preaching career. In his first sermon he explained the nature of the "true" church, its foundation, its inerrancy, and the marks by which it could be ascertained. The first article Knox and John Rough were accused of teaching by Dean Winram was the assertion that no mortal man can be head of the church. In the ensuing debate with Winram and Friar Arbuckle, the major point at issue was the church's responsibility to adhere strictly to Scripture. The debate closed with Knox's assertion that there is a church of malignants, which exists "without the word," as well as a true church.[2]

The general theme of the first sermon and the debate were resumed by Knox in his short treatise against the mass. Rejecting the church's power to honor God in any manner except that expressly commanded in Scripture, he insisted that "all the power of the Kirk is subject to Godis Word."[3] The church does not have the power to establish practices that are expedient for promoting the glory of God, for the establishment of any doctrine or manner of worship that lacks specific biblical sanction is a rejection of Christ's headship of the church. As king and head of the church it is his office to guide, rule, and defend the church, and to make its laws. Such laws are expressed in Scripture and must be obeyed in every detail. The church does not have the power to overlook or alter these laws, nor does it have the right to formulate additional laws of its own.[4]

As a Marian exile Knox continued to express these views. Reflecting the English Protestant apocalyptic tradition launched by John Bale, he used Jeremiah as his authority in 1554 to prove that the Roman Catholic church was malignant and "the Congregatioun of the Antichryst."[5] The true church, on the other hand, must continually suffer the malice of the devil, as manifested in the persecution of believers. God would not, however, allow his church to be oppressed forever; Isaiah had testified to that. Because the true church is composed of the elect, it includes the Hebrew faithful as well as true Christians, hence Knox could refer to the church in the days of Moses and Isaiah as well as in his own time. "Christes holye Church" consists of "the chosen members of Christes mystical body in al ages."[6] This doctrine would presumably comfort the persecuted by establishing their identity with the saints of the past who had suffered and triumphed for the faith.

By 1557 Knox had to deal with a different problem. Because not all the adherents to the Reformed cause in Scotland lived exemplary lives, some of the devout were separating from the movement.

> Sum whilk began with us to follow God, to profess Chryst Jesus and to abhour superstitioun, ar declynit frome the sinceritie and simplicitie whilk is in Chryst Jesus; and have separatit thame selves frome the societie and communioun of thair brethrene, in sectis dampnabill and maist pernicious; being bold to affirme, that amangis us thair is no trew Kirk, be reasone that oure lyvis do not agrie with the Word whilk we profess.[7]

This may indicate the presence of an incipient Separatist movement in Scotland predating that in England. In any case the Scottish Protestants were now the objects of the very argument they had been using against the Catholics. Knox's urging of his Scottish followers not to separate from the church because some of its members were guilty of immoral actions was essentially the argument Roman Catholic propagandists had been using against the Protestants.

There had been a long-standing tendency for the devout to be attracted by movements within or away from the Catholic church which stressed piety and morality. The Protestant movement had capitalized on this tendency by castigating the immorality in Catholicism, particularly among the clergy, but because Scottish Protestantism was not a model of morality and piety, Knox was faced with the possibility of men withdrawing from his movement because of immoral behavior by some of his adherents. He repudiated this course by contending that the lives of church members are no assured sign of a true visible church. Much more significant is the doctrine preached and accepted in a church. If the Word of God is given supreme authority, if Christ is accepted as the sole Savior, and if the sacraments are rightly administered, the church is legitimate. There have always been vices in the true church and virtuous heathen outside it. If virtuous lives are an assured sign of election, Knox argued, Moslems would have to be counted among the elect. Thus the church's status as true or malignant must be determined by doctrine rather than by the morality or immorality of its members.[8]

The doctrine of the church in the coauthored *Scots Confession* reflects the views expressed in Knox's earlier writings. Chapter xvi contains a relatively long description of the invisible church. Throughout the history of the world this church existed, composed of those chosen by God, whom they worshiped through faith. The sole head of the church is Christ, who has never delegated his authority to an earthly vicar. The church is catholic or universal, containing all of God's elect communing together as saints and citizens of the heavenly Jerusalem. Defined in this manner, *extra ecclesiam nulla salus*. It is an invisible church, known only to God and embracing the elect of ages past as well as future, a doctrine common to the Protestant movement. Knox fully embraced it and not only approved it in the *Scots Confession* but also used it in debate with the Catholics. In his response to the letters of the Jesuit James Tyrie, Knox emphasized the importance of the spiritual nature of the church, insisting that it is composed only of the godly elect, and therefore in its visible manifestation has to be holy. No one can tell precisely who is a member of the church invisible, but perceptive men can ascertain which earthly churches generally embrace the members of the church invisible and which do not.[9]

The eighteenth chapter of the *Scots Confession* deals with the problem of distinguishing these two types of churches. Like other Protestants, Knox and his colleagues believed that there are certain visible manifestations which differentiate the church militant from the church malignant. Specifically excluded from these signs are such things as age, titular claim, historical or institutional descent, geographical location, or majority approval. The *Confession* sets forth three signs of the true church of God in its visible form: first, the true preaching of the Word of God; second, the right administration of the sacraments, annexed to the Word of God as seals of confirmation in the hearts of the elect; and third, the administration of ecclesiastical discipline in accordance with Scripture. Where these signs are manifest on a generally continuous basis, there the true church exists. The particular as opposed to the universal nature of these churches is emphasized. The churches — the plural form is stressed — which existed in sixteenth-century Scotland are compared to the churches founded by Paul in Corinth, Galatia, and Ephesus. The *Confession*'s eighteenth chapter concludes with a statement on the significance of Scripture and its proper interpretation. Knox's belief that Scripture must be interpreted by Scripture itself and not in principle by individuals or churches is firmly enunciated.[10]

In the twenty-fifth chapter of the *Confession*, Knox and his colleagues make it clear that they are not willing to equate the elect with any visible church, even if the latter manifests the appropriate signs. They go so far as to indicate that a great number of the members of a true visible church might be reprobate, though temporarily professing faith and partaking of the sacraments, but not persevering to the end.[11] In its practical ramifications this was a difficult problem. Reprobates in the church might on occasion lapse into evil ways, but so might the elect. Discipline could control this problem but not eliminate it, for it was hardly possible to excommunicate all those who did not rigidly adhere to the godly life, particularly when the success of the Reformation was at stake. As the success became more certain, Knox's personal position hardened.

When Knox attempted to refute the arguments of James Tyrie in 1566–67, he placed more emphasis on holiness as a mark of the true visible church than he had in writing to fellow Scottish Protestants a decade earlier. Certainly the circumstances had changed. When the success of the reform movement was in considerable doubt in 1557, Knox could not afford to place great emphasis on the discipline problem, but a decade later the situation was essentially reversed. It had become increasingly imperative to stress discipline in order to prevent his own church from becoming the target of a reforming movement. His letter to Tyrie repudiates Roman Catholicism's claim to be the true church on the basis of its universality or catholicity. Idolatry and Islam, he argued, can claim universality too, but are not for that reason acceptable. The church has to be holy and the communion of saints — the *holy* church universal. Catholicism, Knox charged, does not have the holiness that comes from true faith, hence it is not the true church.[12]

The emphasis on the holiness of the church was fraught with peril for a state institution. This was true even for the state church of Scotland where the emphasis was on the individual congregation more than the national Kirk. The holiness criterion was a major factor in the English Separatist movement in the Elizabethan period, when there is evidence of Separatist activity as early as 1566. Bishop Edmund Grindal wrote to Bullinger on August 27, 1566, that "many of the people . . . had it in contemplation to withdraw from us, and set up private meetings. . . ."[13] The following year the authorities in London discovered the "Privye Churche" of Richard Fitz.[14] There were others as well, drawing their members mostly from lower class females, according to Grindal. They met in fields, on ships, and in private homes. It has been estimated that a thousand persons were involved. Further evidence of Separatist activity appears in the accounts of the Spanish ambassador, De Silva, and John Stowe (1568). Leading Separatists were interested in associating with the Dutch and French congregations in London and with the Kirk of Scotland. After trying to suppress the Separatists by arrest and imprisonment, Grindal sent a delegation of them to Scotland to consult with Knox, hoping that they would either stay in Scotland or be persuaded by Knox to return to the Church of England. Knox replied with a sealed letter.[15]

The reply was made in the aftermath of his rejoinder to Tyrie (though the letter was as yet unpublished), in which holiness was emphasized. To support the Separatists would have been consistent with the general tenor of his remarks on the importance of holiness, but would have been an open invitation to schism in Scotland. In December 1567 the Scottish Parliament, influenced by Knox and his colleagues, passed religious legislation that strengthened the Protestant movement. Even the precarious financial position of the Kirk improved. In July 1567 Mary Stewart abdicated and Knox preached the coronation sermon for James VI. This was no time to risk schism in Scotland or a major break with England by supporting the English Separatists. Yet in view of Knox's position on church-state relations it was very unlikely that he would have supported the Separatists even if conditions had permitted.

Knox refused his support to the Separatists on the grounds that their separation wrongly condemned the ministry of the Church of England. Moreover he opposed rejecting as false prophets and heretics those who disagreed with him or the Separatists on matters of apparel and related opinions, providing they taught "the substance of doctrine and salvation in Christ Jesus."[16] As long as the message of salvation was preached, Christians could not refuse to hear it even if they disagreed with the preachers on some nonsubstantial matters. Knox admitted that there were many in the Church of England who were authorized to preach and yet were Catholics or heretics, but he would not condemn the Anglican ministry and counsel separation on that account. Paul, he pointed out, had been offended with Peter, whom he sharply rebuked, but he did not dissuade people from hearing Peter preach. The advice of Knox was "the equivalent of Bullinger's famous dictum in the case of the more prominent Puritans . . . ,"[17] namely, that a difference of opinion on matters other than fundamental doctrine does not justify schism.

Knox's recommendations were "not in all points liked. . . ." The tenor of his remarks was sharply different from that of his earlier writings, which counseled the suppression of anything in religion that lacked specific biblical sanction. The effect on the Separatists was divisive, and Knox could be quoted by the various parties. Separatism did not die out, despite the discouragement from Knox. In fact, the forms of prayer used by his Geneva congregation continued in use among the left-wing religious groups in England. Moreover, Richard Fitz's London congregation agreed with the three marks of the true church accepted by Knox and his colleagues at Geneva and in Scotland.[18]

Like Luther, Knox mellowed a bit in his later years, moving away from his revolutionary ardor. Certainly his treatment of the Separatists manifests this, if one compares this attitude with that expressed in his early writings. Yet Knox had compromised as an

Anglican clergyman in Edwardian England, so that his advice to the English Separatists was in accord with his own practice in England — if not in Frankfurt — and with his advice to the congregation at Berwick. He also compromised in 1560 with respect to the application of his concept of biblical authority to the church. Although he believed that concept was the best means of preserving the church's holiness and doctrinal purity, he had to agree with his fellow formulators of the *Book of Discipline* that it was sometimes necessary to appeal to expediency rather than Scripture.

In general what Knox had to say about the church accorded with basic Protestant thought. The rigidity of the application of the principle of express scriptural authority to the church in his earlier writings reflects the influence of Zürich. When he was willing to temporize, it was in accord with Bullinger's dictum that schism is not justified because of a diversity of opinions on matters other than basic doctrine. This was also Calvin's position.[19] Reformed influence may also be seen in Knox's repeated emphasis on the true church as comprised of the elect. Luther and the other reformers laid particular stress on the church as the communion of saints, a notion which appears in the *Scots Confession*.[20] This was obviously compatible with the idea of the church as the body of the elect, yet the repeated emphasis on the elect is more common to the Reformed than the Lutheran theologians, and is particularly noticeable in Zwingli[21] and Knox. This does not indicate a doctrinal cleavage, for the two emphases are harmonious. They are combined, for example, in the *First Helvetic Confession*: "The Churche . . . is the congregacion and eleccion of all holy men. . . ."[22] Calvin's *Catechism* likewise defined the universal church as "the body and fellowship of them that beleve, whom God hath ordeined and chosen into life everlasting."[23] The distinction drawn by Knox between the visible and invisible church, and his willingness to admit imperfection in the former but not the latter, was common to the major Protestant reformers.

There is a noticeable distinction among the reformers on the marks of the church. Luther established the basic pattern by making the preaching and hearing of the Word and the correct administration of the sacraments the two signs.[24] Calvin was of the same mind (though in practice it was soon established that discipline was a mark of the true church), as were the formulators of the

Forty-Two Articles of the Church of England.[25] At his trial Wishart took the same position. His translation of the *First Helvetic Confession* had referred only generally to the marks of the church when it spoke of the church as known by "certayne externall [i.e., outward] rytes, institute[d] by Christ, and be one publyke and lawful teachynge, [the] teachynge of the Worde of God. . . ."[26] The *Geneva Confession* of the same year specified the standard two marks.[27]

The importance of discipline was clear to Knox by 1553. When he appeared before the Privy Council in April of that year he criticized the Church of England because its ministers lacked the authority "to divide and separate the leppers from the whole, which was a cheefe point of his office."[28] Nothing has been recorded to indicate that he commented about the marks of the church, but it is clear that he had been impressed with the value of discipline. Conceivably this could have come from knowledge of the emphasis on discipline in the foreign churches of John à Lasco or Valérand Pullain in London and Glastonbury. (Pullain had been Calvin's successor as minister of the French congregation at Strasbourg.[29]) Knox could also have been impressed with the importance of discipline by the discussions surrounding the *Reformatio Legum Ecclesiasticarum* of 1552, which was intended to be the basis for the reformation of discipline in the Church of England.[30] Yet the duty of the minister to exercise discipline was clearly enunciated in the *First Helvetic Confession*: he must "compell and reproue the fautie and vicious; and to exclude from the churche them that stereth to farre, and that by a godly consente and agrement of them whiche are chosen of the ministers and magistrates for correcyon, or to ponyshe them by any other waye conuenient and profytable meanes, so longe untyll they come to a mendement, and so be safe. . . ."[31] Bucer, who (unlike Calvin) formally made discipline a third mark of the church, may have been responsible for this emphasis on discipline.[32]

Discipline appears as the third mark of the church in the 1556 *Confession of Faith* of the English congregation at Geneva.[33] It may be that Knox influenced Whittingham, or that the latter was sufficiently impressed by the importance of discipline in Geneva that he made it a third sign of the church. In December of the following year Knox set forth the signs of the church to his brethren in Scotland: "Whairsoever Godis Word hath supreme autoritie; whair Chryst Jesus is affirmit, preachit, and receavit to be the onlie Saviour of the warld, whair his Sacramentis ar trewlie ministerit; and finallie, whair his Word reuleth, and not the vane fantassie of man, their is the trew Kirk of Chryst Jesus."[34] The third sign may obliquely include discipline, but it is more evocative of Knox's general principle that nothing must be included in the church unless it has express scriptural sanction. If so, perhaps the addition of discipline as the third mark of the church in the 1556 *Confession* is the contribution of Whittingham rather than Knox. Regardless, Knox was very likely responsible for the inclusion of discipline as the third mark in the *Scots Confession*. Willock, the other dominant figure in its authorship, was a disciple of Bullinger, who had asserted only the two traditional marks.[35]

Although it is difficult to pinpoint the sources of Knox's doctrine of the church, his rather heavy dependence on the Old Testament as well as the New Testament is clear. He was fond of linking the remnant spoken of by the Hebrew prophets with the true church of the sixteenth century, and he conceived of a common bond linking the persecuted elect of old with those in his own day. It is hardly surprising to find this emphasis in Knox, for of all the major reformers he most strongly identified with the prophetic tradition.

II. DISCIPLINE IN THE CHURCH

The seriousness with which the Scottish reformers accepted discipline as a mark of the true church is manifested in the *Book of Discipline*. (In the *Book's* title the term "discipline" is used in the sense of church polity and common order rather than the narrower sense of the oversight of conduct.[36]) Studies of the *Book* have demonstrated its parallels with and reliance on a number of sources, including the *First Helvetic Confession*, the Danish *Ordinatio Ecclesiastica*, possibly the *Reformatio Legum Ecclesiasticarum* drawn up but never passed during the reign of Edward VI, Francis Lambert's Hessian constitution of 1526, the writings of Calvin, the *Ordonnances* of the church of Geneva, the polity of the Reformed congregations in France, John à Lasco's *Forma ac Ratio*, the polity of Valérand Pullain's Glastonbury congregation, and

Hermann of Cologne's *Book of the Reformation* (1543).[37] The Scottish reformers did not, of course, admit this dependence. The only pattern they claimed to follow was the primitive church of the New Testament. Knox had been more candid at Frankfurt when he admitted that he wanted the English congregation to be "agreeable in outward rites and ceremonies with Christian Churches reformed."[38] Certainly the Scottish reformers benefitted from their contact with Continental and English ideas, particularly as filtered through Knox and probably Willock, though experience and expedience as well as biblical examples were major factors in the determination of their views of the church and its government.

At least in Knox's case there may have been some psychological factors which contributed to his views, especially on the matter of discipline. Possibly he was influenced in his youth by the attempted enforcement of discipline in Scottish society.[39] More likely, however, the rampant lawlessness that existed throughout much of Scotland in the sixteenth century influenced a man dominated by the idea of a holy God to impose rigid ecclesiastical discipline as a means of curbing some of this lawlessness. Yet discipline was more than mere legalism; it reflected "an inheritance handed down by Augustine from the Greco-Roman ethic of becoming good by exercising oneself in that pattern which is truly good, rational and natural."[40] Knox's concern with discipline and righteousness may also have been influenced by his self-imposed exile on the Continent: "Righteousness was a consolation and a way of organizing the self for survival."[41] Certainly while he was on the Continent he was impressed by the exercise of discipline in Geneva, where Calvin tried to see that morality was actually enforced, essentially through the Consistory. A key feature of this discipline was ecclesiastical excommunication, which provoked considerable controversy in Protestant circles. This practice was rejected by Bullinger, Erastus (who contested it with Olevianus, Calvin's disciple, in the Palatinate), and most Lutherans. Knox's acceptance of ecclesiastical discipline by the session reflects adherence to Calvin on this issue.[42]

Above all, Knox's stress on discipline was theologically influenced. There was a strong emphasis on righteousness and holiness in the prophetic tradition, and it was perfectly natural that Knox's church should embody this righteousness in the highest degree possible. The doctrine of sanctification, with which the exercise of discipline was closely associated, was also basic to Knox's thought. Moreover, the religious experience of the numinous, or holy, was present in the Lord's Supper. Knox sought to avoid the profanation of that sacred holiness by imposing an ecclesiastical discipline that would reasonably guarantee that those approaching the communion table were not wicked.[43] Perhaps most Scots did not really believe discipline was as important as the Word and the sacraments,[44] but Knox did (subject to the fundamental position of the Word in this trilogy).

The authors of the *Book of Discipline* compared the need for laws of ecclesiastical discipline to the need for good laws and proper execution in order to maintain the commonwealth. Just as there would be no commonwealth without such laws and their execution, so there would be no purified church without ecclesiastical discipline. The argument is based on an experiential analogy, not Scripture, but its formulators undoubtedly hoped such an argument would appeal to the Scottish Parliament. The *Book of Discipline* allotted the responsibility for upholding the law to both the church and the state. The civil magistracy was to be responsible for the more open and blatant transgressions of divine law, such as blasphemy, adultery, murder, perjury, and other crimes believed to deserve capital punishment. The church's task was to discipline those guilty of drunkenness, gluttony, excess in apparel, fornication, oppression of the poor, cheating in business transactions, and inappropriate language or licentious conduct.[45]

The draft of the *Book of Discipline* was completed (perhaps in brief form) within a month (May 1560), but was not submitted to Parliament until January 1561. The Great Council approved it that month, but further ratification was not forthcoming. In December 1561 the General Assembly of the Kirk of Scotland requested ratification from the Queen and Privy Council, but was rejected. In spite of the setback the Scottish reformers exercised discipline in their churches. The local kirks through their consistories, comprised of ministers, elders, and deacons, provided an element of government at the local level that Scotland lacked, even though it was, perforce, an extraconstitutional authority. The consistories predated the *Book of Discipline*, as did most of the features of church government and discipline set forth therein. At

St. Andrews in the spring of 1560, Knox himself took part in the session meetings, when over eighty percent of the cases handled concerned adultery or fornication. The church courts also enforced attendance at sermons and punished those who criticized Knox. At Edinburgh in April 1562, for example, a cook was scourged and put in the branks for having slandered the Scottish reformer.[46]

The *Book of Discipline* accused Roman Catholicism of having corrupted the civil magistracy so that virtue was not properly encouraged and vice not severely punished. Consequently the church was obligated "to draw the sword" which it received from God against both those it had a duty to punish and those who should have been punished by the state. The sword which God bestowed on the church is excommunication. To be excommunicated did not mean being assigned to hell, for that was a power residing in God, who exercised it in predestination. Instead, excommunication was banishment from participation in the worship and sacraments of the kirk until such a time as repentance was openly manifested. The *Book of Discipline* does, however, use the phrase "repent and be so saved." Once excommunication was invoked, it was to be maintained with severity, for laxity would only encourage contempt of virtue and result in increased evil. Except for one's family and members appointed by the church to deal with the excommunicate, no conversation or general social intercourse and no commercial dealings were permitted. The purpose of this virtual isolation was to encourage the impenitent person to repent. The judgment imposed on him was to be publicly proclaimed throughout Scotland. Because of the seriousness of excommunication, specific steps were set forth in the *Book of Discipline* to ensure that no hasty and regrettable action was taken. Ample warning was given and no practical effort was spared to persuade the accused to repent — at least in theory.[47] Knox and his colleagues sought to develop and maintain a holy society, but they were also concerned to do everything reasonable to keep the members of that society from being expelled.

Because the seriousness of the respective offenses differed, four modes of discipline ultimately were used. The most serious was greater excommunication, which was imposed for such crimes as murder, incest, open blasphemy, railing against the sacraments, incorrigible contumacy, and apostasy to Catholicism. An offender had to be cited three times before sentence could be pronounced. The guilty were outlawed and suffered social ruin. Lesser excommunication, which was not excommunication proper, involved suspension from participation in the Lord's Supper for less serious offenses until satisfactory retribution was made and absolution received. The third mode of enforcing discipline was the refusal of communion tokens to those who lacked adequate knowledge or grace to be worthy communicants, or to those who had not contributed to the poor. The final mode was the "fencing" of the communion table, which was a challenge to the prospective communicant to examine his conscience before partaking.[48]

Knox and his colleagues have been criticized for their medieval and tyrannical disciplinary practices.[49] In considering the merit of such criticism two factors must be borne in mind: first, the practical factor — the need for rigorous discipline to maintain the effectiveness of a revolutionary organization until it was firmly entrenched; and, secondly, the theological factor — the conjunction of biblical demands for holiness with the continuing conviction, so strong in the medieval period, that the soul's welfare was the primary criterion in all matters. To be sure, Knox was intolerant, but discipline was nevertheless exercised with discretion. Like à Lasco, Knox was concerned not to exclude anyone from the church until every reasonable effort had been made to return him to the faith, but unlike à Lasco, he was willing to make excommunication involve social ostracism.[50] The punishment for violations could be severe, but it was not imposed by ministerial authority alone. Discipline was a matter that pertained to the whole church, and its enforcement was consequently entrusted not only to the ministers but also to the duly elected representatives of the congregation.

III. A PROGRAM FOR CHURCH REFORM

Knox's blueprints for ecclesiastical and doctrinal reform are reflected in the *Book of Discipline* and the *Scots Confession*. Indeed, the bulk of his writings deal with various aspects of church reform. There is, however, a very concise summation of what he considered to be the essentials of church reform in his *Brief Exhortation to England*, completed in January 1559. Mary Tudor had died, and Knox, in Geneva, was anxious that Elizabeth and the English people embrace the Reformed faith. He was preparing to return to Scotland to aid the Reformed movement at the request of the Earl of Glencairn, Lord James, Erskine of Dun, and others. It must have been an exciting moment for Knox, for there was renewed hope that both nations might embrace Protestantism. As he understood it, his prophetic vocation required that he work toward this goal.

Knox gave specific advice to the English for the reform of their church, insisting first that the English refuse to allow any Catholic or former persecutor of Protestants to be placed in any position of authority in the church. Because of the close relationship between church and state, this implicitly extended to officers of the state as well. Secondly, Knox warned of the abuses resulting from pluralism. Each minister was to have one benefice and an ample stipend. Men were not to be free to preach wherever they wished, but only where they were assigned by the church, for only in this manner could all of England have sufficient preachers. Thirdly, Knox proposed that the bishoprics be divided, so that each existing see would become approximately ten smaller but more manageable bishoprics. Each city and "great town" was to have a bishop and subordinate clergy. Fourthly, Knox urged diligence in making certain that ministers discharged their responsibilities. It was not enough that they chant Psalms, read chapters for Matins or Evensong, or recite homilies. Ministers must preach. The "lyvinge voice," Knox reminded, was so much more effective than simple reading.

Fifthly, Knox sought the prohibition of ministers' involvement in civil affairs, except when the civil magistrate and the ministers met for the purpose of executing discipline. There was no need for ministers to attend Parliament, Knox argued, once the true faith was properly established and religious controversy ceased. Sixthly, Knox reminded his readers of the importance of discipline, which was to be maintained by ministers and magistrates working together without respect to any persons, including the monarch. Seventhly, Knox asserted that schools must be erected in all chief towns and cities for the purpose of maintaining the Protestant faith, with their oversight committed to magistrates and godly learned men.[51] *Mutatis mutandis*, Knox and his colleagues subsequently applied this reform program to Scotland. When Knox wrote the *Brief Exhortation to England* the Scottish situation must, because of the circumstances, have been in his mind. When he and five colleagues were appointed by the Great Council of Scotland in April 1560 to draw up the *Book of Discipline*, he had already outlined the essential features in his *Brief Exhortation to England*. Knox must have discussed this outline with his Scottish friends before they set about their task of composition.

IV. THE CHURCH AND THE SABBATH

The Sabbatarian views associated with the Scottish Covenanters in the seventeenth century were foreign to the views and practice of Knox. This is rather surprising in view of the laxity with which the Scots observed the Lord's day. Most towns had a Sunday market, sports activities were commonplace, folk dances were enjoyed, and clowns entertained in the streets. Archbishop Hamilton's *Catechism* expressed the chagrin of the Catholic Church at such happenings and included exhortations to observe the Lord's day. The spread of reforming ardor was subsequently responsible for the enactment by the town council of Dundee in October 1559,

> that the Sunday be keepit in the meditation of God's Word, and that na merchants, craftsmen, nor hucksters, open their buiths nor use ony manner of traffic, and in special that na fleshers brek flesh upon the samin. Also, that na taverners, browsters, nor baxters open their buiths nor sell breid, wine nor ale during the time of the preaching upon the Sunday; and quhasoever beis apprehendit doing the contrair sall pay eight shillings unforgiven.[52]

The town council of Edinburgh enacted a similar statute the following October. Neither the residents of nor the visitors in Edinburgh were allowed to engage in business activities on Sunday, and everyone had to attend the church services in the afternoon as well as the morning. In December 1560 the town council of Peebles prohibited work on the sabbath. Thus the church, whether Catholic or Reformed, was concerned with curtailing activities that seemed irreligious on the sabbath.

In formulating the *Scots Confession*, Knox and his colleagues did not reflect a Sabbatarian outlook. The fourth commandment, prescribing remembrance of the sabbath, is summarized as requiring hearing of and believing in the Word and participating in the sacraments. Thus, the essential requirement of the fourth commandment was worship.

The *Book of Discipline* reveals more about the views of Knox and his colleagues toward the sabbath. In notable towns (a size smaller than great towns), a church service with sermon and prayers was to be held twice a week. The town, during the time of the service, "must be kept free from all exercise of labour, as well of the master as of the servants." Even in smaller towns, where only Sunday services were possible, "Sunday must straitly be kept, both before and after noon. . . ." This also applied, of course, to the larger towns.[53]

Knox did not interpret reverence for the sabbath to mean that all forms of enjoyment were excluded. On a Sunday evening in November 1562, he was present at a dinner party with the English ambassador, Thomas Randolph, and the Duke of Châtelherault. On an earlier occasion he visited Calvin on a Sunday evening during a game of bowls.[54] Calvin's own *Catechism* explained that the fourth commandment was given "to represent our spiritual rest . . .: for a comely order to bee used in the Church: And . . . for the refreshing of servants." Christians were bound to spiritual rest one day a week, by which Calvin meant that "we cease to doe our own workes, that the Lord may bring foorth his works in us." The fourth commandment bound Christians to observe the order appointed in the church for the sermon, prayer, and the administration of the sacraments.[55] Elsewhere Calvin had written that Christ abrogated the Jewish sabbath, and that Christians were not to have anything to do with "the superstitious observance of days."[56]

The position of Knox and his colleagues on the sabbath reflects the Swiss view generally and Calvin's position more specifically. When, in 1566, the Kirk of Scotland received a copy of the *Second Helvetic Confession* to see if the Kirk was in agreement with the Swiss Protestants, the Scots replied affirmatively, "albeit in the keeping of some Festival days our Church assented not, for only the Sabbath-day was kept in Scotland." The Scots agreed with the Swiss belief that the Lord's day was consecrated for religious exercises and a holy rest, but was not to be regarded superstitiously or as holier than any other day. Moreover it was to be observed freely.[57]

The Kirk manifested continuing concern with the sabbath on several occasions in the 1560s. At the session of the General Assembly in July 1562, the Kirk sought punishment for breakers of the sabbath. At the June 1565 session, further concern was evinced with respect to "manifest breaking of the Sabbath Day" as well as witchcraft and sorcery.[58] There was as yet, however, nothing like the rigid Sabbatarianism of the following century.

Knox's eclectic inheritance is well manifested in his views of the church, its discipline, and the sabbath. In these areas alone the influence of Zwingli, Bullinger, Calvin, Wishart, the Danish Lutherans, the leaders of the Edwardian Church, à Lasco, and others is visible.

THE MINISTRY AND GOVERNMENT OF THE CHURCH

I. THE NATURE OF THE MINISTRY

There was always a latent tendency in Protestantism to devalue the importance of the ministry because of the concepts of the perspicuity of Scripture and the sole mediatorship of Christ (or, from another perspective, the priesthood of all believers). Knox, like the other principal reformers, opposed this tendency. His most striking apology for the ministry (which excluded women) was written in December 1565, when Protestant ministers throughout Scotland were in financial distress. Writing to the Scottish Protestants, he outlined the benefits they received from their ministers, including the proclamation of the gospel, the exposition of Scripture, the bestowal of the means of spiritual strength, and the knowledge of the spiritual blessedness derived from the inner awareness of justification *sola fide*. The ministers administered the sacraments and taught the elect how to pray and be of service to God. In a statement rather reminiscent of medieval sacerdotalism, Knox asserted that these benefits, including the proclamation that calls the elect to salvation, cannot be bestowed without the ministry. "If we thinke that al these things may be due without ministers or without preaching, we utterly deceyve our selves." Faith comes only by hearing the declaration of the Word, and that declaration does not come immediately from God (as the radical

Protestant tradition argued), but from divinely appointed ministers acting as agents of the Holy Spirit. It was a simple matter for Knox: no ministers, no gospel, no salvation.[1]

From what is known of Knox's sermons, he stressed the element of proclamation rather than the expository or homiletic aspects. This was a minister's first responsibility, the shirking of which was the betrayal of the fundamental reason for his divine vocation. Yet the minister had other major responsibilities for his flock, including teaching. When Knox preached in Edinburgh on November 9, 1572, on the duty of a minister and the responsibility of a congregation to him, he "made the mariage" between his successor, James Lawson, and the congregation because he was "now vnable to teiche. . . ."[2] Teaching was a *sine qua non* of the ministry. Although Scripture was intelligible even to laypeople, it had to be interpreted in its own light, which required time to read widely in the Scriptures and to compare relevant passages. More time was needed to formulate confessions of faith based on this biblical analysis. All of this was preparatory to giving intelligent guidance to laypeople in their interpretation of Scripture, especially in the weekly assemblies. Ministers also were urged to spend time searching the Bible for answers to the various spiritual problems posed by their congregations. The minister, as Knox pointed out to Mrs. Bowes, also had to guard his flock from the dangers of heresy and idolatry. Failure to do this could not cause the damnation of the elect, but they could be led astray by false doctrine and wander aimlessly in the darkness of doubt.[3]

Another major function of ministers posed by Knox was the evaluation of the government from the pulpit, a task especially significant in the sixteenth century because of the close relationship between church and state. Knox did not fail to underscore the public nature of this criticism. He personally preached publicly and fearlessly at St. Andrews in 1547 and subsequently before Edward VI and his court. On December 13, 1562 he preached, from the pulpit of St. Giles', one of a number of public sermons criticizing Mary Stewart. When he was summoned to Holyroodhouse two days later to answer for his preaching, he refused Mary's request to be admonished privately in the future, informing her that she could either attend his sermons or establish a regular time each week for him to preach to the court. On August 19, 1565 he again preached in St. Giles', with Darnley present. The sermon was on Ahab and Jezebel — an implicit reference to Darnley and Mary. Knox continued to criticize the state from the pulpit in the twilight of his life. Following the St. Bartholomew's Day massacre on August 24, 1572, he publicly denounced Charles IX as a traitor and murderer. "Godis vengeance sall neuer depairt from him nor his house, bot that his name sall remaine in execratioune vnto the posterities to cum; and that nane sall come of his loynes sall enjoye that kingdome in peace and quyetnes, vnles repentance prevent Godis judgmentis!"[4] The outraged French ambassador, Philibert du Croc, protested to the Privy Council, but was informed that it was not within the Council's power to restrict preachers in the pulpit. Thus from the earliest days with the Castilians in St. Andrews to the ebb of life in victory at Edinburgh, Knox, true to his prophetic vocation, called all persons into account.[5]

II. KNOX AS SPIRITUAL COUNSELOR

Knox's pastoral role received relatively little attention in his writings. He was virtually consumed by the prophetic task which involved him in the English and Scottish Reformations. The most documented aspect of his pastoral work is his role as a spiritual counselor and casuist, primarily to Mrs. Elizabeth Bowes. In this capacity he has been justly compared to Luther because of their common concern with the pastoral and homiletic application of theology rather than with systematic theology *per se*.[6] At the same time the tenor of Knox's letters indicates his connection with another religious tradition — Puritanism and its casuistry. His letters were akin to those of the English Puritans Edward Dering and Thomas Wilcox, the predecessors of William Perkins who first formally treated casuistry.[7] The recurring theme of most of Knox's letters of spiritual counsel was assurance of election. In attempting to dispel Mrs. Bowes' doubts, Knox was faced with the difficult enigma posed by the doctrine of predestination to the psyche of a devout but insecure person.

Edwin Muir's analysis of Knox's relationship with Mrs. Bowes is intriguing. His assessment of Knox's personal needs and their fulfillment in this relationship appears to be incisive, though certainly speculative: "As a relief from the knocks of a reformer's life, amid which he had to be perpetually the stern, objective instrument, he needed a feminine intimacy, an intimacy on the one side almost maternal, on the other almost filial, in which the instrument could with a good conscience be laid aside, and the man with all his weaknesses might appear."[8] Knox found in Mrs. Bowes someone to whom he could express his own feelings as well as someone who relied on him for spiritual courage. Because Mrs. Bowes was older and his (prospective) mother-in-law, he could experience the maternal relationship that Luther seems to have found through rebirth in the matrix of Scripture and his personal dispensing of the milk of spiritual life. Having forsaken Mother Church, several of the reformers had to fill the maternal void psychologically. In Knox's case Mrs. Bowes met that need, and in turn he sought to give her assurance of election.

Knox dealt with the problems of assurance in theological terms in his treatise on predestination, emphasizing that it was grounded on the doctrine of election. Practically, however, it was precisely the assurance of this election that was needed. He was forced by experience to acknowledge that not all believers could achieve full assurance in their mortal lives. Instead, therefore, of berating Mrs. Bowes because she lacked assurance, he repeatedly cited her doubts as evidence of election. Her faith was weak, Knox was forced to admit, but the very fact that she turned to him for aid was a sign of election, for the reprobate by their nature despised ministers. Doubt had, after all, remained in Jesus' disciples even after being with the master. Complete assurance was not, therefore, a normal state. In Knox's judgment the bitterness of doubt was divinely implanted to keep believers from becoming either negligent in their spiritual life or content with their earthly existence. Yet if a believer embraced Christ, refused idolatry, confessed the truth, and loved others, he had, according to Knox, the gifts of God bestowed only to the elect, and was guaranteed perseverance to the end.[9]

Mrs. Bowes could not rest assured with such advice. She was, as Florence MacCunn aptly observed, "a weariful Mrs. Much-Afraid," with a character akin to that of John Bunyan's Mr. Fearing.[10] As she read Scripture, she became more concerned about her status. Jesus had said that many would seek but would not find salvation, and that many were called but few chosen. Knox explained that the former passage only meant that many would seek salvation by various means, but that only those seeking it by Christ alone would find it. The calling to which Jesus referred, Knox informed Mrs. Bowes, was the general call of all men to obey God, not the special call of election. The continual assaults of the devil ought not bother her either, for as Chrysostom had counseled, the devil would not bother to assault the reprobate. This theme had to be reiterated, for Mrs. Bowes was unconvinced. God himself, Knox explained, chastised his elect, but never permanently, and such chastisement coupled with assaults from the devil were certifications of election. Knox was actually arguing that a Christian should rejoice because of the presence of doubt even while recognizing the assurance of election. Perceiving by introspection the work of the devil within, the believer had to flaunt the great adversary and profess faith grounded on Scripture. The very turning to Christ in time of crisis was a sign of election, for the reprobate fled from him. Mrs. Bowes was safe. Knox finally wrote to her that he was pleased "that the enemy assaltis yow with dyvers and new assaltis, for that is the maist sure prufe that by his ald trickis he has not prevalit." One did not continue to attack a fortress unless there was something in it that had not been overcome. As long as Mrs. Bowes continued to fight and to sob for divine assistance she was assured of election, for once chosen, there was no way to lose election. Knox was assured of her eternal fate, though Mrs. Bowes was probably never as convinced of her election as was Knox.[11]

One of Knox's ministerial letters to her, written from London and dated June 23, 1553, dealt at some length with the matter of repentance. Mrs. Bowes was counseled that she had to acknowledge her sin, which she could not do until her conscience was enlightened and divine judgment concerning her sin was revealed. She must hate both the actual offense and herself for contemning God, for only then could her troubled conscience seek mercy and be assured of forgiveness. To give her further comfort, Knox specified the signs which indicate divine forgiveness: her confession, lamentation, and a desire to live a better life. Introspection was urged. Following this advice Knox briefly applied theology to the practical spiritual question, asserting that because God is just, he must forgive the elect. Sin demands satisfaction, but this has already been rendered by Christ, and a just God cannot demand more than is rightfully due.[12] It is a simple argument, but it manifests Knox's ability to apply theological doctrines to everyday problems. He was perhaps more adept at dealing with the spiritual qualms of a hypersensitive conscience than with problems of state.

Occasionally Knox's casuistical responsibilities were manifested in works other than letters. In his exposition of the sixth Psalm, addressed to Mrs. Bowes in 1554, Knox developed the thesis that those who "exercised" themselves in the Law would be less likely to have weak faith than those who refused to follow his admonitions. His discussion of the importance of the Law in the Christian life, in fact, followed his counsel to Mrs. Bowes on the problem of weak faith. The elect know by experience how difficult it is when God appears to be angry with them. When they are tempted by material and bodily considerations to swerve from strict obedience to God and his Law, Satan is swift to accuse them that they have nothing to do with God. They cannot help agreeing because their faith is so weak. Especially in times of adversity Satan pounds away at the theme that they are being divinely punished for their iniquity, for they have rejected the precepts of the Law and must be punished without hope of mercy or relief. A weak faith, Knox warned, is simply unable to cope with such accusations. The problem had special meaning for Knox because of his belief that the elect are normally subject to adversity in the present life. Not only was it his task to warn of such adversity, but it was also part of his prophetic responsibility to prepare the elect for it. Ideally, of course, Knox would have preferred that the elect strengthen their faith by the continual study and practice of the Law, but in actuality he found it necessary to comfort those of weak faith. If they could only sob to God for assistance, he counseled, they were assured of salvation. Even martyrdom could not signify what that basic sob did — the fact of election. Yet as Mrs. Bowes would undoubtedly have testified, Knox's advice was not as simple to practice as it was to state: sob and fight.[13]

In the last year of his life Knox published a synopsis of their relationship in which he indicated that her conscience was troubled continually except when she was in the presence of fellow believers (with whom she presumably could compare spiritual experiences). Knox wanted it known that of all the Christians he had known in Scotland, England, France, and Germany (he omitted Switzerland), he had met none whose spiritual conflict equaled that of his mother-in-law. After reading their correspondence there is no inclination to dispute him, and he was candid enough to admit that she had been something of a burden to him, spiritually as well as physically. She was also, despite her age and her fifteen children, something of a physical attraction to him. (He had a marked preference for the company of married women with children.)[14] His account of Mrs. Bowes reveals love as well as sympathy. "Her company to me was comfortable (yea, honorable and profitable, for she was to me and myne a mother). . . ."[15]

Knox's ministerial responsibilities of a casuistical nature were fulfilled for others besides Mrs. Bowes. He urged his correspondents in London not to attend mass, counseled his friends in Edinburgh about his views on women's clothing and fellowship with idolaters, and described the progress of his reforming work in Scotland to Mrs. Anne Locke. Idolatry and political matters were also frequently discussed. At the request of Mary Stewart he wrote to the Earl of Argyll asking that he treat her half-sister, his wife, in a better manner. Some of these letters were not casuistical, but they illustrate from a practical point of view Knox's conception of ministerial responsibility in this area.[16]

III. THE ELECTION OF MINISTERS

The basis of Knox's personal status as a minister was a matter of dispute in his own lifetime. He was ordained in Edinburgh on April 15, 1536, but did not receive a benefice, and by 1540 was acting as a notary or registrar (which was not uncommon for ordained men) in the Haddington area.[17] Thereafter he took up tutoring. Around 1543 he was living in Longniddry, a village near Haddington, where he tutored the two sons of Sir Hugh Douglas. Following his involvement with Wishart, he was subsequently persuaded to join the Protestants in the castle at St. Andrews. There he continued his tutoring work, but was soon prevailed upon by Henry Balnaves and John Rough, the preacher, to take up the preaching task. When Knox demurred on the grounds that he had no lawful calling to do so, Balnaves, Rough, and Sir David Lyndsay set out to provide that call. Rough preached on the election of ministers and the sovereignty of the congregation, in the name of which he charged Knox to accept the vocation of the public office and charge of preaching. Knox was not eager to accept and for many days kept his own counsel. Finally, his opposition to the Catholic views expressed by Dean John Annand prompted the people to insist that he preach, and he agreed.

There are many factors that must have weighed heavily on his mind in those days of doubt. There was the obvious danger to his life, as witnessed by Wishart's recent martyrdom, and there was probably a feeling of insecurity, since he was not accustomed to public preaching. There may have been doubt as to the validity of his vocation by the congregation. He had been ordained, but as a priest in a church he publicly denounced to Annand. Could he preach in a Protestant church on the basis of the old ordination? If it was invalid, could he preach without new ordination simply because the congregation called him to preach? In any case, his first desire was not to be at St. Andrews at all, but to visit the Protestant churches of Germany.[18]

Shortly after Knox's return to Geneva in 1556, the provincial council at Edinburgh condemned and excommunicated him, degrading him from his priest's orders and burning his effigy. He denounced the sentence as unjust and the men who imposed it as false and ungodly. To prove his innocence he demanded the calling of a general council, as Luther had done, and like Luther he also requested the support and protection of the nobility and estates.[19] The seriousness of the official action was apparent in June 1559 when the Lords of the Congregation were undecided as to whether Knox should be allowed to preach. In reply to attempts to persuade him to stay out of the pulpit, he retorted: "I cannot of conscience: for in this town and church began God first to call me to the dignity of a preacher . . . from the which [office] most unjustly I was removed. . . ."[20] It is worth noting that he attributed his call directly to God and did not include the St. Andrews congregation. The following year he was undoubtedly one of those who presented a Supplication to the Estates in which the petitioners offered "evidently to prove that in all the [rabble of the] clergy there is not one lawful minister, if God's word, the practice of the Apostles and their own ancient Laws shall judge of lawful election."[21] While this obviously referred to the Catholic clergy, the overt attack on Catholic ordination may indicate that Knox by this point had repudiated his own ordination. Certainly his joint authorship and approval of the *Scots Confession* is evidence of his repudiation of Catholic ordination no later than 1560, for it asserted that Catholic clergy are "no ministers of Christ Jesus. . . ."[22]

The basis of Knox's call was raised by Catholic disputants in 1562 – 63. In March 1562 Ninian Winzet asserted that there were only two lawful bases for the ministry: episcopal ordination and an extraordinary call from God. There could be no doubt of the properness of Knox's ordination, but his repudiation of Catholicism involved a repudiation of the ordination of the Catholic church. While he made it amply clear that his baptism in the Catholic church was not to be repudiated in favor of rebaptism, ordination was not treated in the same manner. Winzet accused him — and Knox never denied the accusation — of repudiating his Catholic ordination, but not his baptism:

> [Authority] wes geuin to zow in the sacrament of ordinatioun be auctoritie of preisthed. Quhilk auctoritie geue ze esteme as nochtis, be reasoun it wes geuin to zow (as ye speik) be ane papiste bischope, and thairfor renunceis it, and seikis ane vther ordinatioun of secularis, — it followis consequentlie that ze (quhilk God forbid) sulde renunce zour baptism also, geuin to zow be ane papist preist. . . .[23]

Winzet pressed Knox to declare the basis for his ordination, "sen ze renunce and estemis that ordinatioun null, or erar wickit, be the quhilk sumtyme ze war callit Sehir Iohne."[24] An extraordinary call, Winzet claimed, had to be proved by the working of miracles, as the Hebrew prophets had done. Knox chose to debate rather than make his personal position explicit. When, in a sermon at St. Giles', he retorted that Amos and John the Baptist had not worked miracles, Winzet replied that signs and miracles had occurred when John the Baptist was in his mother's womb; Knox could not claim this. The validity of Amos' extraordinary call had been verified by the fulfillment of his prophecies. Knox, of course, considered himself to have been called to the prophetic vocation, and his closest followers agreed.[25]

The basis of Knox's call was again a matter of dispute in September 1562, when he debated for three days with Quintin Kennedy, Abbot of Crossraguel. The principal subject of their disputation was the mass, but Kennedy taunted Knox as one *"quia est sacerdos Dei altissimj secundum ordinem Caluini."*[26] Kennedy also charged that Knox and his fellow Protestant ministers were unsure of the basis of their ordination. There was undoubtedly some truth to the general substance of the accusation. Knox repudiated Catholic ordination, claiming that Protestant ministers received their ministerial authority directly from God. He was aware of the enigmatical, practical implications of his position, for if the ministerial vocation was received directly from God, there was no way for the organized Protestant church to control admission to the ministry. Knox therefore appealed to extenuating circumstances in his case and that of his colleagues, arguing that historically God had temporarily suspended the traditional order of calling men when the established ministry had become corrupt. At such times God called directly upon simple and obscure men to rebuke the elect and convict the organized ministry of their negligence, idolatry, and unworthiness to continue as ministers. As examples Knox pointed to Elijah, Jeremiah, Amos, and the other prophets, and in modern times to Zwinglians, Lutherans, Oecolampadians, and Calvinists. These men had not usurped the authority of the church; rather, the organized clergy had usurped the authority of God and his church.[27]

Knox's argument could have been used, as it was on the Continent, to support more radical reformers. As early as December 1557 he wrote from Dieppe to the Protestants in Scotland, cautioning them about the dangers of men claiming immediate divine vocation. No man was to be allowed to preach or assemble congregations without first undergoing trial and examination, both of life and of doctrine. Knox was worried less about the effects of ungodly preachers upon the elect than about the danger of men spewing out envenomed doctrine. He sought to steer a middle course between formal ordination in the old orthodox manner and unrestricted preaching in the manner of the Waldensians and Anabaptists. He had not forgotten his summary of the twenty-fourth chapter of Balnaves' treatise, where he had described the vocation common to all the elect, distinguishing it from the special vocation of ministers. Only those possessing the latter could preach or administer the sacraments. The door was left open even then, however, to immediate calling from God. What obviously concerned Knox was that a number of the elect confirm the immediate call before a man began preaching.[28]

Knox rejected the traditional doctrine of apostolic succession, as did other reformers. Calvin representatively charged that "in the organization of the church nothing is more absurd than to lodge the succession in persons alone to the exclusion of teaching."[29] The *Scots Confession* rejected the doctrine, and Knox dealt with it in his reply to James Tyrie. It was repugnant to Knox to think that a line of descent might be an essential link between the elect and God, hence he stressed God's free sovereignty in drawing men to himself without regard to ecclesiastical formality. He also argued that the doctrine of apostolic succession lacked biblical sanction, though he went on to contend that the Scottish Kirk and ministry were in fact in apostolic succession inasmuch as they admitted nothing which did not have explicit apostolic sanction.[30]

Late in life Knox wrote to the General Assembly meeting at Stirling and warned them not to admit unworthy men to the ministry. Mindful of the abuses of the medieval period, he specifically cautioned them to beware of men seeking admission to the ministry for purposes of financial gain.[31] Actually, the authors of the *Book of Discipline* had already established a sound procedure for the selection of ministers. Its provisions in this regard were largely based on *The Forme of Prayers and Ministration of the Sacraments*, which was more widely used in Scotland in Knox's lifetime than the *Book of Discipline*, due to the latter's not being printed in this period.[32] According to the *Book of Discipline*, ordinary calling consisted of a threefold process of election, examination, and admission, providing a careful screening process for ministerial candidates. The responsibility for the selection of the minister was basically that of the local congregation, which was given forty days to choose a candidate. If it failed to select one, the superintendent and his council were empowered to intervene. Candidates were required to undergo an examination of their knowledge and ability by the ministers and elders of the

Kirk and the congregation. Specific attention was paid to matters of doctrinal dispute between the Reformed churches and Catholics, Anabaptists, Arians, and others. If the life, doctrine, and abilities of a candidate were found acceptable by the ministers and elders of the Kirk and by the local congregation, the latter was normally obligated to accept the candidate as its minister. The *Book of Discipline* sought to ensure the liberty of a church to select its own minister, but was equally concerned that this liberty not be abused by the rejection of fully qualified candidates. The threefold process of selection — election by the congregation, examination by ministers and elders, and admission or public approbation by the church — reflected the general manner of selecting ministers used in the Reformed churches. The polity of Calvin, Pullain, à Lasco, and Francis Lambert were its direct sources.[33]

The *Book of Discipline* specified the kind of persons that were not to be admitted to the ministry, especially those who had a reputation of infamy and those who lacked the ability to edify the church by sound doctrine. Public edicts were to be sent to all parts of Scotland where a ministerial candidate was known, demanding that any knowledge of improper conduct be communicated to the church issuing the edicts. The *Book of Discipline* asked specifically for knowledge of wilful murder, adultery, fornication, thievery, drunkenness, fighting, and contentious bearing.[34] Clearly, Knox and his colleagues were determined to create a group of ministers that was not subject to the prevalent immorality that had characterized the medieval clergy. They were not altogether successful.

The section in the *Book of Discipline* on the admission of ministers is particularly interesting. Admission — the traditional term "induction" was not used by the Scottish reformers — was a twofold process, requiring consent of the congregation and approbation of the ministers and elders responsible for the examination. No other ceremony was approved, including the laying on of hands. The new minister was charged, as Knox had been at St. Andrews, to care for his church and to obey God, while the congregation was required to respect its minister and to obey the commandments he uttered from the Word of God. No conception of ordination was implied or stated.[35] There is no indication, as Gordon Donaldson points out, that the framers of the *Book of Discipline* recognized "any state of being 'in orders', [or] any clerical character, apart from the holding of a particular charge."[36] For the Catholic concept of the sacrament of ordination — a term the Scottish reformers avoided — the reformed Kirk of Scotland substituted the inauguration of ministers. Having repudiated the doctrine of apostolic succession and the sacrament of ordination, Knox and his colleagues were consistent in repudiating the laying on of hands which, like Calvin,[37] they found to be of no use. Curiously, however, when the Scottish Kirk was asked to approve the *Second Helvetic Confession* of 1566, it gave its approval, noting only its exception to the observance of festivals. Knox and his colleagues did not object to the statement in the *Confession* that "those who are elected are to be ordained by the elders with public prayer and laying on of hands."[38]

Once a minister had accepted his charge, the *Book of Discipline* forbade him to leave it or his church to reject him without due cause. The Scottish Kirk as a whole was free to approve the transfer of ministers, but the arbitrary decisions of ministers or congregations to change was explicitly condemned. Neither were the churches, because of the scarcity of acceptable ministers, permitted to select those who could not meet the high standards imposed by the *Book of Discipline*. Better to have no minister than to have ill-equipped or immoral men in the pulpit who could not proclaim the divine message or rightly administer the sacraments.[39] Their failure to fulfill those functions, the reformers believed, would endanger the very existence of the church in view of the Protestant conviction that right preaching and the administration of the sacraments were, with discipline, the *sine qua non* of a true church.

Until such a time as there were sufficient godly ministers to fill the pulpits, Knox and his colleagues provided for the interim office of reader. The reader's responsibility was to read the Bible and the common prayers, working to foster the spiritual growth of the church and himself. A reader who attained the ability to preach could be admitted to the ministry. The office of reader was also used in Zürich and Basle, where Knox probably learned of it. During the winter of 1554 he traveled throughout Switzerland visiting the Reformed churches, and in the course of those travels he undoubtedly was introduced to the reader's office.[40]

IV. SUPERINTENDENTS AND THE EPISCOPAL QUESTION

One of the more disputed aspects of Knox's thought is his position on episcopacy. Extant evidence from his life, his writings, and the *Book of Discipline* is not fully clear, but it is reasonably sufficient to conclude that Knox did not oppose episcopacy in some form. In October 1552 he was offered the bishopric of Rochester, but refused. There is no reason to believe that his rejection involved opposition to episcopacy in all forms (though he clearly opposed the Catholic understanding of episcopacy). He had his congregation in the North, which enabled him to maintain contact with incipient Protestantism in Scotland. To have taken the bishopric of Rochester would have removed him from that strategic position, and he may have been aware of the trouble that might descend on English Protestantism in the near future. Edward was in ill health, and the heir apparent was clearly Mary Tudor, an avowed Catholic. As a bishop Knox would also have had the responsibility of enforcing all aspects of the *Book of Common Prayer*, including the ceremony of kneeling at communion. There is, however, no indication that he opposed the office of bishop itself. In fact, in 1559 he urged an increase in the number of bishops and dioceses in England in order to administer discipline more effectively.[41] He was never reticent to speak his mind, and if he opposed episcopacy *per se* in 1559, he surely would have said so. Writing from the Continent he had nothing to fear.

Knox steadfastly refused to accept the office of superintendent in the Scottish Kirk, but not because he was opposed to the institution of superintendency. This time he occupied the most influential pulpit in Scotland — St. Giles' — and was in a position to observe and influence the affairs of state that were crucial to the success of the Scottish Reformation. In a letter to Sir William Cecil, Randolph commented that "Mr. Knox thinks his state honourable enough and will receive no other."[42]

In 1572 Knox was caught up in a controversy that involved episcopacy in the Kirk of Scotland. Because the *Book of Discipline* had not been given parliamentary approval, ecclesiastical affairs in Scotland were still anomalous. In addition to the superintendents provided for by the *Book of Discipline*, there were still bishops. As the Catholic bishops died, they were replaced by Protestant bishops selected by the lords. The problem was compounded by the fact that these bishops were receiving two-thirds of the tithes, with the remaining third being divided between the government and the Kirk.

In January 1572 the Kirk and the Privy Council compromised, with the Kirk agreeing to accept bishops providing the lords appointed only men whom the Kirk sanctioned. For their part the lords were permitted to take a substantial portion of the revenues paid to the bishops. Like most ministers, Knox must have been less than content with this arrangement. The situation quickly worsened for Knox when the Earl of Morton nominated John Douglas, Knox's friend and Rector of St. Andrews University, for the post of Archbishop of St. Andrews. In accordance with the recent agreement between the Privy Council and the Kirk, Douglas and Morton determined that the latter would receive all the revenues from the office. When Knox was requested to inaugurate Douglas on February 10, 1572, he refused, undoubtedly disappointed that his friend was involved in such an arrangement. More important, Knox feared undue influence in ecclesiastical affairs from the universities and the individual lords. That same year he was involved in a controversy at St. Andrews in which he made his position on university interference in church matters manifest. He was also aware of the conflict created by lay investiture, to which the then-current practice of appointing bishops was not altogether unrelated.[43] Yet during the course of the controversy Knox never objected to episcopacy *per se*, but to the abuses associated with it in Scotland.[44]

In August 1572 Knox wrote to the General Assembly meeting at Perth. While most of his attention was directed to problems associated with the bishops, at no point did he call for their abolition in the Kirk of Scotland. He was definitely not opposed to episcopacy *per se*, though he would not have approved any form of episcopacy that had as a concomitant the doctrine of apostolic succession. Neither would he have approved a system of episcopacy that did not recognize the underlying equality of all ministers, including bishops, whose only superiority was the exercising of delegated supervisory powers. He was adamant on the point that every bishop had to be first and foremost a preacher, and he and Rough had been accused of teaching that there are no bishops unless they preach themselves. No bishop was to engage in "temporall or seculer busines" but was to devote his entire energy to his principal task, the proclamation of the gospel.[45] Knox was not strongly concerned with details of polity, whether episcopalian or protopresbyterian, a point that has too often been missed by later writers who mine his writings seeking for evidence to shore up their own conception of church government.

There are certain affinities between the office of a bishop and that of superintendents in the Kirk of Scotland. "Generally it may be said that the superintendents performed most of the administrative, disciplinary and judicial functions which in an episcopal system pertain to bishops and in a presbyterian system to the presbytery."[46] Had it not been for the special circumstances in which the *Book of Discipline* was drafted, superintendents might have been called "bishops." The *Book* was completed before the success of the revolt was assured, hence an ecclesiastical constitution was developed which could operate regardless of the status of the Catholic church. As it was, the success of the revolt and the Reformation did not result in the removal of the traditional bishoprics.[47] The basic function of the superintendents — in contrast to the practice of the existing bishops — was to preach, to found churches, and to appoint ministers. At least eight or nine months out of the year the superintendents were to travel throughout their districts, preaching at least three times a week and remaining in one place no more than thirty days. In the course of their visitations they were to examine the life, diligence, and behavior of the ministers, the order of the churches, and the conduct of the people. Their duties also extended to supervision of care for the poor and the education of young people. Superintendents were required to give admonition and counsel where necessary, and report serious offences which required the censure of the Kirk.[48] Unlike the Catholic bishops, they were not given the sacramental powers of confirmation and ordination. Their position and responsibilities were evocative of the principles of polity discussed in the primitive church. Like their primitive predecessors they were not to manifest the pomp and power, let alone the idleness, laxity, and secular concerns, that had characterized the bishops of more recent centuries. As conceived by Knox and his colleagues in the *Book of Discipline*, superintendents were "reformed bishops," that is, bishops as the Scottish reformers believed them to be in the primitive church.

Historians have often regarded the institution of the office of superintendent as a temporary expedient,[49] but this is not the case.[50] The passage in the *Book of Discipline* upon which the misunderstanding is based states that the superintendents be chosen "for this time" to ensure that all areas of the kingdom be reached by qualified preachers (i.e., the traveling superintendents).[51] But the *Book of Discipline* subsequently goes on to indicate numerous other functions of the superintendents which continued to be necessary regardless of how many ministers were available. The supervisory and disciplinary aspects of their work could not be rendered unnecessary by the future provision of sufficient ministers to staff churches in all areas of the kingdom. The assumption of that work by committees associated with a hierarchy of courts — a distinctive feature of presbyterian polity — did not occur until some twenty years later, or well after Knox's death. The Register of the St. Andrews Kirk Session underscores the intention that the superintendency be permanent by its affirmation that "wythowt the cayr [of] superintendentis, neyther can the kyrk be suddenlie erected, neyther can th[ey] be retened in disciplin and unite of doctrin. . . ." Furthermore "o[f] Crist Jesus and of his apostolis we have command and exempill to appoynt me[n] to sic chergis. . . ."[52] Permanency is also evinced in the provisions of the *Book of Discipline* for the selection of future superintendents. After the Kirk had been established for three years, no man was to be allowed to become a superintendent without first serving as the minister of a church for at least two years. From the modern perspective it is obvious that the superintendents were only temporary, but from Knox's standpoint there is no evidence to indicate that this was the intention of the authors of the *Book of Discipline*.[53]

Precedent for the office of superintendent was found in numerous places. The Scottish reformers might have considered the use of superintendents in the Lutheran churches of Denmark and Germany.[54] The term itself was used at times in England as an equivalent of bishop or rural dean, and the importance of preaching attached to the office had been manifested in connection with the Edwardian bishops. The foreign churches in London had a superintendent during Knox's English sojourn. The administrative duties of the superintendent in the Kirk of Scotland were akin to those of a "visitor" in the Swiss Reformed churches.[55] Essentially, Knox and his fellow reformers were seeking to establish a preaching and administrative office that embodied the characteristics of the primitive ἐπισκοπή, which men of the sixteenth century were translating "superintendent" as well as "bishop."

Reformed leaders were in general agreement on the need for such an office, regardless of the title attached to it. Calvin was not opposed to a reformed episcopate, and approved episcopacy in Poland. Moreover, he sent Knox a copy of John à Lasco's church order, which included the office of superintendent. Rudolf Gualter of Zürich and Martin Bucer also approved a reformed episcopate.[56] It is noteworthy that "the description of a superintendent in Martin Bucer's *De Regno Christi* is wholly applicable to the office established in Scotland,"[57] for it is yet another indication that Bucer's influence on Protestantism in Scotland has been underestimated. The *Second Helvetic Confession* of 1566, approved by Knox and his colleagues, sanctioned bishops, and John à Lasco's *Forma ac Ratio* asserted the divine origin of the office.[58] The Scottish Kirk was therefore neither unusual nor out of step with the general Protestant tradition in establishing an office that endeavored to approximate the episcopate of the early church. Yet Geneva, especially under Beza, became increasingly chary of episcopacy. Beza was clearly concerned about Knox's more moderate attitude when he warned, in April 1572, that "as Bishops brought forth the Papacy, so will false Bishops . . . bring in Epicurism into the world. . . . When in process of time you shall have subdued that plague in Scotland, do not, I pray you, ever admit it again, however it may flatter by the pretence of preserving unity. . . ."[59] Knox and Willock, the two dominant figures in drafting the polity and doctrine of the reformed Kirk of Scotland, were certainly no supporters of an unreformed episcopate, but neither did they fail to appreciate the supervisory advantages that reformed bishops or superintendents could provide.[60]

The first superintendents were selected by the Great Council, reflecting the practice of the English and German Protestants. Subsequently, however, the superintendents were to be selected in the manner used in the primitive church. When a vacancy occurred, the ministers, elders, deacons, and magistrates or council of the principal town in the district were to nominate two or three suitable candidates from the whole of Scotland. All candidates had to be thoroughly examined by all the ministers of the province and by the neighboring superintendents, with final selection by election. Each superintendent was subject to censure and correction by the ministers and elders of the province entrusted to his care.[61] In practice only five superintendents were appointed, and after their death or retirement the office was discontinued.

V. ELDERS AND DEACONS

The polity envisaged by Knox and his fellow reformers had various democratic elements. The people had a voice in the selection of ministers and were to have had a voice in the selection of superintendents. They were given additional responsibility for the governing of the church through the eldership and diaconate. This was another indication of the reformers' desire to restore the pristine simplicity of the primitive church, and it underscored their determination to bind the ministers and laypeople more closely together, bridging the chasm that separated the Catholic clergy from their flock. The ideal was leadership and order in unity.

The *Book of Discipline* specified that elders be elected annually by the congregation, with no limit on the successive number of terms as long as the freedom of the annual election was preserved.[62] The elders' responsibility was to assist the minister in governing the church, particularly with respect to the conduct of the members. The elders' scrutiny was also to be directed to the conduct of the minister, whom they had the power to admonish, correct, or, with the consent of the church and superintendent, depose. Annually an elder and a deacon were to report to the superintendents on the conduct of their minister. The life of the minister's family was also to be scrutinized, especially the manner in which they spent the stipend accorded them by the church. Ministers also had to be watched to see that they did not spend excessive time at the Royal Court or engage in local politics.[63] Knox and his friends were concerned lest the reformed ministry degenerate into a state like that which characterized much of the later medieval clergy and destroyed their spiritual effectiveness.

The eldership in the Kirk of Scotland was generally akin to that of the Geneva church. In Geneva, however, elders had to be members of one of the councils, which somewhat restricted the democratic implications of the office.[64] Furthermore, when the elders and ministers of Geneva sat as a court to deal with disciplinary cases, the court was not purely ecclesiastical but was a special branch of the city government. Calvin's personal preference for a purely ecclesiastical eldership was realized not in Geneva but in Scotland. Reformers in Switzerland and Germany had been interested in the eldership prior to Calvin, and it may be that Wishart instituted the eldership in the churches of the Dundee area during his ministry. In Edinburgh as well as Dundee and elsewhere, elders were definitely being used to help administer discipline by 1558, and were working with the minister at St. Andrews on the problem of alms no later than 1559. The authors of the *Book of Discipline* must have been satisfied with the results, for they regularized the practice for all Scottish churches in 1560.[65]

It has been remarked that Knox's reliance on the Lords of the Congregation and other laymen in reforming the Kirk of Scotland "launched the Reformed Church into a tradition which has meant an impressively large share of leadership being exercised by the elders in church courts."[66] Such claims for Knox are overstated, for there was substantial lay participation in the churches of the Reformed tradition on the Continent, as well as in the churches of the foreigners and the Puritans in England. Moreover, the tradition of the Scottish eldership was established in practice before Knox and his colleagues formalized it in the *Book of Discipline*. It is doubtful if Knox had any substantial influence on this aspect of ecclesiastical polity, except perhaps for the provisions relating to the disciplinary control of the elders, which may reflect the influence of the Reformed churches of France and thus may have been introduced in the Scottish Kirk through Knox.[67]

Deacons were to be elected annually, but had to wait three years before being elected again. Their responsibility was the handling of the financial affairs of the church, including the distribution of alms to the indolent. The rigid rules prescribed for their care of church funds was the outcome of the reformers' desire not to revert to the traditional mishandling of church property. Because such property belonged to the people, it had to be administered by their representatives according to their regulations. Deacons were allowed to assist the ministers and elders in administering discipline, and could serve as readers if qualified. Neither they nor the elders received monetary compensation for their endeavors. Both groups, however, were subject, with their families, to the same censure prescribed for the ministers.[68] Knox and his colleagues could not afford to tolerate laxity, idleness, immorality, or generally improper conduct at any level of church leadership. Not only were the biblical precepts of holiness and righteousness to be obeyed, but there was also the pragmatic consideration that the success of their movement with the people depended to a significant degree upon the ability of church officers to demonstrate their spiritual superiority to the Catholic clergy and their officials.

The procedure for the election of deacons in the Kirk of Scotland was patterned after the election of elders by Pullain's congregation. The duties assigned to the deacons were akin to those of the Reformed churches of France and perhaps reflect the influence of Knox's travel there.[69]

Certainly a study of the ministry and government of the reformed Kirk of Scotland underscores the fact that its polity, like its theology, was not merely a replica of Geneva. In polity the Kirk of Scotland owes a broad debt to the Reformed churches scattered throughout Europe.

CHAPTER
‡ FIVE ‡

THE SACRAMENTS

I. BAPTISM

In 1555 Knox left Geneva for Scotland, arriving about late September. Because Mary of Lorraine desired their political support, the Scottish Protestants were being treated well. That autumn, Knox preached in and around Edinburgh, and then spent the winter preaching in the West. His attacks on the mass and key Catholic doctrines resulted in a summons to appear before the Archbishop of St. Andrews and a special commission at Edinburgh in May 1556, but Mary's intervention resulted in a quashing of the summons. Knox nevertheless went to Edinburgh and preached for ten successive days, spurring the Protestant movement in the capital. Six weeks later, after a personal rebuff from the regent, he accepted the call of his Geneva congregation and returned to the Continent. It was probably during his 1555–56 sojourn in Scotland that he wrote his little tract on baptism, which was apparently intended for private circulation among his supporters.[1] Because his sermons had been a frontal assault on Catholicism, his followers were inquiring about the validity and efficacy of their baptism at the hands of the Catholic clergy. Knox's tract was primarily an answer to these queries.

At the outset of the tract[2] Knox made it known that he did not regard Catholic baptism as the true baptism initiated by Jesus. Catholic baptism was a profane, adulterated version of the pure original, and was therefore to be shunned by Christians. His reasons for this judgment were based on his conceptions of the sole authority of Scripture and the necessity of the conjunction of the preached Word with the sacraments. Catholic baptism did not preserve the original simplicity of Jesus' institution, and Knox refused to accept anything not expressly sanctioned by Scripture. In Catholic baptism "many thingis be addit, besydis Chrystis institutioun; and all manis additioun in Godis perfyt ordinance, especiallie in his religioun, ar execrable and detestable befoir him."[3] Moreover, the Catholic observance of baptism was not conjoined to the proclamation of the Word to enable the people to understand the meaning of the sacrament. Consequently the people were misled into placing their confidence in a ceremony rather than understanding the proper significance of the sacrament. Apart from these reasons, Knox also cited the Pauline admonition (1 Cor. 10:20−21) not to fellowship with unbelievers. Those who submitted their children to Catholic baptism were signifying their approbation of Catholic doctrine and fellowship with Catholics. In short, Knox accused such persons of offering their children to the devil.

Knox's position would seem to be *prima facie* evidence for requiring Protestants to be baptized again in Reformed churches, yet he followed the other Protestant reformers in repudiating the Anabaptist insistence on the need for new baptism. Arguing that the Holy Spirit purged true believers from the dross which they received in their Catholic baptism, he insisted that it was not the external sign of baptism that mattered but the faith of the believer, "for be faith, and not be externall signis doith God purge oure hartis. . . ."[4] By this faith God purged the impurities of the corrupt ceremony. It was now more important, Knox urged his followers, to manifest faith by a plain and continual confession than by undergoing another baptismal ceremony. He was also unwilling to discount the element of proper intent on the part of parents who had sincerely believed Catholic baptism to be valid, nor would he totally reject its validity, since it had been administered in the name of the Trinity. He admitted only that the adulterated form of Catholic baptism caused it to be of no "profit" to individuals, but this problem was altered by the Spirit's purging activity, making the original baptism efficacious without a repetition of the external ceremony.[5] Knox's position was thus consistent with his theology. The ceremony in itself meant relatively little, and without the working of the sovereign Spirit through electing grace it meant nothing.

Knox knew by personal experience that his followers were quick to draw two conclusions from his premises. Whereas some concluded that sacraments were practically unnecessary for the elect, others concluded that because of the inward working of the Spirit it made no difference whether a child was baptized in a Catholic or a Protestant church. Knox rejected both conclusions. In answer to the first contention, he retorted that no believer was so strong spiritually that he could ignore the divinely instituted means — the preaching of the Word and the right administration of the sacraments — to preserve him in the faith. He rejected the idea that baptism was necessary for salvation, but he asserted that it was the duty of a regenerate man to be baptized if he had not already been. Thus, people were to be baptized not so much because of what baptism did for them but because Christ commanded it. It is wrong, therefore, to place excessive emphasis on the sacraments in assessing Knox's theology. The role of the sacraments in the life of the Christian and the church was wholly based on what Knox believed to be their divine institution in the Word, which retained primacy. It is also inaccurate to argue that Knox emphasized the sacraments because of the role accorded to them in the modern Church of Scotland. More than one worthy scholar has fallen into the trap of attributing his own sacramental views to Knox.[6]

Both sacraments, Knox believed, were seals of "the justice of faith" and a profession to one's fellow human beings of belief in God.[7] The sacraments also attested one's fellowship in doctrine and community with others who shared in those sacraments, but care was to be had, Knox warned, not to attibute too much significance to the external sign, which was neither the cause nor the effect of virtue. Once received, the seal of baptism was not to be repeated lest the illuminating, regenerating, and purging of the Spirit associated with it be wrongly attributed to the external act itself. The Lord's Supper, on the other hand, had biblical precept to be repeated, and to violate that precept would be to reject the Word, the basis of Christianity.

According to Knox, baptism was the sign of regeneration and the elect's entrance into the Christian fellowship. It signified the acceptance of the believer into a covenant relationship with God. Baptism is a sign that believers "ar ressavit in league with him. . . ."[8] Acceptance into this league is a testimony that the recipient has been justified with the righteousness of Christ. Because both that righteousness and the covenant are permanent, the promise of mercy made in baptism can never be frustrated. Thus Knox concluded that it was not necessary to receive the sign of baptism more than once, which would imply that before rebaptism the individual was not justified and in league with God. This relationship could only be established once in life, after the first baptism, making any reiteration superfluous and misleading. Knox was careful in developing this argument not to involve himself in the enigmatical question of whether all who were baptized were in league with God and therefore elect. Logically he was not forced to adopt this position because of his emphasis on the inner working of the Spirit rather than the external sign, yet his words, taken literally, make it appear that he believed this. He would, of course, repudiate such a conclusion. Baptism could signify regeneration only if the recipient were elect and therefore justified.

A basic question of convenant theology in the late sixteenth and seventeenth centuries was whether the covenant made with God could be broken. Knox's Scottish followers put the question to him in the context of baptism. Some believed that the league could be broken and the benefits of Christ's righteousness lost; consequently they concluded that it was necessary to repeat the sacrament of baptism to restore the covenant relationship and its benefits. Knox, in reply, asserted the permanence of the league: once made, it could not be broken. Man's assurance of the covenant's continuity could be disturbed, but Knox would not accept a second baptism as a sign to reassure troubled consciences. "The iteratioun of baptisme is not the meane whilk God hath apoyntit to assure oure consciences that the league betwix God and us is permanent and sure."[9] Working through the Lord's Supper, it is the task of the Holy Spirit to provide reassurance. Participation in this sacrament is a visual manifestation of continuity in the league, and those who transgress from the godly path are restored through the fellowship of the table. They were also urged by Knox to study the meaning of their baptism — reception into the household of God through grace and mercy alone. Once, however, apostolic baptism as opposed to Catholic baptism was available, parents could not have their children subjected to the latter without running the considerable risk of being deprived of the benefits offered by God through proper baptism.

Two other aspects of Knox's thought on baptism indicate the rather strict view he took of the doctrine. The authors of the *Book of Common Prayer* authorized the baptism of children in private homes only when their lives were endangered: "The Pastors and Curates . . . shall warn them [the people] that, without great cause and necessity, they baptize not children at home in their houses."[10] Knox evinced some displeasure with this practice, probably at least partly because he did not believe baptism was essential for salvation, because he opposed baptism by women (including emergency baptism by midwives), and because of the importance he attached to the baptismal service in the church. His position is noted by Bishop Nicholas Ridley in a letter to Bishop Grindal in 1555:

> As for private Baptism, it is not prescribed in the Book; but where solemn Baptism, for lack of time and danger of death, cannot be had, what would he in that case should be done? Peradventure, he will say, It is better then to let them dye without Baptism. For this his 'better,' what word hath he in the Scripture? And if he have none, why will he not rather follow that that the sentences of the old ancient writers do more allow? from whom, to dissent without warrant of God's Word, I cannot think it any godly wisdom.[11]

According to Jaspar Ridley, Knox's opposition to private baptism was an original contribution to sixteenth-century theology,[12] but such is not the case. Pullain and probably Calvin rejected the tradition of private baptism that can be traced back to Cyprian and Augustine. Knox apparently was influenced on this point by Calvin, for it was at Frankfurt that he began manifesting some displeasure with this practice.[13]

Knox did not agree with Calvin on another matter relating to baptism. In August 1559 Knox wrote to Calvin inquiring whether the bastard children of idolaters and excommunicated persons should be baptized. Knox's position was negative, but he was criticized on this point by Catholics and Protestants alike. Calvin had taken a similar position to Knox's in the *Institutes*, but his reply to Knox urged the Scottish reformer to allow such children to be baptized if they had suitable sponsors who would promise to provide them with a Christian education. Calvin's justification was basically one of expedience: the practice of using sponsors in baptism was to continue "while better progress is expected."[14] Once again this reflects Knox's more radical application of the principle of express scriptural sanction in religious matters.

Knox's stricter position enabled the church to use baptism as a tool of discipline. Errant parents could be brought to heel by refusing their child baptism until they conformed. Despite the fact that all parents were required to present their children for baptism, a Reformed minister was not compelled to baptize those presented if they were disqualified. Calvin's position, however, undercut the use of baptism as a disciplinary tool by permitting the use of sponsors. Even more lenient was Calvin's belief that infants should be baptized even if they are only the progeny of holy and pious ancestors "a thousand generations" ago. Intervening apostasy in the ancestral line would not abrogate "the perpetual covenant of God."[15] Quite apart from the impossibility of tracing ancestry as far as Calvin would permit (thus making a sham of the whole concept), his position destroys the nexus between baptism and faith which Knox at least attempted to maintain more substantially. The *Book of Discipline*, it might be added, notes that "if any think it severe that the child should be punished for the iniquity of the father, let them understand that the sacraments appertain only to the faithful and to their seed. . . ."[16]

There is another example of some strictness in Knox's attitude toward godparents in baptism. From the writings of Ninian Winzet it appears that the Scottish reformers initially allowed the presence of both godfathers and godmothers: "Quhy half ze godmotheris in the beginning, and now repellis the samin?"[17] The *Book of Discipline* allowed a mother or godly friend to present a child for baptism if the father was impenitent.[18] During his Genevan pastorate, however, it appears that Knox began to feel doubts even about the use of godfathers. Toward the end of the list of baptisms "witnesse" replaces godfather. This is true, for example, of the baptism of Knox's second son, Eleazer, on November 29, 1558, when Coverdale was the witness. It may be that Knox influenced Mrs. Anne Locke on this subject, for at the baptism of her child in the parish of Bow, Cheapside, London, on February 12, 1561, there was no godfather or godmother. Nevertheless the more moderate position taken in *The Forme of Prayers and Ministration of the Sacraments* prevailed in the reformed Kirk of Scotland, which specified the use of godfathers but not godmothers. This was in keeping with Calvin's position. *The Draft Ecclesiastical Ordinances* of September and October 1541 specify the use of godparents, but the *Ordinances for the Supervision of Churches in the Country* of February 1547 mention only godfathers.'[19]

The coauthored *Scots Confession* depicts baptism as a divinely instituted sacrament which demarcates those within and those without the league with God. Baptism was said to exercise the faith of the elect and seal in their hearts the assurance of the divine promise of salvation and of union with Christ. It is not simply a naked and bare sign. "By Baptism we are ingrafted in Christ Jesus to be made partakers of his justice, by the which our sins are covered and remitted. . . ."[20] It has often been remarked that the teaching of the *Confession* on baptism reflects Calvin's influence, and certainly there is nothing in the *Confession* on baptism that Calvin could not have said. One could also say the same of Bullinger.[21]

It is difficult to trace the antecedents of Knox's doctrine of baptism, for he has left little indication of his views on the subject prior to 1556. It is therefore virtually impossible to ascertain whether or not there were any differences between his pre- and post-Genevan thoughts on baptism. The *First Helvetic Confession* defined both sacraments as tokens of secret, godly, and spiritual things, and repudiated the idea that they were naked signs, insisting that they were tokens of "sygnes and verities together."[22] The repudiation in the *Scots Confession* of sacraments as mere naked signs[23] is thus hardly conclusive evidence of Calvinist influence, for the *First Helvetic Confession* had earlier made the same point in Scotland. The *First Helvetic Confession* also taught that the sacraments were signs of grace and badges of Christian society. The *language* of the twenty-first article, which deals specifically with baptism, is nevertheless markedly different from that of Knox's baptismal tract and the *Scots Confession*:

> We affyrme Baptym to be by the institucion of the Lorde, the lauer of regeneracion, the whiche regeneracion the Lorde exhibiteth to his chosen by a visible sygne by the ministracion of the congregacion, as is aforesayde. In the which holy lauer we wasshe oure infantes, for this cause, because it is wyckednes to rejecte and cast out of the felowshyp and company of the people of God them that are borne of us, whiche are the people of God, excepte them that are expressely commaunded to be rejected by the voyce of God; and for this cause chefely, bycause we shulde not presume ungodly of theyr election.[24]

To this can be added Wishart's belief in the importance of getting believers to understand what is promised to God in the name of the infant in baptism. Apparently Knox's view of baptism was influenced at the outset of his reforming career by Wishart and the *First Helvetic Confession*. There is also the possibility that he could have been influenced by the *Shorter Catechism* of Leo Jud, Zwingli's colleague at Zürich. Certainly Knox was using a catechism at the St. Andrews castle in 1547, and that catechism was probably either Jud's, which he could have received from Wishart, or, less likely, a Lutheran catechism that could have been given to him by Thomas Gilyem.[25]

While preaching in the Edwardian church Knox believed that the sacraments were instituted by Christ in the church "for sealing up and better memorye to be had of those benefitts, that we have resaived by the communion that we have with Christ Jesus in his bodye and bloode."[26] This sounds very much like the doctrine evinced in the baptismal tract of 1556 and the *Scots Confession*, hence there appears to be a continuous development of Knox's doctrine of baptism from his conversion through the Genevan period and into the 1560s. When, in December 1565, the General Assembly discussed the doctrine of baptism, it reflected the position asserted by Knox in his 1557 tract. Catholic baptism was not to be reiterated, and when children came of age, they were to be rightly instructed about baptism. The Assembly also noted something that is stressed in Calvin's writings, namely, that the Holy Spirit "makes baptisme to work in us be proper effects thereof, without any declaration of the externall signe."[27] Calvin's *Catechism* stated that "the efficacie of the Sacraments doeth not consiste in the visible signe, but wholly in the working of the Spirite of God."[28]

One other aspect of Knox's doctrine of baptism requires notice: his discussion of baptism in conjunction with the league or covenant with God. Zwingli had done this in his defense of paedobaptism, for he was more concerned with man's responsibility to fulfill the obligations of the covenant than with the sacramental importance of baptism as a covenant seal. "They who do not keep the covenant glory in the symbols in vain."[29] Bullinger too developed the notion of the covenant in relationship to infant baptism. Baptism enrolls the infant in the covenant, the signs and seals of which are the two sacraments. The following passage from Bullinger's *Fifth Decade* blends very well with the views expressed in Knox's baptismal tract:

> As in making leagues, or in confirming promises in earnest and weighty matters, men use signs or tokens of truth, to win credit to their words and promises; even so the Lord, doing after the manner of men, hath added signs of his faithfulness and truth in his everlasting covenant and promises of life; the sacraments, I mean, wherewith he sealeth his promises and the very doctrine of his gospel.[30]

Usually Bullinger's concept of the covenant emphasizes man's reciprocal responsibility, but here he sounds not only like Knox but also like Calvin, who conceives of the covenant as God's promises and the sacraments as tokens of these promises.[31]

While it is probable that Knox's view of the relationship of the covenant or league and baptism is at least partly due to the influence of Continental theology (notably the views of Bullinger and Calvin), there is a distinct possibility that he was led in this direction by English sources. William Tyndale, one of the early English Lutherans,[32] closely associated the covenant with baptism. Copies of his *Briefe Declaration of the Sacraments* (1536?) were circulating in Edwardian England, and Knox may have read one. For Tyndale, sacraments were signs of the covenant divinely instituted in order to stir up faith in the participants, but they were also seals of the obligations which the faithful were to perform and to which they were bound by the covenant. The sacraments served "to keep the promises and covenants better in mind, and to make them the more deep sink into our hearts, and to be more earnestly regarded."[33] Coverdale, incidentally, was influenced by Tyndale's views,[34] and may well have discussed them with Knox in Geneva, especially since Knox selected him as the witness for the baptism of his second son.

Knox's doctrine of baptism was thus developed against the background of the thought of Wishart, the *First Helvetic Confession*, Bullinger, Calvin, Tyndale, and perhaps such others as John Hooper and John à Lasco. (The latter's views on the sacraments, which reflect Swiss teaching, were published in London in 1552, in the *Brevis et dilucida de Sacramentis Ecclesiae Christi Tractatio*.)[35]

II. THE LORD'S SUPPER

The richness of the sources of influence on the thought of John Knox is rarely manifested as clearly as in his doctrine of the Lord's Supper. He was exposed to a variety of Protestant concepts of this sacrament early in his career. Lutheran views were propagated in Scotland,[36] though there is no evidence that the Lutheran doctrine of the Lord's Supper was ever accepted by Knox. In fact, Knox specifically states in his *History of the Reformation in Scotland* that the first communion service he celebrated at St. Andrews in 1547 was exactly the same as that he was celebrating in the 1560s. "Not only all those of the Castle, but also a great number of the town, openly professed, by participation of the Lord's Table, in the same purity that now it is ministered in the churches of Scotland, with that same doctrine that he [Knox] had taught unto them."[37] This indicates that the catechism he used at St. Andrews was not a Lutheran one, for all his existing doctrinal statements oppose the Lutheran interpretation of the Real Presence in the Eucharist.

Knox could have had contact with Zwinglian views through Leo Jud's *Shorter Catechism*, perhaps given to Knox by Wishart, or the writings of Oecolampadius. Oecolampadius was being read in Scotland as early as 1540, and in 1558 Quintin Kennedy, Abbot of Crossraguel, wrote of Oecolampadius as a man "quhais opinioun men in thir dayis praysis sua hichlie. . . ."[38] Yet Knox did not accept the Zwinglian doctrine of the sacrament, at least in his published writings. His views instead reflect the doctrine of the Lord's Supper set forth in the *First Helvetic Confession*, which was translated and taken to Scotland by Goerge Wishart.

Wishart, born around 1513, had been educated at Louvain before returning to Scotland to teach the Greek New Testament at Montrose. He was charged with heresy and fled to England. He appears in the old Lollard center of Bristol in 1539, allegedly teaching that Christ could not merit salvation for man. For such teaching he was again charged with heresy and forced to recant. Thomas Cromwell (who assisted other Scottish Protestants) apparently helped him make his way to the Continent, where he traveled in Germany and Switzerland. It was during this sojourn on the Continent that he became acquainted with the *First Helvetic Confession*. In 1543 he was at Corpus Christi, Cambridge, but returned to Scotland around 1544. His remaining years were spent preaching in Dundee, Ayr, Kyle, Mauchline, Perth, Leith, and Haddington — areas likely to be receptive to Protestant teaching. Knox joined him in Lothian, listened to him preach, very likely discoursed with him on theological matters, studied his manuscript of the *First Helvetic Confession* (first published, apparently, in 1548), and was with him just prior to his apprehension in January 1546. (Wishart was martyred on March 1, 1546.)[39]

The *Confession* which Wishart brought to Scotland had been drafted in 1536 by Heinrich Bullinger, Leo Jud, Oswald Myconius, and Gaspard Grossmann, all of Zürich, and Simon Grynaeus of Basle. The conferences requesting and approving the *Confession* were held at Basle in February and March of that year. Although Calvin was in Basle early in 1536, he did not take part in drafting the *Confession*. Martin Bucer and Wolfgang Capito of Strasbourg arrived in Basle in time to influence the final draft of the *Confession*. As a result of their influence the wording of the article on the Lord's Supper was altered in order to make it less offensive to Luther. The other theologians agreed, but on the condition that they could interpret the article in accordance with their own beliefs. When Wishart saw this *Confession* he was possibly impressed by its ecumenical nature, particularly the attempt to bridge the gulf between the Reformed and the Lutherans on the Lord's Supper. It is, however, erroneous to associate the *Confession* with Calvinism.[40] It is a compromise of the views of Bucer and Bullinger (who did the compromising), with an eye to concord with the Lutherans. It also prepared the way for the 1549

Consensus Tigurinus, which brought the churches of Zürich and Geneva together.[41]

Bucer in the 1530s believed that Christ was truly present in the Lord's Supper by faith. The bread and wine exist unchanged, but Christ is equally there, though not physically and not mingled naturally with the elements. "It is one Christ who is always present to all believers and is their food. But it especially belongs to this sacrament that in it the gospel is really preached, the death of Christ is proclaimed, with the sacraments as seals of the promise of God, the body and blood of Christ are equally visibly presented and thereby faith is awakened. . . ."[42]

The bread and wine are not mere symbols. Christ is undoubtedly present and is spiritually eaten by the communicant who receives him worthily and with faith through the work of the Holy Spirit. *Only* believers feed on the body and blood of Christ. The relationship between Christ and the elements is a sacramental union which the human understanding cannot comprehend. Bucer subsequently opposed the notion that Christ could not be present in the Lord's Supper because he was in heaven. Yet neither did Christ leave heaven, though he is "now truly present to us by faith; even as the sun, in whatever part of the world we behold him, is truly present to us by sight."[43] The emphasis in Bucer's doctrine is on the inner working of the Spirit through faith, for it is by faith that Christ is present and by faith that his body is fed on. When the sacrament is received by faith, the bread is a communication of Christ's body, the wine a communication of his blood. This communion with Christ, Bucer emphasized in the 1530s, also involves a communion with fellow believers, uniting them together in divine love.

Calvin's view is close to that of Bucer. For Calvin the symbols of bread and wine are means through which spiritual good is communicated to men. Professor Brian Gerrish has called this view "symbolic instrumentalism."[44] It could also apply to Bucer. Like Bucer, Calvin believes Christ is really present in the sacrament. He is not present corporeally but by a "secret communication" (*arcana communicatio*). He is present in the act of believing, through the work of the Holy Spirit, and through the Word. The Supper for Calvin is a gift of Christ bestowed through the signs by the Holy Spirit to all who communicate. Yet although Christ's body is offered to all, only believers eat it spiritually. The faithful are nourished and sustained in their communion with Christ. But Calvin, unlike Bucer, held that in the sacrament believers enjoyed the presence of Christ because the Spirit lifted them to heaven. At the same time he modified this idea by using the sun, like Bucer, to illustrate Christ's presence: "If we see that the sun, shedding its beams upon the earth, casts its substance in some measure upon it in order to beget, nourish, and give growth to its offspring — why should the radiance of Christ's Spirit be less in order to impart to us the communion of his flesh and blood?" So Calvin could also say that "Christ descends to us both by the outward symbol and by his Spirit. . . ."[45] The closeness of Calvin's views to those of Bucer explains why previous historians have argued either that Knox was a Calvinist as early as 1547 with respect to the Lord's Supper, or that his statement in the *History of the Reformation in Scotland* about the continuity of his doctrine and practice was a mistake. In fact it was neither. The continuity in Knox's doctrine of the Lord's Supper is due to the early influence on him of Bucer's views through the medium of Wishart and the *First Helvetic Confession*.[46]

The twenty-second chapter of the *Confession*, influenced mostly by Bucer and translated by Wishart, explained the "sacrament of the aulter" as a mystical supper in which Christ offers his body and blood to his faithful, "for this entent he myghte lyue more and more in them, and they in hym." The body and blood are not "communed naturally to the bread and wyne, or closed in them as in one place; or put in them by any carnal or meruelous presence. . . ." The body and blood must be received by faith. Zürich influence is reflected in the statement that the bread and wine are tokens by which "the very communion or participacyon of the Lordes body and blode are exhibited of the Lorde himselfe . . ." as nourishment and refreshment for eternal life. The sacrament provides "spiritual lyuynge and eternall foode" so that "we all and whole are effused with all our power and strength. . . ."[47] Like Zwingli, the authors of the *Confession* believed that the Lord's Supper symbolized and commemorated the death of Christ, moved believers to give thanks, and bound them by loyalty to Christ and fellow members of the church. Unlike Zwingli, however, they also believed that this sacrament is the means by which God gives what he promises. The significant parts of the article are those which reflect the true presence of Christ and the eating of his body. This is as far as Bullinger was willing to go.[48]

Bullinger's own doctrine of the Lord's Supper has been described by Professor Gerrish as "symbolic parallelism." The emphasis is on the symbols as testimonies that a spiritual occurrence is taking place simultaneously with the physical eating of the elements. Christ is truly present, though not corporeally. Outwardly the believer partakes of bread and wine; inwardly he eats the body and blood of Christ. The faithful eat the elements; "*at the same time* by the work of Christ through the Holy Spirit they also inwardly receive the flesh and blood of the Lord. . . ." Bullinger views the sacrament primarily as a present communion rather than the remembrance of something past. The element of recollection is indeed present, but at least equally important is the idea that in the Supper believers have communion with Christ.[49] By "communion" Bullinger means "the society, conjunction, or partaking of the Lord Christ, by the which through his Spirit he doth wholly knit and join himself to us, and we are made partakers of him by faith. . . ." Bullinger places great emphasis on the *spiritual* presence of Christ, and is reluctant to say any more than that this presence is the same apart from the Supper as in the Supper. He too uses the sun as an illustration: "The sun, which is absent from us in the heavens, is notwithstanding effectually present among us. How much more is the Sun of Righteousness, Christ, although in his body he is absent from us in heaven, present with us, not corporeally, but spiritually. . . ."[50] Bullinger is saying rather less[51] than Calvin, who uses the same illustration to indicate the more substantial impartation of Christ's body and blood to the faithful. Bullinger also used the illustration of the sun in the *Second Helvetic Confession*, which he authored. In this *Confession* he taught a sacramental union of sign and reality, while retaining his symbolic parallelism. Believers eat bread outwardly and, simultaneously, eat Christ's body inwardly. But Bullinger did not go as far as Calvin; the outward event did not convey, cause, or give rise to the inward occurrence, but indicated that it was transpiring. Thus in 1566 Knox and the Kirk of Scotland approved Bullinger's doctrine of the Lord's Supper when they sanctioned the *Second Confession*.[52]

Knox's first major statement of the Lord's Supper appeared in his 1550 *Summary, according to the Holy Scriptures, of the Lord's Supper*. In 1549 – 50 he had been preaching in northern England, directing most of his sermons against the mass. His diocesan bishop was Cuthbert Tunstall, Bishop of Durham and Catholic in his theological sympathies. In April 1550 Knox was summoned to appear before the Council of the North at Newcastle to answer for his attacks on the mass and his rejection of the doctrine of transubstantiation. It was in connection with this defense that he probably composed the *Summary* of his doctrine of the Lord's Supper. That *Summary*, coupled with the evidence in his *History*, indicates that he never accepted the Lutheran doctrine of consubstantiation. With respect to the Lord's Supper, from the outset of his Protestantism he adopted a viewpoint akin to that of Bucer and Bullinger, as expressed in the *First Helvetic Confession*. He was basically unconcerned with pursuing the minor doctrinal divergencies between those positions, conserving his energy for the more fundamental task of repudiating the mass and its concomitant doctrines.

In his *Summary* of the doctrine of the Lord's Supper,[53] Knox began by asserting the Supper's divine ordination and use of visual elements to enable the believer to be lifted up "unto hevinlie and invisibill thingis. And that when he [Christ] had prepareit his spirituall banket, he witnessit that he him self was the lyvelie bread, whairwith our saullis be fed unto everlasting lyfe." Partaking of the visual elements is a confirmation and seal of the divine promise of salvation and communion, manifesting God's gifts to his elect. Christ himself is present and is spiritually eaten in the sacrament, but must be received by faith; there is no transubstantiation. He "giveth unto us him self, to be receaveit with faith, and not with mouth, nor yit by transfusioun of substance." Through the work of the Spirit the believer, "being fed with his flesche, and refrescheit with his blude, may be renewit both unto trew godlines and to immortalitie." There is also, as Bucer stressed, a strong element of fellowship on the horizontal level in the Lord's Supper. The sacrament binds believers together in a visual band or covenant under the sole headship of Christ. It reminds believers of the sacrifice of Christ that made this possible, and assures them of Christ's promise to preserve his elect.

The Lord's Supper binds believers together in a covenant of mutual love, manifesting their common faith and doctrine. None but believers are to participate, for the Lord's Supper is a seal and confirmation of faith as well as of the divine promise.

Knox condemned Catholics for stressing the importance of transubstantiation. What mattered was not Christ's presence in the bread and wine but his presence in believers through faith. "For it is not his presence in the bread that can save us, but his presence in our hartis through faith in his blude. . . ." Scripture reports Christ as saying, "This is my body," hence Christians must accept this statement. Nevertheless, according to Knox, Christ spoke these words in a sacramental, not a literal sense. Christ is present in the elements spiritually, not physically. "For in the Sacrament we receave Jesus Chryst spirituallie, as did the Fatheris of the Old Testament, according to St Paulis saying [1 Cor. 11]. And yf men wald weill wey, how that Chryst, ordeyning this Halie Sacrament of his bodie and blude, spak theis wordis Sacramentallie, doutless thai wold never so grosslie and foolischlie understand thame. . . ." Knox called not only on the Apostle Paul to support his assertion, but also on such patristic fathers as Augustine, Jerome, and Origen.[54]

In the same year that Knox's brief tract on the Lord's Supper was written, John Hooper and John à Lasco in England were opposing the practice of kneeling during the Lord's Supper. Preaching the Lenten sermons (with John Ponet) before Edward VI and his Council, Hooper, a disciple of Bullinger, castigated kneeling as a sign of worshiping the elements. Since "heretofore hath grievous and damnable idolatry been committed by the honouring of the sacrament, I would wish it were commanded by the magistrates, that the communicators and receivers should do it standing or sitting." His preference was sitting inasmuch as "the Paschal lamb was eaten standing, which signified Christ yet not to be come, that should give rest, peace, and quietness." Moreover, Christ and his disciples had eaten sitting at the Last Supper.[55] In the fall of 1550, à Lasco wrote to Thomas Cranmer, objecting to kneeling because the Last Supper was partaken sitting and because sitting declared the believer's rejection of idolatry and symbolized his rest in Christ.[56]

Like à Lasco and Hooper, Knox preferred sitting during

the Lord's Supper. If his testimony in the *History* is correct, he followed this practice from the beginning, in which case the views of Hooper and à Lasco would have done no more than reinforce his opinion. In any case his English congregations sat rather than kneeled. This was not illegal inasmuch as the *First Book of Common Prayer* did not stipulate kneeling during the Lord's Supper, though it was assumed that this would be the practice. The proposed *Second Book of Common Prayer*, however, stipulated that the sacrament be received kneeling. Knox preached before Edward at Windsor in September 1552, objecting to the rubric requiring kneeling. Hooper and à Lasco were in agreement, but Cranmer, Nicholas Ridley, and Peter Martyr, a disciple of Bucer, were opposed to Knox's views.[57] The Council, however, considered Knox's arguments sufficiently noteworthy to request Cranmer to reconsider the issue with Ridley and Peter Martyr. Cranmer responded quickly, arguing that Knox's contention that nothing be commanded without express scriptural warrant was the error of the Anabaptists and other sectaries.[58] "For what should men travail to set an order in the form of service, if no order can be set but that is already prescribed by the Scripture?" Besides, Cranmer argued, Scripture did not specify standing, kneeling, or sitting at the Last Supper, and the prevailing custom of the time was to eat lying on the ground.[59]

After reading Cranmer's letter to the Council, Knox renewed his arguments. Despite the fact that kneeling was an indifferent matter, it tolerated idolatrous worship, offended the consciences of weak Christians, and comforted Catholics. Kneeling was a gesture of grief and supplication, not thanksgiving; it did not symbolize the believer's rest in Christ—a point also made by Hooper and à Lasco. Primarily due to Knox's contentions, the Black Rubric was drawn up, probably by Cranmer or Peter Martyr.[60] Kneeling was retained, but it was expressly stated that this gesture did not imply adoration of the elements or "any real and essential presence there being of Christ's natural flesh and blood." Kneeling signified only "the humble and grateful acknowledging of the benefits of Christ given unto the worthy receiving, and to avoid the profanation and disorder which about the Holy Communion might else ensue. . . ."[61] The Council ordered the rubric affixed to the *Book of Common Prayer* and gave Knox a payment of £40.[62]

Neither Parliament nor Convocation was requested to sanction the rubric. Dr. Weston of Lincoln College later referred to the incident in testimony before Hugh Latimer: "A runagate Scot did take away the adoration or worshipping of Christ in the sacrament, by whose procurement that heresy was put into the last Communionbook: so much prevailed that one man's authority at that time."[63]

Approval of the *Second Book of Common Prayer* with its mandatory kneeling put Knox in an awkward situation. He had taught his congregation at Berwick that kneeling was wrong, but the state now required kneeling. He believed in obedience to the state in all matters not contrary to God's commands. The matter did not, however, seem serious enough to advocate disobedience to the state. Knox wrote to his Berwick congregation, reaffirming his earlier opposition to kneeling. Kneeling, he reminded them, was often associated with superstition, that is, the adoration of the Real Presence in the physical sense. Kneeling was also not commanded in Scripture, and therefore could not be sanctioned. Yet Scripture also required obedience to magistrates, who now commanded kneeling at communion. To refuse their order would disrupt the unity of the church, which Knox said he wished to avoid. Despite his belief in the unity of scriptural principles, Knox was forced to choose between two of those principles, for both could not be simultaneously obeyed. He deferred to the magistrates as the wisest course, but clearly on biblical grounds. Kneeling would therefore be acceptable, but only on three conditions: First, it had to be made clear that kneeling did not imply adoration of the elements, and was only a temporary requirement to preserve order in the Church of England. Second, it had to be recognized that kneeling was not stipulated by Jesus, but was adopted by men as a ceremony thought to be good. Third, Knox wanted it made absolutely clear that he was in no way responsible for the rubric requiring kneeling. Having satisfied his conscience, he informed his congregation to comply with the new regulations.[64]

Three years later Knox dealt, in action if not in words, with the relationship of the administration of the Lord's Supper to the establishment of an organized church. James McEwen, in his Croall Lectures, developed the thesis that Knox believed the visible church was founded on the sacrament of the Lord's Supper.

"None in the Reformed world made the Sacrament basic for the Church itself, as Knox did." McEwen argued that in Knox's stress on the sacraments, particularly the Lord's Supper, he departed significantly from Calvin. McEwen did not overlook the importance of the Word in Knox's theology, but argued that Knox made the Scottish Kirk a church of the table as well as of the Word. The church was founded on the Word and sacraments together, not the Word alone.[65] Lord Percy earlier made the same point, regarding Knox's achievement as his making the Lord's Supper the central act of Christian worship and the Kirk of Scotland "a Eucharistic Church."[66] Percy and McEwen are correct in perceiving some difference between Knox and Calvin concerning the Lord's Supper; nevertheless, care must be taken not to overemphasize this difference by elevating the Lord's Supper to a position that Knox would have repudiated.

Knox's activities during his travels throughout Scotland in 1555–56 and his visit to Kyle in 1562 are used to support the contention that he placed extraordinary emphasis on the sacraments. During these travels he preached at numerous private residences, including those of the Earl of Glencairn and Dun Castle. McEwen contends that Knox was administering the sacraments without waiting for the establishment of organized kirks, thus supporting his argument that Knox believed the church was founded on the sacraments.[67] Percy, on the other hand, argues that Knox organized churches during the course of his travels, in large measure to restore the correct observance of the Lord's Supper.[68] Jasper Ridley recently found in Knox's actions far more than theological significance: Knox's "new communion service, at which everyone sat together with the minister around a table, and which was so unlike the mass, was not only a symbol of unity among the congregation; it was the method by which Knox was forming the first national political party in modern history."[69] There is an element of truth in each of these positions.

Knox did not administer the sacraments to a body he did not believe was part of the kirk. The church was at once visible and invisible. The former was not rigidly constructed. There were three signs by which it could be recognized: the preaching of the Word, the right administration of the sacraments, and the enforcement of ecclesiastical discipline. But a church also existed, as

Jesus had proclaimed, wherever two or three believers were gathered together to worship. When Knox administered the sacraments during his travels in 1555—56, he *was* administering them to visible kirks. His congregations were, at least for the most part, believers, and he was proclaiming the Word and administering the sacraments. Only ecclesiastical discipline was lacking. In this sense one cannot speak of the sacraments being the foundation of the visible church. Both had to exist simultaneously, and both were grounded on the Word. Where the Word was preached and the sacraments were rightly administered, there the visible church existed.

Knox differed from most of his fellow reformers in administering the sacraments before establishing an *organized* visible church. Calvin, for example, recommended that the Huguenots delay instituting the celebration of the Lord's Supper until they had organized their churches in an orderly manner.[70] Knox had no time for this in 1555—56. Knox certainly did not underestimate the value of an organized kirk. Neither did he equate that value with the underlying reality of the church as a body of believers gathered to hear the Word and receive the sacraments. In essence, Knox did not absolutely equate the visible church with the organized church. The latter was obviously visible, but there was also a visible church which could totally lack the elements of ecclesiasticism. It was not until Knox's visible kirks of 1555—56 became organized kirks that he added the element of discipline as a necessary mark. The significance of Knox's position, however briefly it was expressed, was that visible churches could exist where ecclesiasticism was absent. Knox had broken through centuries of stultifying ecclesiasticism to return to the simple experience of spiritual worship shared by Jesus and his disciples — but the breakthrough was only momentary.

Approximately six years after he wrote his short tract on the Lord's Supper, Knox replied to some questions on baptism, eating animal blood, and tithes. In the course of his remarks on baptism he made passing references to the Lord's Supper. As sacraments "besyd uthir ussis and endis, ar ordeynit to be seallis of the justice of faith, sa ar thai also a declaratioun of oure professioun befoir the warld, and ane approbatioun of that doctrine and religioun, which is taught be sic as with whome we communicat, in ressaving the sacramentis." In the Lord's Supper believers profess "that we ar the houshald of God. . . , receavit in the league of his mercie. . . ," hence "espresselie in his word [he] setteth befoir us the bread of lyfe whilk discendit fra the heavin, to assure our consciences. . ." of his immutable love toward his elect.[71] There is nothing here that would indicate Calvin's influence, though such influence was exerted on Knox's views on baptism by this date. Neither, of course, is there anything in these few remarks about the Lord's Supper that Calvin could not accept. In the same year (1556) that these statements were made, Knox was admitted to membership in and elected a minister of the English congregation at Geneva. This church used the *Order of Service* drafted the previous year by Knox and four colleagues at Frankfurt. It did not use Calvin's *La Forme*, though the *Order of Geneva* (properly *The Forme of Prayers and Ministration of the Sacraments*) was, of course, approved by Calvin, and owed much to him. In this sense, Knox therefore begins to reflect Calvin's influence on his concept of the Lord's Supper.

When Knox and his fellow ministers drafted the *Scots Confession* in 1560, they depicted the Lord's Supper as a divinely instituted sacrament to demarcate those within the league (or covenant) with God, to exercise the faith of the believers, and to seal in their hearts the assurance of the divine promise and union with Christ. The Lord's Supper was not a naked sign. It has usually been assumed that the Scottish reformers were attaching Zwingli on this point, but they were more likely repudiating Abbot Quintin Kennedy's conception of extreme Protestant teaching on the Lord's Supper.[72] Knox and his fellow reformers believed that in the Lord's Supper Christ was so joined with the faithful communicants that he became food for their souls. Transubstantiation was repudiated. The union and communion which they experienced with the body and blood of Christ was wrought by the Holy Spirit, who made it possible to feed spiritually on Christ's body. Like Bucer and Calvin, the Scottish reformers emphasized the idea of communion with the body and blood. "The faithful, in the right use of the Lord's Table, so do eat the body, and drink the blood of the Lord Jesus, that He remaineth in them and they in Him: yea, that they are so made flesh of his flesh, and bone of his bones, that as the Eternal Godhead hath given to the flesh of

Christ Jesus . . . life and immortality, so doth Christ Jesus his flesh and blood eaten and drunken by us, give us the same prerogatives." The reformers were careful to distinguish between Christ in his natural substance and the elements in the sacramental signs.[73]

The authors of the *Confession* stop just short of Calvin's symbolic instrumentalism, and appear to reflect the Bucer-Bullinger compromise worked out in the *First Helvetic Confession*. Eating the bread and wine is a mystical action for believers if the sacrament is rightly administered. It will bring forth fruit, as good seed sown on fertile ground. This does not necessarily occur simultaneously, however, for if the faithful are "oppressed by negligence, and manly infirmity" they will profit less than they should, though the full benefits will ultimately become theirs because the Holy Spirit "will not frustrate the faithful of the fruit of that mystical action." The benefits of this mystical action — life and immortality — are not given to the elect "at that only time, neither yet by the proper power and virtue of the Sacraments only. . . ." The Spirit plays a key role, for it is the Spirit's operation that enables the faithful to have union and communion with the body and blood of Christ when the sacrament is rightly administered. Care is taken to state that the spiritual feeding on the body and blood of Christ takes place in heaven, where the Spirit "by true faith carries us . . . and makes us to feed. . . ."[74]

With respect to the administration of the Lord's Supper, the ideal of Knox and his colleagues was the practice of the primitive church. Thus they favored the frequent administration of the sacrament. In 1561, when Knox was ministering to his congregation in Edinburgh, he once held communion services daily for a week. Yet just three years later such services were held only when nobility were in the town.[75] Knox's preference for frequent celebrations is akin to Luther's feelings, for the German reformer preferred weekly communion. Calvin was of the same mind, though the Geneva *Ordinances* prescribe only monthly celebration in Geneva and quarterly celebration in the outlying parishes. (The Genevan Council, however, would accept only quarterly celebration.) The English reformers also preferred weekly communion, though the laxity of the people forced the church in the *Second Book of Common Prayer* to require the laity to attend communion at least three times a year. In populous parishes it was celebrated monthly, but only quarterly in other parishes. Unlike Luther, Calvin, Knox, and the English reformers, Zwingli believed only in the quarterly celebration of the supper, at Easter, Whitsun, Autumn, and Christmas.[76] Clearly Knox was in sharp disagreement with Zwinglian practice on this point.

Knox was unable to have the Lord's Supper celebrated as frequently as he desired. When he returned to Scotland from the Continent in 1559 he brought with him the *Order of Geneva*. Before this, Scottish Protestants had used the *Second Book of Common Prayer* (which indeed continued to be used in some kirks as late as the 1570s).[77] *The Genevan Order*, adopted for use in Scotland in 1562 as the *Book of Common Order*, recommended monthly celebrations. The *Book of Discipline*, however, specified only quarterly celebrations, and an act of the General Assembly in December 1562 required only semiannual celebrations in the country kirks. Yet as late as 1565 the Assembly determined to try and censure ministers "for not ministring the communioun for six yeeres bypast. . . ."[78] This is the kind of abuse for which Protestant writers, both contemporary and modern, have castigated the Catholics, yet there is ample evidence of corruption in the reformed Kirk of Scotland. The shortage of ministers is not the only reason for Knox's failure to have the Lord's Supper celebrated frequently in Scotland. It might also be noted that even in Edinburgh between 1560 and 1564, the Supper was normally celebrated only triennially.[79]

Knox and his colleagues emphasized the importance of preparation before partaking of the sacrament. The sacrament had to be conjoined with a sermon of exhortation. "Wher Christ Jesus is not preached," Knox wrote to Mrs. Anne Locke in 1559, "(marke well that I say, preached), that there hath the Sacrament neither life nor soule. . . ."[80] The *Book of Discipline* likewise required the plain instruction of the people prior to the administration of either sacrament. No one could be admitted to the Lord's Supper who had not heard this exhortation.[81] In conjunction with this practice the Scottish reformers also instituted the Saturday sermon as a preparation for the sacrament. This idea was likely borrowed from Archbishop John Hamilton's *Ane Godlie Exhortatioun*, more commonly known as *The Twapenny Faith*.[82]

Adequate preparation before the Supper was also the purpose of catechetical requirements imposed by Knox and his fellow reformers. The religiously ignorant were to be barred from the communion service. A week or so before celebration of the sacrament the kirks held special public examinations of potential communicants. They were required to recite the Lord's Prayer, the Ten Commandments, and the articles of belief by memory. If anyone failed, he had to find a worthy member to stand surety for him that he would know the required material by the next communion. Preparation also required reconciling persons at odds with one another or barring them from the table.[83]

Knox's doctrine and practice of the Lord's Supper thus reflect elements drawn from Bucer, Bullinger, Calvin, Wishart, and possibly Hooper, à Lasco, and *The Twapenny Faith*. Doctrinally the heaviest debt is to Bucer and Bullinger, and to the conveyor of their views, Wishart. The practice of Knox was originally based on the same sources, but on the Continent he helped draft and used the *Order of Geneva*, patterned largely on Calvin's *La Forme*. The latter itself had an eclectic background. Calvin had substantially taken it from Bucer, who in turn had borrowed it from Diebold Schwarz, a Dominican monk who reformed the mass after becoming impatient with Luther in 1524.[84] Knox may even have been influenced somewhat by the *Second Book of Common Prayer*. Its treatment of the Lord's Supper, as Professor C. W. Dugmore has demonstrated, reflects the influence of late medieval English piety, notably in the memorial aspect of the Supper. Its concept of the Real Presence of Christ, who is spiritually eaten by faith, was expressed in the fourteenth-century manuals for parish priests, the *Pupilla Oculi* and the *Manipulus Curatorum*, which in turn reflected the views of Augustine.[85] Knox himself attested his debt not only to Augustine but also to Jerome, Origen, Fulgentius, and Vigilius.[86]

As the leading theologian of the Scottish Reformation, Knox imparted to the reformed Kirk of Scotland the rich diversity of his doctrinal heritage. He personally acknowledged this debt following his debate with William Maitland of Lethington in the General Assembly's June 1564 meeting: " 'I myself am not only fully resolved in conscience, but also I have heard the judgments in this [question of the obedience of subjects to their sovereigns], and *all other things* that I have affirmed within this Realm, of the most godly and most learned that be known in Europe. I come not to this Realm without their resolution; and for my assurance I have the handwritings of many. . . .' "[87] In particular the debt of Knox and Scottish Protestantism to Martin Bucer has never been adequately recognized.[88] Heinrich Bullinger has not fared much better. The key to Knox's concept of the Lord's Supper, which is reflected in the *Scots Confession*, is Bucer's teaching more than Calvin's. To the extent that Knox's theological views on the sacrament are akin to those of Calvin, the primary reason is that both men are, at least on this subject, disciples of the ecumenical Strasbourg reformer.

THE CHRISTIAN
COMMUNITY:
Political Considerations

The medieval world view, which envisaged church and state co-existing harmoniously in an integrated commonwealth under God, was embraced by the major Protestant traditions, though not always expressed in the same manner. In keeping with the relationship he saw in the Pentateuch between Moses and Aaron, Knox believed church and state could and should work together. Both were subject to divine Law and, ideally, magistrates were loyal members of the church, sharing its goals and applying its precepts in their governing work. Despite the doctrine of predestination, Knox, like Richard Hooker, tended to view church and state as comprising the same community.[1] Thus the question of relations between the two involved no more than the relationship between two governing bodies ministering to the related needs of one commonwealth. For his vision of the ideal Christian commonwealth Knox did not look to Geneva[2] but, like Bucer,[3] to the Old Testament, and to a lesser degree to the recollection of the commonwealth ideal in the Epistle to the Ephesians (2:12).[4] At the conclusion of his first interview with Mary Stewart in September 1561 he departed, saying, "I pray God, Madam, that ye may be as blessed within the Commonwealth of Scotland, if it be the pleasure of God, as ever Deborah was in the Commonwealth of Israel."[5] As he intimated to Mary, he wanted not only the prim-

111

itive simplicity of the apostolic church, but also a church existing in a politico-religious commonwealth of the kind he believed the early Hebrews developed. Like the Hebrew prophets before him, he sought to recall people to this idealized state, and his career in Reformation Scotland was always one of tension created by his longing for this utopian ideal and his pragmatism. Like any successful reformer, he was forced to temper his idealism through compromise in order to accomplish in part that which he envisioned as a glorious whole.

Knox firmly developed the position that no power on earth was superior to that of the state. All ecclesiastical personages, no matter what their rank, were subject to the secular authority. Yet from the very beginning he qualified the duty of obedience by exempting matters that repugned the glory and commands of God. Balnaves' treatise (like the formularies of Henry VIII's bishops) had not made that qualification, though it was common to most Protestants. Knox added it in his summarization of Balnaves' views,[6] and again asserted it in his 1557 *Apology* for the French Protestants, citing Tertullian to substantiate clerical subservience to secular authority:

> With Tertulian, we affirme, that the Emperour and everie Prince within his awn dominiouns, hath his haill autoritie of God, and is inferiour to none but to God onlie. And farther, that neither Bischope, Cardinall, nor Pope, aught more to be exemptit frome giveing obedience, paying of tribut, and of other dewteis aperteanyng to Kingis, than ar the commoun sort of peple.[7]

The same argument was used the following year against Castellio's disciple. This was the year of *The First Blast of the Trumpet* and the *Appellation* to the nobility and commonalty of Scotland. There was no change in his basic position, but simply a stronger clarification of the principle of superior, divine sovereignty (coupled with a change in the nature of disobedience to ungodly rulers): "We desire the people and the Rulers to be subject unto God, and unto his holy will plainly reveled in his most sacred Worde."[8] The *Appellation* itself stresses the duty of magistrates to supervise religious matters. Knox specifically claimed the right to appeal sentences imposed by the church to secular authorities, citing Jeremiah as his authority. The continuing vision of the Hebrew commonwealth was used in his argument as well. The divinely instituted laws which the Hebrews received did not exempt Aaron and the priestly caste from the jurisdiction of Moses, but specifically committed both secular and religious authority to him (Exodus 21, 24, 25, 28).[9]

In 1561 Mary Stewart shrewdly used these arguments against Knox in the course of their informal debate. Mary might well have quoted from Knox's own writings, ranging from the summary of Balnaves' treatise to the well-known 1558 tracts, but Knox, without rejecting any of the principles he had formally professed, had a ready reply for Mary. He recognized the duty of subjects to obey their sovereigns, but he insisted that subjects were not obligated to follow the religious dictates of their rulers if those dictates contradicted what was manifestly revealed in Scripture. Without intending personal insult, Knox informed the Queen that secular princes were often the most ignorant of all with respect to true religion. Using scriptural and historical evidence, he also pointed out the dangers of unqualified obedience in religious matters if the Hebrews in Egypt had accepted the religion of the Pharaoh or the apostles had accepted the state religion of the Roman Empire. The church must be subservient to the state as long as the latter pursues a godly course.[10] In essence if not in theory, "Knox, in failing to fence off the Church from the State, had meant only to provide for the absorption of the latter."[11] The governors of the state should, according to Knox's ideal, be so imbued with godly principles that their program reflects the commitments of the true church. Like Bucer, Knox "assigned the magistrate a spiritual responsibility and demanded that he be a Christian."[12] The responsibilities of both rulers and subjects were developed by Knox in a covenant context, and it was the violation of covenant duties by a sovereign that ultimately provided grounds for popular resistance.

THE COVENANT TRADITION

Modern scholarship on John Knox has tended to ignore his development of the covenant concept and his place in the covenant tradition. This is especially surprising because of the significance of the covenant idea for seventeenth-century Scottish history. The covenant, moreover, became a basic theme of English and American Puritan thought in the century following Knox's death. During the early years of the formulation of the covenant concept in English Puritanism, Knox was a revered figure. Following his various preaching activities in Edwardian England and his association with English exiles on the Continent during Mary's reign, he continued to maintain his interest in and contact with English Protestants, even while playing a major role in the establishment of the Reformed faith in Scotland. In 1568–69, for example, he was called upon to give advice respecting the question of separation from the Church of England. It is thus quite possible that his views on the covenant influenced English Puritan thought, as well as the thought of the Scottish Protestants. A study of Knox's views on the covenant is also important because of the place of the covenant in the development of his position on the legtimacy of active rebellion against tyrannical, idolatrous sovereigns. Finally, an examination of Knox's covenant thought is significant because it reveals that he was not as dependent on John Calvin as has been commonly supposed.

The covenant (or its synonyms band and league) was not treated systematically by Knox in his writings, but its development and application to theology and politics can be traced. As early as

1550, Knox depicted the Lord's Supper as "a band of mutuall love amangis us,"[1] but he did not make additional use of the covenant theme in his brief tract on the Lord's Supper. It was not until late in 1553 and early in 1554 that he returned to the idea of a league in his writings. In February 1554, after arriving as an exile on the Continent, he completed his exposition of Psalm 6, which he had begun in England. In this exposition he noted the "leag and felowschip that is betuene God and his elect," the seals of which were love of life and tranquility.[2] During the same period he wrote *An Admonition or Warning That the Faithful Chris-tiās in London, Newcastel, Barwycke & Others, May Auoide Gods Vengeaūce*. Like the exposition of Psalm 6, *An Admonition or Warning* was also begun in England and completed in France. This work contains Knox's basic treatment of the covenant. It is worth noting that this work was completed prior to Knox's initial meeting with Calvin, and contains his first mention of Calvin's name. As will be shown, however, the concept of the covenant reflected in this work does not indicate Calvin's influence on Knox's thought.

Knox was motivated to develop his exposition of covenant obligations by the accession of Mary Tudor to the throne in 1553. When Edward died in July, Knox was preaching in Bucking-hamshire at the behest of the Privy Council. Knox returned to London, arriving the same day (July 19) that the Council, the Mayor, and the citizens declared their support for Mary in op-position to Lady Jane Grey. Knox, true to his prophetic task, preached against popery. Mary's arrival in London and subse-quent ban (August 12) on preaching without royal consent forced Knox out of the pulpit. Soon faced with the choice of attending mass, being martyred, or taking flight, he left for Dieppe in January 1554. It was in these circumstances that he wrote *An Admonition or Warning*. It was not a systematic work, and hardly could have been, given the circumstances surrounding its com-position. After enjoying the favor of Somerset and Northumber-land and preaching before Edward and the royal court, Knox had been driven into exile. The cause of Protestantism was being submerged by the Catholic revival. His fellow Christians who elected to remain behind were faced with conformity or the stake. The woman to whom he was engaged — Marjory Bowes — had been unable to flee with him. Knox's enemy had all the power of the throne at her disposal in addition to support from Spain, the Holy Roman Empire, and the papacy. Knox had only a pen, but he used it as best he could to continue his prophetic mission. If anything, that mission was intensified by recent events. His prophetic fervor is unmistakable as one turns the pages of the *Admonition* and reads of the covenant obligations.

To be a party to the covenant was to avoid idolatry — specifically Catholicism. "This is the league betuixt God and us, that He alone sall be oure God, and we salbe his pepill: He sall communicat with us of his graces and gudness; We sall serve him in bodie and spreit: He salbe oure saifgard frome death and dampnatioun; We sall seik to him, and sall flie frome all strange Godis." This was the kernel of the *Admonition's* message. Those who succumbed to idolatry openly declared that they had no true faith and were not party to the covenant. Because they did not continue in league with God they had to suffer eternal damnation. Knox's phraseology definitely implied the idea that once in the covenant a man might subsequently reject it and so be condemned. The following phrases indicate this conditional element: "yf the league betuix God and us stand inviolatit"; "gif we will haif the league to stand betuix God and us"; "we cannot keip the league betuix him and us inviolatit gif we favour, follow, or spair idolateris"; "such is the condition of the league betwene me and my God."[3] Yet Knox's doctrines of predestination and perserverance make this theologically impossible. A man truly in league with God could not permanently leave that band and be damned. At the same time, a man apparently in covenant with God could forsake it and be condemned, yet even if such a person continued his apparent adherence to the covenant, he could not be saved because he would always have been reprobate. In the *Admonition* Knox was thus using some rhetorical warnings that his theology could not support.

The basic provisions of the covenant — and these were commonly stated by covenant writers — were that God would be the believer's God if they would be his people. From God came grace and goodness; from man, service in body and spirit. God would preserve his elect from damnation, and man would refuse to worship other gods. Knox then became more specific, reflecting his views on the sole authority of the Bible and the commands expressly stated therein. As a covenant obligation man had to swear never to have fellowship with a religious group whose worship was not expressly authorized by Scripture. Specifically, Knox referred to idolatrous worship, the very worship he believed was being restored by Mary at that moment in England. God would not tolerate idolatry, but commanded judgment to be executed severely against idolaters, and required that members of the league should accuse idolaters of their crime, even if the idolaters were members of one's own family. (Knox was quite aware that his prospective father-in-law, Richard Bowes, captain of Norham Castle, would conform to Catholicism.[4] The admonition to his fiancée and future mother-in-law was thus harsh: they must accuse Richard Bowes of idolatry because of their covenant obligations.) "Neither suld blude nor affinitie . . . save suche as offendit; neither yit . . . the husband suld conceill the offence of his awn wyfe; neither the father the iniquitie of his sone or of his dochter, but that the father, husband, or brother, suld be the first to accuse sone, dochter, brother, or wyfe."[5]

Further developing the covenant obligations with respect to idolatry, Knox put forth three reasons why men of the band were to avoid idolatry. First, idolaters intended to lure believers from God; hence they had to be denounced and punished if the covenant was to remain firm. Second, God's wrath could never be quenched until all idolaters were destroyed. By destroying idolaters God demonstrated his love for the elect by opposing their enemies; believers were required to do the same. Third, divine mercy and love were given as rewards to those who took vengeance upon idolaters in a manner prescribed by God. Knox specified that manner. It was not the duty of the individual to punish idolatry — a position Knox reversed in 1558. In 1554 he confined the punishment of idolatry to civil magistrates. It was the duty of every "Civill Magistrate" in England to slay all idolaters. Believers were not to take it upon themselves to engage in armed rebellion against Mary Tudor, but if the magistrates were to undertake armed rebellion against her, the logic of Knox's position of obedience to secular authority in all matters not contravening divine precepts would require Christians to obey the magistrates rather than the idolatrous sovereign.[6] As a specific covenant obligation, however, one had only to avoid the company of idolaters and participation in idolatrous worship. Knox pointedly indicated that this obligation held true even when the Christian was in a country full of idolaters. No Protestant was to participate in Roman Catholic worship. He was bound by his covenant responsibilities to avoid the mass.[7]

Two years later, in his baptismal tract of 1556, Knox discussed the league in the context of baptism. The baptismal ceremony signified reception into the league with God. This time Knox stressed the permanence of the covenant: "The league of God is of that fermitie and assurance, that rather sall the covenant maid with the sonne and moone, with the day and nycht, perische and be changeit, then that the promeis of his mercie maid to his elect salbe frustrat and vane." The covenant made with the elect is manifest and sure. Iniquity does not break it. Assurance of its permanence comes through the internal testimony of the Holy Spirit and repentance. The Lord's Supper is also associated with the band, for it "is the declaratioun of oure covenant, that be Chryst Jesus we be nurissit, manteanit, and continewit in the league with God our Father."[8] *The Forme of Prayers* used by the English congregation in Geneva used the notion of a covenant in its *Order of Baptism*. The baptismal ceremony must be given to the children of believers, according to the *Order*, because "our infantes apperteyne to him by covenaunt. . . ." The *Order* also remarks on the conditions of the covenant in that standard phraseology, that he will be our God and father, and we his people and children. The fact that Knox first associated the covenant with baptism in 1556 (according to extant evidence), the year in which the English congregation published its *Order of Baptism*, would indicate that this aspect of his thought was derived from the *Order*. The *Order* itself was borrowed by the English congregation from Calvin, who had compiled it while in Strasbourg.[9]

Unlike most later writers on the covenant, Knox thus developed the covenant concept largely in a political context, and then also applied it to the sacrament of baptism. From an early stage in his Protestant career the politico-religious situation in Marian England prompted him to write on covenant responsibilities. In exile he broadened his understanding of the league to include baptism. Two years later, in different circumstances and with more specific political connotations, he broadened the covenant obligations of the Christian. When, in 1558, he pursued his political conclusions to their end by advocating active rebellion by individual believers as well as by godly nobles and magistrates, it was the covenant idea that served as a principal theological force in his mind. Idolatry was roundly damned because it was a covenant obligation to do so. Idolatry in princes was the reason for rejecting their rule. The Hebrew prophets had been strenuous in their denunciation of idolatry. Fittingly enough, the notion of the covenant was itself Hebrew, and the prophet Jeremiah — one of Knox's favorites — had announced a new covenant. The covenant concept was congruous both with Knox's prophetic task and with his belief. The league aptly met his need for a biblical vehicle to channel his thought into productive action.

The Hebrew background for the idea of the covenant is amply manifested in Knox's 1558 *Appellation* to the nobility, estates, and commonwealth of Scotland. He cited the covenant made by Josiah on behalf of the Hebrews that they should observe the divine Law (2 Kings 23). This covenant provided Knox with the idea of a league between the king and God or between the nobles and magistrates on the one hand and God on the other. Because of this covenant, Knox argued, rulers were responsible for the reformation of religion and the punishment of idolatry. The existence of a covenant between God and temporal authority was also implied by Knox during his interview with Mary Stewart in September 1561. If princes exceeded the bounds imposed on them by God, subjects had to disobey because of their duty to obey God.[10]

In his *Appellation* of 1558 Knox also called attention to the covenant made by Asa with the Hebrews to serve God and maintain his religion (2 Chron. 15) — an example of yet another kind of covenant, namely, one between the sovereign and his subject.[11] The idea of a covenant or social compact between the people and their rulers was also the basis of Knox's statement in his outline of a proposed *Second Blast of the Trumpet* (which was never written) that a ruler who contravened divine Law might justly be deposed and punished by those who gave him authority. "Neither can othe nor promesse bynd any such people to obey and maintein Tyrantes against God and against his trueth knowen." That ruler who manifests himself unworthy of governing can be overthrown: "moste justely may the same men depose and punishe him, that unadvysedly before they did nominate, appoint, and electe."[12] Knox reiterated this idea during his interview with Mary Stewart in 1563. There was, he informed her, a mutual covenant between sovereigns and subjects. The latter could disobey if monarchs did not fulfill their obligations, namely, protection and defense against evildoers. "Consider . . . what it is that ye ought to do unto them by mutual contract. They are bound to obey you, and that not but in God. Ye are bound to keep laws unto them. Ye crave of them service: they crave of you protection and defence against wicked doers." If Mary failed to fulfill her duty to her subjects, she would not receive their full obedience.[13]

In the 1558 *Appellation*, Exodus 34 provided a suitable example of a covenant between God and his people (which was the concept of the league that Knox had initially developed in his *Admonition or Warning* four years earlier). In Exodus 34 the biblical account portrays God as warning the Hebrews not to make any covenant with the inhabitants of Palestine, but rather to destroy the latter's idolatrous worship. The point Knox wished to make was that "the Gentiles . . . be bound to the same leage and covenant that God made with his people Israel. . . ."[14] The covenant between God and his people was also the implicit basis of Knox's 1558 letter to the commonalty of Scotland in which he argued that it was the responsibility of the people as well as the kings, nobles, and magistrates to see that Christ was truly preached. If the civil authorities were negligent or tyrannical, the people were obliged to provide and defend preachers against any who would persecute them.[15] Knox's extension of the principle of active resistance to the people in 1558 thus occurred in a covenant context and because of covenant obligations. Knox reiterated this point in his 1564 debate with William Maitland of Lethington in the General Assembly of the Kirk of Scotland. Referring to the commandment to the Hebrews not to make a league with the Canaanites (Exod. 34), Knox wrote of "the people assembled together in one body of a Commonwealth, unto whom God has given sufficient force, not only to resist, but also to suppress all kind of open idolatry. . . ."[16] The Old Testament was thus a fertile source to illustrate and support Knox's covenant conceptions.

Apart from the Old Testament there are several sources which influenced Knox in his formulation of the idea of a league.

One of these appears to have been the ancient Scottish custom of banding, usually undertaken for the common defense of lives and property. Its origins are in medieval feudalism, involving the oath of fealty and the clan-family realtionship. Because Scotland lacked strong central government, groups banded together by sworn pledges of fidelity, contrary to royal legislation. Some of these bonds were temporary political alliances. Others were bands of manrent entered into by such individuals as small landholders or freemen in order to get protection from powerful lords. These were not, however, known as covenants prior to Knox's time.[17] It appears that Knox, in applying the Hebrew notion of covenant to the band in his *Appellation*, was the first to introduce a change in the terminology. Even more significant, of course, was Knox's reorientation of the band; in lieu of an agreement among men it became a covenant with God.

Numerous bands were made in the course of the Scottish Reformation. Knox's *History of the Reformation in Scotland* records a number of them. The first occurred in 1556 when he was visiting the laird of Dun. The gentlemen of the Mearns "bound themselves . . . to maintain the true preaching of the Evangel of Jesus Christ. . . ."[18] There is no evidence to indicate that this band assumed written form. This is not the case with the band subscribed to on December 3, 1557, in response to Knox's urging of the reforming party to get on with their work. The signatories, including the Earls of Argyll, Glencairn, and Morton, the Lord of Lorne, and John Erskine of Dun, bound themselves to do everything in their power to further the reform cause. There were subsequent bands at Perth in May 1559; at Edinburgh in July 1559; at Stirling in August 1559; at Leith in April 1560; at Ayr in September 1562 ; at Newcastle in March 1566; at Edinburgh in July 1567 and May 1568; and at Leith in July 1572.[19] Knox was already writing of a league before any of these bands were formulated, but the tradition of banding that lay behind them was known to him before he began writing of the covenant in 1553–54. Nevertheless, it would appear that the notion of a political band did not influence his theological notion of a covenant until 1557 or 1558, when he began to urge the nobility to act in concert on the basis of the same covenant that God had made with Israel.

By 1558 the Hebrew idea of covenant and the traditional Scottish practice of banding blended in Knox's mind as manifested in his *Appellation*.

There are also theological sources for Knox's development of the covenant idea. One of these — the influence of the Genevan *Order of Baptism* — has already been noted in connection with the relationship of the covenant to baptism. The fact that Knox began writing about the league in England at the outset of Mary's reign indicates that a major theological source of his covenant notion is to be found in his associations or readings there. Certainly England had a native covenant tradition, the earliest exponent of which, in religion, was William Tyndale. Although it has been suggested that Tyndale borrowed his concept of the covenant from Bullinger,[20] there is insufficient evidence to indicate the possible degree of dependence on Continental sources.[21] Tyndale is known to have read the works of Zwingli and Oecolampadius, both of whom made some use of the covenant conception.[22] By the mid-1530s Tyndale had developed the idea of the covenant as a bipartite, divine-human contract binding God and man. God would fulfill his promises to man on the condition that man would endeavor to keep God's Law. The emphasis was on the conditional nature of the divine promises: "God bindeth himself to fulfil that mercy unto thee only if thou wilt endeavour thyself to keep his laws. . . ." For Tyndale, the Sermon on the Mount was the embodiment of God's laws and promises, set forth in contractual terms. It provided the model for the life of faith. Tyndale's treatise on the Sermon, *An Exposition upon the V. VI. VII. Chapters of Mathew*, was reprinted several times during the reign of Edward VI, and may have been known by Knox. Despite its fundamentally Lutheran outlook the *Exposition* contains several key passages on the covenant. Matthew 6:14–15, according to Tyndale, embodies the covenant and manifests its conditional nature. Tyndale warns that "if, when thou hast professed it, and received the sign thereof, thou cast the yoke of the Lord from off thy neck," there will be no divine forgiveness. "Comfort thou thyself with the hope of a better life in another world, ever assured that thou shalt have here sufficient, only if thou keep covenant with the Lord thy God. . . ." Of special interest is Tyndale's statement of the responsibilities of kings and nobles as well as preachers to restore the people to their covenant obligations. "And if the people come again [to the covenant], let the priest or bishop, after the ensample of the prophets and high priests of the Israelites, take an oath, in God's stead, of the kings and lords. And let the king and lords receive an oath of the people. . . ." Certainly Knox's emphasis in *An Admonition or Warning* on contractual responsibility is in keeping with the tenor of Tyndale's developed views on the subject.[23]

Tyndale is known to have influenced Miles Coverdale, for the latter's preface to his Bible reflects Tyndale's views on the covenant. Coverdale also corresponded with Bullinger and translated two of his works, so that he may have been acquainted with the covenant views of Bullinger, as well as Tyndale, when he arrived in Geneva in 1558.[24] By that time, however, Knox had already written of the league in distinctly contractual terms. If, therefore, Tyndale's views were a motivating force in Knox's development of the covenant concept, the medium of that influence probably came through the writings of Tyndale directly, especially the exposition of the Sermon on the Mount.

There is also the possibility that Knox's use of the covenant theme in *An Admonition or Warning* resulted from contact in Edwardian England with the views of John Hooper. As a disciple of Bullinger, Hooper — like Tyndale — emphasized the contractual nature of the covenant. God's promises were conditional on man's obedience. These conditions are set forth in the Ten Commandments. God is bound "to aid and succour, keep and preserve, warrant and defend man from all ill, both of body and soul, and at the last to give him eternal bliss and everlasting felicity." For his part, man contracted "to obey, serve, and keep God's commandments; to love him, honour him, and fear him above all things."[25] A similar view of the covenant is propounded in the writings of Oecolampadius, which were circulating in Scotland as early as 1540, and could, therefore, have been one of the earliest sources of influence on Knox. Oecolampadius emphasizes the contractual nature of the covenant and man's responsibility, defining the covenant in terms of the *charitatis lex* in his commentary on Isaiah.[26] On this basis, then, it is reasonable to conclude that the contractual emphasis in Knox's *Admonition or Warning* resulted, at least in part, from the views of Tyndale, Bullinger (as expressed by Hooper), or Oecolampadius, as well as the Hebrew idea of the covenant. Simultaneously, it is well to remember that, in view of Knox's normal lack of references to his sources, finality in determining those sources can never be attained.

It has already been noted that *An Admonition or Warning* contains Knox's first mention of Calvin, "that singular instrument of God. . . ."[27] The mention of Calvin in this work, particularly the fact that the reference is to Calvin's commentary on Jeremiah, the prophet who announced a new covenant, would seem to be *prima facie* evidence that Calvin was the source of Knox's earliest expression of covenant thought. Yet Calvin's concept of the covenant differs from that developed by Knox in 1554. Calvin depicted the covenant as God's promise to man, which had been fulfilled in the Incarnation, death, and resurrection of Christ. Man's obligations in the covenant were not ignored, but they were subjugated in importance to the promissory aspect. "The covenant is at the outset drawn up as a free agreement, and perpetually remains such."[28] Even when discussing the covenant duties imposed by God on man, this was the element stressed by Calvin. Knox, on the other hand, was closer to Tyndale, Bullinger, Hooper, and Oecolampadius, who dealt with the covenant essentially as a conditional promise calling for man's reciprocal obedience. Knox, not Calvin, repeatedly stressed the point that *if* man wished to remain in the covenant he had to fulfill his obligations. To be sure, Calvin admitted that uprightness and sanctity of life were required to those in the "covenants of . . . mercy," but he did not threaten divine abrogation of the covenant if those conditions were not met, whereas Knox did. Calvin was concerned with promises; Knox, in 1554, with contractual obligations.[29] Knox's view of the covenant in relation to the sacraments was influenced by Calvin through the *Order of Geneva* and perhaps his commentaries, but this influence is not apparent until 1556.

Before Knox left Geneva he had transposed the religious covenant or league freely and smoothly into the political realm, where it became allied with the traditional Scottish band and the natural law-social contract theory, which was of major significance in British and American political history in the following centuries. The ultimate divergence of Knox and Calvin on the nature of lawful rebellion against temporal sovereigns can be traced to their differing interpretations of the covenant. It was Knox, not Calvin, who was willing to contend for the right of the people actively to resist a tyrannical monarch.[30] The covenant was an idea with awesome political potency, as Knox demonstrated, and as the French Huguenots and the English Puritans as well as Knox's Scottish followers subsequently discovered.[31]

THE LEGITIMACY OF RESISTANCE

In a recent study assessing the influence of Calvinism on the Scottish Reformation, Professor James Kirk, the Scottish historian, argued that one of the principal contributions of this tradition "was its ability to provide to Knox and his colleagues the necessary religious justification for a rebellion in a way in which submissive Lutheranism did not. . . ."[1] In view of the fact that Knox expressly cited the Lutheran Magdeburg *Bekenntnis* (1550), which embraced the legitimacy of active rebellion against a tyrannical, idolatrous sovereign, it is difficult to accept Professor Kirk's rejection of the Lutheran influence on Knox in this area. Moreover, Knox's assertion of rebellion was, as his most recent biographer reminds us, a revolutionary departure from the views propounded by Calvin prior to 1560.[2] It is the purpose of this chapter to reexamine Knox's position on resistance as it developed in the course of his reforming career, particularly in the context of the Reformed ministers with whom he consulted in Switzerland.

Knox's views on disobedience *per se* to secular authority never changed. Throughout his career he maintained that obedience to higher powers was due as long as those powers did not command things contrary to divine precepts. When such things were commanded, disobedience was justified. Knox changed, however, in his development of a doctrine of active disobedience to or rebellion against secular authority, particularly at the popular level. While this development was consistent with his earlier view of the right of disobedience *per se*, it required a major reversal of the *nature* of the disobedience permissible for the common people. There is nothing in Knox's theology itself—or in Reformed or Protestant theology in general—that made such a reversal inevitable, although his conception of covenant responsibilities made it extremely likely. The reversal, of course, also involved political factors and Knox's personality. Yet the importance of theology must not be discounted. The Protestant doctrine of obedience to higher powers, when qualified by a statement limiting obedience to matters not contravening divine precepts, made the road to rebellion psychologically inevitable in some territories. Where either a majority of the people or a disciplined, strong minority were convinced of their right to disobey an ungodly monarch, it was only a matter of time before they would refuse to accept passively either the punishment for their disobedience or flight into exile.

Knox's earliest position on the matter of disobedience was a practical affirmation of the right of rebellion. Surely no other meaning can be attached to his involvement with the Castilians at St. Andrews in 1547. "Sheltering among a company of murderers and treaty-breakers, he propounded what he had fully convinced himself was the true Gospel of Christ, and he quite approved of the crime which had brought them together."[3] His experience on the galleys did not temper his spirit, for he deliberately added a statement to his summarization of Balnaves' treatise exempting Christians from obeying higher powers when they commanded things opposed to divine law. In Edwardian England Knox became more conservative, even reluctantly agreeing to the rubric commanding kneeling at communion. In his 1552 letter to his Berwick congregation he specifically urged obedience to secular authorities, even if they were personally wicked or commanded ungodly things. Disobedience was acceptable only if a chief point of religion was violated. Even then, Knox deliberately ruled out rebellion, restricting his followers to passive disobedience.[4] He probably trimmed his sails because he believed that the English Reformation would be dynamic, not static. Moreover, at this juncture there was nothing of consequence to be gained by advocating rebellion against the Protestant Edwardian government. Then came Edward's death, the fiasco involving Lady Jane Grey, and England's return to Catholicism under Mary Tudor.

Knox's mind was now unsettled. He had rebelled once, and

he was pondering the possibility again. In January 1554 he left Dieppe and went to Switzerland. He broached the question of disobedience to Calvin, who sent him to Zürich to meet with Bullinger, and to Lausanne to talk with Pierre Viret. Knox subsequently traveled throughout Switzerland, undoubtedly raising the issue with other Reformed ministers. Four specific queries were submitted by Knox to Calvin, Bullinger, and presumably Viret:

> 1. Whether the Son of a King, upon his father's death, though unable by reason of his tender age to conduct the government of the kingdom, is nevertheless by right of inheritance to be regarded as a lawful magistrate, and as such to be obeyed as of divine right?
>
> 2. Whether a Female can preside over, and rule a kingdom by divine right, and so transfer the right of sovereignty to her Husband?
>
> 3. Whether obedience is to be rendered to a Magistrate who enforces idolatry and condemns true religion; and whether those authorities, who are still in military occupation of towns and fortresses, are permitted to repel this ungodly violence from themselves and their friends?
>
> 4. To which party must Godly persons attach themselves, in the case of a religious Nobility resisting an idolatrous Sovereign?

Calvin's responses were not given in writing to Knox, but in reply to the crucial third question he rejected the right of subjects to rebel actively against an idolatrous ruler.[5]

Bullinger responded in writing, giving a positive answer to the first question, with a specific affirmation of the lawfulness of Edward VI's royal position. In response to the second question, he asserted that divine law ordained that a woman be a subject, not a ruler, though according to temporal law women could rule. There was no apparent biblical sanction for the godly to rebel. Yet Bullinger clearly gave Knox room to maneuver by stating that "the Lord will in his own time destroy unjust governments by his own people, to whom he will supply proper qualifications for this purpose, as he formerly did to Jerubbaal, and the Maccabees, and

Jehoiada." To the critical third question Bullinger admitted the lawfulness of using force to oppose idolatrous sovereigns, but urged caution. Under no circumstances, however, would he tolerate obeying a king or magistrate whose commands were opposed to God. In reply to the fourth question, Bullinger wrote that the answer depended on the circumstances in any given case, particularly as assessed by men knowledgeable in Scripture and inspired by the Holy Spirit.[6]

Bullinger was obviously not trying to discourage Knox from considering armed rebellion, though he was definitely concerned that the matter be approached cautiously. He did not want to provoke a breach that would divide the Reformed churches in Switzerland. Such a doctrine might, in fact, be dangerous to the Reformed cause in Switzerland because of its religious dominance there. Yet Bullinger certainly had no intention, based on the known evidence, of paralyzing Knox's action, nor was Knox restricted by what Bullinger told him.[7] After his earlier meeting with the more reticent Calvin, Knox must have been encouraged by the tacit but cautious approval accorded by Bullinger. Never, in fact, did Knox "pursue a wholly independent line of thought" from Bullinger or even Calvin, as J. H. Burns has suggested.[8]

Bullinger's views on disobedience were more fully stated in the *Second Decade*. Although he specifically called attention to David's refusal to kill Saul, and Jeremiah's prayers for Joachim and Zedechiah, he did not teach "an almost unqualified doctrine of submission."[9] Jeremiah obeyed wicked kings, but only as long as they did not command things directly contrary to God's precepts. Likewise Christians "ought not to obey the wicked commandments of godless magistrates, because it is not permitted to magistrates to ordain or appoint any thing contrary to God's law, or the law of nature." Indiscriminate tyrannicide by individuals was not, however, acceptable to Bullinger. He was willing to acknowledge that tyrannicide was sometimes legitimate, and even that it could be accomplished by persons other than magistrates, provided they were divinely called. But without that calling, he warned, "he is so far from doing good in killing the tyrant, that it is to be feared lest he do make the evil double. . . ."[10] This was harmonious with Knox's beliefs in 1554.

In spite of Calvin's conservative temperament and juristic

mind and his attempts to restrain Knox, his position was also akin to Knox's in 1554. Calvin developed his view of magistracy in Book IV, chapter xx of the *Institutes*. In the penultimate section of the chapter he expressly sanctioned the kind of disobedience Knox had approved in a tract written just prior to his meeting with Calvin. Earlier in the twentieth chapter Calvin had argued that magistrates, as vicars of God on earth, must pursue righteousness and administer the judgments of God, using the drawn sword when necessary. After carefully cautioning that it was not the right of subjects to overthrow a ruler, he admitted that sometimes God raised up "open avengers from among his servants" and armed them "with his command to punish the wicked government and deliver his people. . . ." Such men were not violating the divinely implanted majesty in kings, but — as Knox also argued — were obeying a higher sovereignty. In the following section Calvin likened the power of magistrates to the Spartan ephors, the Athenian demarchs, and the Roman tribunes — all elected officials, and all possessing legitimate authority to check tyrannical governments. Zwingli had made the same point in his 1524 treatise, *The Pastor*.[11]

Calvin applied these historical precedents to the sixteenth-century magistrates and broadened their check on higher powers to include religion.

> If there are now any magistrates of the people, appointed to restrain the willfulness of kings . . . , I am so far from forbidding them to withstand, in accordance with their duty, the fierce licentiousness of kings, that, if they wink at kings who violently fall upon and assault the lowly common folk, I declare that their dissimulation involves nefarious perfidy, because they dishonestly betray the freedom of the people, of which they know that they have been appointed protectors by God's ordinance.

Calvin preferred that the magistrates exercise their function of controlling errant monarchs through representative bodies or parliaments, though he did not restrict them to this form of activity. The closing paragraph in the *Institutes* drives home the point that "obedience to man must not become disobedience to God." This applies to individuals as well as to magistrates. Daniel is commended for his refusal to obey an impious edict of Darius. Hosea,

Calvin pointed out, condemned the Israelites for obeying Jeroboam's commands to participate in idolatrous worship.[12]

In practice, Calvin was conservative, for when it came to definite issues he often counseled nonresistance. He did not approve of the 1558 tracts of Knox and Goodman dealing with rebellion (and female sovereignty). He later apparently refused to support the anti-Guise plot (the Amboise Conspiracy) on the grounds that such a revolt, though led by some nobles, would result in massive shedding of blood which would scandalize the cause of Christ. Yet recent scholars have shown a credibility gap in Calvin with respect to this whole affair and related events. "He was by no means unsympathetic, despite his retrospective disclaimers. . . ."[13] Even more, "although Calvin constantly preached patience and obedience, it is also clear from his own correspondence that he did envisage the use of force, if necessary, to install [Antoine de Bourbon, King of] Navarre in power at the end of 1560." Calvin's behavior moved N. M. Sutherland to remark that "his political philosophy allowed for successful rebellions; their success made them legitimate."[14] But the Amboise Conspiracy failed and Calvin issued his retrospective disclaimers. As he explained in a letter to Coligny after the Conspiracy, active resistance could be sanctioned *only* if the princes of the blood and the parliaments took joint action to maintain legal rights, in which case they could receive popular support. But in reality, as Calvin knew, there was no united front on the part of the princes and the parliaments. Yet in the same year (1561) that he wrote about the Amboise Conspiracy, he published a lecture on Daniel 6:22 which sanctioned popular defiance against princes who opposed God. "Earthly princes lay aside all their power when they rise up against God, and are unworthy of being reckoned in the number of mankind. We ought rather utterly to defy than to obey them whenever they are so restive and wish to spoil God of his rights. . . ."[15] Since this position was taken by Calvin in the *aftermath* of the successful Scottish revolution, there is a possibility that he was influenced by Knox. As his reaction to the Amboise Conspiracy indicates, however, he was reluctant to practice his theory. After 1562 his reluctance waned somewhat, for he helped raise funds to support the Huguenot cause. Although lacking the support of the French parliaments, it was led by Louis de Bourbon, Prince de Conde, and Gaspard de Coligny, thus meeting Calvin's precondition that it be led by lesser magistrates. But in 1554 Calvin and Knox were at least agreed on this principle, namely, that magistrates, to whom the godly owed obedience, could legitimately rebel against a monarch who contravened divine Law.[16]

No records survive of Knox's meeting with Viret, but the latter's advice to Knox can be tentatively reconstructed. Viret, a personal friend of Calvin, spent two years in Geneva following his exile from Lausanne in 1559. He had visited Geneva periodically in the years 1553 to 1559, during which time he would have met various British refugees. After the latter returned to England, Viret maintained ties with such former exiles as Miles Coverdale, Christopher Goodman, Laurence Humphrey, Thomas Sampson, and Edmund Grindal. Foxe thought highly enough of Viret's work to include it in his *Acts and Monuments*. Viret's works received increasing attention in England and Scotland following the publication (in English) of his *A Verie Familiare and Fruiteful Exposition of the xii Articles of the Christian Faieth Conteined in the Comune Crede, Called the Apostles Crede* (1548). In 1561 Viret left Geneva for France, where he died a decade later. His views continued to have an impact in England, especially on the more radical Protestants.[17]

Viret's views differed from Calvin's in several areas, including the issue of resistance. The clearest advocacy of Viret's views on this subject appear in his *Remonstrances aux fideles qui conversent entre les Papistes*, published at Geneva in 1547 (and not subsequently translated into English). These views were later reaffirmed in works published in the 1560s and 1570s. Like Calvin and Bullinger, Viret affirmed the importance of the subject's obedience to his sovereign, but the stress is on obeying *good* magistrates and *true* kings and princes. Tyrants were another matter. Viret conceived of tyranny in both religious and political terms: a tyrant was one who transgressed divine or civil laws, or persecuted the church. Tyrants are continuously warned of the punishments in store for them. Viret called their attention to the Old Testament to prove, in Professor Linder's words, that "God frequently chastened tyrants by popular uprisings . . . with rulers becoming subjects and subjects becoming rulers in many cases."[18]

Christians were to obey their rulers in secular matters, according to Viret, as long as conscience was not violated and consent was not given to idolatry. If, however, the authorities acted against matters of purely religious concern, resistance was justifiable. Initially this was to be passive in nature, involving prayer and patience. Yet it was also acceptable to disobey cruel political edicts which were opposed to God's will. One could likewise withhold information from the authorities in order to protect the faithful. As a last resort armed resistance was justifiable, but only if two preconditions had been met. First, all other expedients, beginning with prayer and patience, had to be tried. Secondly, armed resistance would have to be led by legitimately constituted lesser magistrates, with authority based in the people. In 1547 Viret argued that resistance could be undertaken to overthrow political as well as religious tyranny, thus making his views distinctly more political in tone than those of Bullinger or Calvin. Of crucial importance to Knox was Viret's contention that magistrates have the *duty* — not just the right — to depose tyrants who threaten to ruin the cause of the gospel by force.[19]

The state of Knox's mind just prior to and after his meetings with Calvin, Bullinger, and Viret can be determined by comparing his *Admonition or Warning* (written in December — January 1553 — 54) with the 1554 tracts penned after those meetings. The thesis of the *Admonition or Warning* is that Christians should flee in body and in spirit from all fellowship with idolaters in their worship. Mass must not be attended, even if commanded by the sovereign herself. Traditionally, Knox recognized, this would be regarded as treason, but he cited Jeremiah 37 as an example that God's prophets could advocate treason against secular authority and not offend God. Neither would those who obeyed the prophets in committing this treasonous activity be offending God. Knox prophesied that if Catholicism were maintained in England because the people refused to resist, the kingdom would be subject to divine vengeance and the city of London made a desert. Just as the Hebrews were collectively punished for tolerating idolatrous governments, so would the English be punished if they acquiesced in the restored Catholicism. Christians had made a covenant with God in which they agreed that they would avoid the worship of false gods and never have fellowship with any religion not expressly confirmed by Scripture. Covenant obligations did not, however, require more than passive disobedience. Knox made it quite specific that believers were not to take it upon themselves to undertake armed rebellion. But Knox, in 1553—54, apparently called for open resistance against an idolatrous monarch, for it was the duty of every "Civill Magistrate" in England to "slay all ydolateris."[20] The logic of Knox's position required Christians to be loyal to secular authority in all matters not opposed to God. If the English magistrates were to engage in armed rebellion against Mary, would it not be the duty of Christians to obey those magistrates, not the sovereign? The key phrase "Civill Magistrate" is unfortunately ambiguous. J. H. Burns takes it to mean only the sovereign, in which case Knox would not be thinking of active resistance in any form. Knox does speak of sovereigns as magistrates, but he also refers to princes and nobles defending Jeremiah. Jeremiah, of course, had to be defended primarily from the "pestilent preistis," not the king.[21] The key to the passage is likely the rebellion at St. Andrews in 1547. For Knox to say in 1553—54 that no one but kings had the power to slay idolaters would incriminate the Castilians who had executed Cardinal Beaton. If, however, the Castilians were justified because civil magistrates were among their number, then Knox in 1553—54 was probably using "Civill Magistrate" in a broad sense, thus justifying active resistance by specified persons.

When Knox returned to Dieppe from his travels throughout Switzerland, he wrote two epistles to his friends in England. The first epistle, dated May 10, 1554, urged hope and promised divine vengeance against the Catholics. "Whome God sall use to execute his wraith, I can not say . . . ," though Knox was certainly not thinking of the common people to whom he wrote as being the divine agents for this undertaking. The advice of the *Admonition or Warning* for Christians to suffer patiently but not to have any fellowship with idolaters was repeated. Knox also reiterated his belief that it was not treasonous to disobey sovereigns whose laws were opposed to those of God. "All is not lawfull nor just that is statute be Civill lawis, nether yet is everie thing syn befoir God, whilk ungodlie personis alledgeis to be treasone. . . ."[22] The second letter was dated May 31, 1554, and returned to the theme of vengeance against Mary Tudor and her Catholic supporters. Again Knox admitted that he did not know who would be appointed by God to wreak the promised vengeance, but he cautioned that his readers not seek vengeance themselves, that is, he wanted no popular revolution. Yet he urged more than patient suffering, encouraging his readers spiritually to hate their Catholic rulers and earnestly to pray for their destruction, not their salvation. Soon God would "styr up one Jehu or other to execute hys vengeaunce uppon these bloudde-thyrsty tyrauntes and obstinate idolators."[23] England must be ready.

Knox published his *Faithful Admonition* in July 1554, openly denouncing Edmund Bonner, Bishop of London, Cuthbert Tunstall, Bishop of Durham, Stephen Gardiner, Bishop of Winchester, and Mary Tudor herself. His antipathy to Mary knew no bounds. With unconcealed rancor he blasted her as a false, dissembling, proud, and deceitful monarch who was an open traitoress to the English crown. By virtually all standards — religious, legal, national, economic, strategic, and social — she stood condemned by her acts as a traitoress. Knox unabashedly appealed to English nationalism to gain support for his accusations, charging that Mary and her bishops had betrayed England into the arms of Spain. He did not appeal for a popular insurrection, but repeated the theme of his previous letters, calling to God to provide a Phinehas, Elijah, or Jehu to overthrow the Catholic regime. The inclusion of Elijah, to whom Knox often referred, is significant, for Knox conceived of himself as a prophet and compared himself to his Hebrew predecessors. In 1554 he was hoping that he would be the prophet called by God to overthrow Mary Tudor and her Catholic cohorts in conjunction with the English nobility. In the meantime his readers were warned not to attend mass, even if this meant martyrdom or exile. His position was consequently unchanged as a result of his meetings with Calvin, Bullinger, Viret, and other Swiss ministers. If anything, Bullinger and Viret had strengthened rather than paralyzed his resolve. He was not yet calling for resistance by the elect as a whole, but he was not willing to rule out any means of deliverance God might provide. "By what meanes that he shall performe that his merciful worke, it neither apperteyneth to thee to demaunde, nor to me to defyne." He went so far as to praise Jeremiah's admonition to cease obedience to and defense of one's native princes, and to render obedience to the enemies of one's state.[24]

In his *Admonition or Warning* Knox had stated his views on the nature of the covenant between God and the elect. In the *Faithful Admonition* he implied the existence of a league between king and people. Mary violated her covenant with the English people by rejecting the laws of the realm and marrying a Spaniard, thus utterly subverting "the whole publicke estate and common wealth of Englande."[25] In his *Appellation* of 1558 Knox applied this notion of a covenant between sovereign and people to Scotland. He warned the nobility and estates that no idolater would be exempted from divine punishment, citing the "solemned othe and convenante" made by Asa with his people to serve God and execute idolaters (2 Chron. 15). Knox obviously believed that the nobility and estates were part of such a covenant; like the monarch, they too had obligations to the people to preserve and support true worship.[26]

In the *Appellation* Knox also discussed a third form of covenant. The reformation of religion and the punishment of idolatry was the responsibility of nobles and magistrates not only because of their covenant with the people but also because of their covenant with God. As proof he cited the covenant made with Josiah on behalf of the people (2 Kings 23).[27] But Knox never relinquished the idea of a direct covenant between God and the people. It appeared in the *Appellation* and it provided the implicit foundation of his 1558 letter to the commonalty of Scotland. In that letter he argued that it appertained to the people no less than to monarchs or princes to see that Christ was truly preached. If the civil authorities were negligent or tyrannical, the people were obliged to provide and defend preachers against any — including the civil authorities — who would persecute them.[28] In 1564 Knox reasserted this principle in his debate with William Maitland in the General Assembly. Referring to the commandment to the Hebrews in Exodus 34 not to make a league with the Canaanites, Knox discussed "the people assembled together in one body of a Commonwealth, unto whom God has given sufficient force, not only to resist, but also to suppress all kind of open idolatry. . . ."[29] Thus he conceived of a covenant between sovereign and people; sovereign and God; magistrates, nobles, estates and people; magistrates, nobles, estates and God; and the people and God. To be sure, these forms of the covenant are not systematically devel-

oped in his writings, but they are there, and his concept of disobedience cannot be properly understood without a knowledge of
covenant obligations and relationships.

Knox applied his views on obedience and resistance to the
Scottish scene in a letter written to the lords and other believers
in December 1557. He carefully cautioned his readers not to
disobey the established government in any lawful matter. At the
same time they were to profess their Protestant faith openly and
seek from the government either the promotion of Protestantism
or, failing that, its toleration. If the government refused their
petition, they were advised to profess again their obedience in all
things lawful, but to proceed to provide for the furtherance of the
Protestant cause in defiance of royal authority. They were also
exhorted by Knox to use every means at their disposal to defend
the Scottish Protestants from persecution and tyranny (an obligation to which they were bound), provided only that they continued to yield obedience to the government in lawful matters and
not seek their own glory.[30] This was essentially the position which
Knox had consistently advocated, barring his Edwardian period.
If there was a change, it was in the specific appeal to the nobility
rather than to magistrates. It is not likely that Knox attached any
significance to the change, but considered the Scottish nobility as
the magistrates responsible for suppressing a tyrannous or idolatrous monarch. Both lords and magistrates gained their power
directly from God. The nobles often held governmental positions
subordinate to the sovereign as would magistrates in the technical
sense. Knox was no political theorist, and it is quite likely that
these similarities were sufficient for him to equate nobility and
magistracy in the context of his views on obedience and resistance.

About the same time that Knox was writing his letter to the
Scottish lords, he was also composing *The First Blast of the Trumpet
against the Monstrous Regiment of Women*, which was secretly published in Geneva in the spring of 1558. The tract contains another
statement of the duty of the nobility to overthrow an idolatrous
sovereign. Knox demanded that they acknowledge government by
a woman to be odious to God and refuse to serve as Mary's
officers. Even more, they were commanded to repress her pride
and her tyrannical rule. Athaliah was cited as an incitement to
action. Jehoiada the high priest (a prototype of Knox) had called

upon the captains and chief rulers of the people to depose Athalia (Mary Tudor) and promote Joash to the throne. Knox specifically called the attention of the nobility to the fact that Athaliah was executed, as was the high priest of Baal (Stephen Gardiner?). In a major innovation in his teaching Knox then argued that this was the duty of both the estates and the people. Not only was Mary to be removed, but all those who supported her were also to be executed.[31] "Knox's social conservatism faded before his prophetic fury. . . . Tyrannicide was no longer the special mission of an inspired man [more accurately, the magistrates or nobility]; it had become the ordinary vocation of any man ['who understood the ordinary vocation of a saint'] who would assume it."[32] Knox made it a sin — rebellion against God — *not* to kill an idolatrous sovereign.

That summer Knox issued an expanded version of the letter he had written two years earlier to the Scottish regent, Mary of Lorraine. It was a general statement of the right of rebellion and an attempt to justify it against a second female ruler whom he detested. It was blasphemy, he contended, to assert that God commanded any man to be obeyed above God himself. He repeated his assertion that real treason was *not* to oppose an idolatrous monarch to the death. Christ came, he ominously pointed out, not to bring peace but a sword; not to unite, but to divide. Historically it had always been the duty of prophets and apostles to pit one half of a people or nation against another.[33] The regent had undiplomatically referred to his original letter of 1556 as a pasquil, and what she now read was a clarion call to revolution.

Knox was incensed. Not only had Mary of Lorraine sneered at him, but he had also been hanged in effigy. Mary Stewart, moreover, was about to wed a Frenchman of royal blood, directly threatening his hopes for reformation in Scotland. Religious persecution continued in England — persecution for which his fellow Protestants were blaming him.[34] His personal and family life had been repeatedly troubled because of the religious controversy, and he had experienced four and a half years of exilic turmoil. Consumed with prophetic indignation, he poured his feelings into his summer tracts of 1558. God must be avenged. Knox, his prophet, must be avenged, and idolatry destroyed. If the nobility would not act, God's people must. Calvin, complacent in Geneva, would not approve, nor would Theodore Beza. Neither, for that matter, would most of Europe,[35] but Knox was not deterred, for his vision was not theirs. Like the Hebrew prophets, he dared alienation and castigation to proclaim what he considered to be the truth.

In his *Appellation* of July 1558 he stressed the thesis that no one who imposed idolatry on the people should be exempt from death. The personal status of such a person was of no consequence, be he monarch or commoner. The punishment of idolaters and blasphemers, who desecrated the majesty of God, was not simply the concern of kings and chief rulers, but of every person in the state in accordance with his Christian vocation and the possibility afforded to him by God to wreak vengeance. Deuteronomy 13 provided the biblical sanction for Knox's call to revolution. As noted, Knox evoked the covenant motif: God's covenant with his people required that they obey his law, which called for the execution of idolaters without respect to status. Knox's extension of the principle of active disobedience to the people (i.e., the saints) thus occurred in a covenant context and because of covenant responsibilities.[36]

This theme also appeared in the letter to the commonalty of Scotland that accompanied the *Appellation*. Subjects might lawfully require from their temporal superiors the provision of true preachers and the expulsion of false prophets. If the temporal powers refused, the people could provide their own ministers and defend them against governmental persecution. Furthermore, believers were not obligated to render tithes to false bishops and clerics. The core of Knox's argument was based on the thesis that people who acquiesced in the rule of idolaters were themselves guilty of idolatry. In religion all men were equal and must therefore bear the responsibility for the propagation of the faith. The letter made it clear that he desired the commonalty to work with the estates and nobility in the repression of tyranny rather than against them.[37] Knox did not seek anarchy or democracy, but religious reform in accord with divine law and the covenants, and in the context of the existing social and political structure of sixteenth-century Scotland. He did not seek to harness the nobility to the mob or to place the mob "at the disposal of an aristocratic *fronde*."[38] Rather, he sought harmonious unity between the saints, whatever their social class and political status, in the accomplishment of reform.

With the *Appellation* and letter to the commonalty Knox published an outline of a proposed *Second Blast*, which he never completed. Unlike the *First Blast*, its concern was with the lawfulness of rebellion, not primarily with a woman sovereign. No manifest idolater or notorious transgressor of the divine law, regardless of birth and lineage, was to hold a position of authority in a Christian state. The people of such a state were not bound by any oath or promise to obey tyrants who contravened divine law. Any such ruler might justly be deposed and punished by those who granted him authority. Although Knox had earlier stated that temporal rulers received their authority from God, he clearly implied here that the people or estates were the agency through which that authority was bestowed. The idea of a covenant or social compact between the people and their rulers was again present.[39] Undoubtedly Knox would have developed his ideas more explicitly if he had been a political theorist rather than a prophet.

Knox wrote again to England early in 1559. His *Brief Exhortation to England*, completed in January, urged Elizabeth's subjects to accept only those aspects of religion that were commanded in Scripture. If the queen or any other authority sought to alter or ignore the least jot in religion commanded by God, they were to be reputed enemies to God and unworthy to reign. If they sought to establish idolatry (Catholicism) they were to be executed. Elizabeth herself was not to be excepted. Negligence of this duty in the Marian period had, according to Knox, made the English guilty of murdering their fellow humans, denying Christ, and committing treason to God. Knox's heavy indebtedness to Hebrew conceptions was perhaps nowhere so keenly manifested as in his insistence that subjects were responsible for the religious policies of their sovereigns, a concept that completely ruled out the idea of religious toleration for him. Neither "power nor libertie [may] be permitted to any . . . either to lyve without the yoke of discipline by God's Worde commaunded; either yet to alter, to chaunge, to disanull, or dissolve the least one jott in religion, which from God's mouthe thow hast receyved."[40] For Knox, resistance against idolatrous monarchs was a duty for conscientious Protestants, but if conscientious Catholics should resist they would be rebelling against God.

In May 1559 Knox and his colleagues wrote to Mary of

Lorraine stating the right to resist for the sake of conscience. "Except this cruelty be stayed by your wisdom, we will be compelled to take the sword of just defence against all that shall pursue us for the matter of religion, and for our conscience sake. . . ."[41] Obedience would be rendered to the regent's government only if the Protestant faith were tolerated. A subsequent letter was sent to the nobility who opposed the Protestant cause, reminding them that it was their duty to bridle the actions of wicked men, including princes and emperors. Knox and his colleagues pointed out that there was a difference between the authority which was divinely commanded and the persons who exercised that authority. Whereas the former was always right, the latter could become corrupt, in which case it was wrong for Christians to obey their commandments. Resistance was a duty.[42] Two months later Knox summarized the position of the Scottish Protestants in a letter to Sir Henry Percy, a leader of the English army in Scotland the ensuing year: "We mean neyther sedition, neyther yit rebellion against any just and lauchfull authoritie, but onlie the advauncement of Christes religion, and the libertie of this poore Realme."[43]

Knox continued to maintain these ideas in his interviews with Mary Stewart. In September 1561 Mary inquired of him if subjects could resist their sovereigns. Knox's reply implied the existence of a covenant between God and temporal princes. If the latter exceeded the bounds imposed on them by God, subjects had to disobey because of their duty to obey God. Princes who persecuted Protestants were, in their blind zeal, subject to a mad frenzy, and had to be restrained by their subjects until their minds became sober. Knox tactfully steered away from the divinely prescribed punishment for idolaters in Deuteronomy 13.[44] He repeated his beliefs to Mary again in 1563, but explicitly warned her that idolaters could be lawfully executed by believers. In his list of examples he pointedly included a reigning monarch (Agag) executed by a religious leader (Samuel). If Mary knew her Old Testament well, she would have found Knox's remarks not only offensive but chilling: a cheerful King Agag was hewed in pieces by Samuel in God's name (1 Sam. 15:33). Knox also called attention to the mutual covenant between sovereigns and subjects, and clearly affirmed the right of subjects to disobey if sovereigns did not fulfill their obligations, which he summarized as protection and defense against evil doers. "Consider . . . what it is that ye aught to do unto them by mutual contract. They are bound to obey you, and that not but in God. Ye are bound to keep laws unto them. Ye crave of them service: they crave of you protection and defence against wicked doers."[45] If Mary failed to fulfill her duty to her subjects, she would not receive their full obedience. On that note the interview concluded.

In the debate in the General Assembly in June 1564, which primarily involved William Maitland and Knox, the latter emphasized the covenant between God and the people. Knox expressed to Maitland the same views he had been putting forth since 1558 — the duty of subjects to obey temporal authority, but also their duty to rebel if that authority opposed divine law. Maitland, who agreed only to passive disobedience, cited Luther, Melanchthon, Bucer, Musculus, and Calvin to support his thesis. Knox's retort indicated that he was aware of the arguments of these men. He rejected the references to Luther and Melanchthon on the grounds that they were writing against the Anabaptists and were attempting to refute the Anabaptist position on church-state relations. The remaining writers, according to Knox, were providing counsel for dispersed minorities of Christian subjects who had no opportunity to rebel. Knox thereupon declared that his concept of rebellion applied only where believers were "assembled together in one body of a Commonwealth, unto whom God has given sufficient force, not only to resist, but also to suppress all kind of open idolatry: and such a people . . . are bound to keep their land clean and unpolluted."[46]

For his authority in the 1564 debate Knox cited not only Scripture but also the *Apology (Bekenntnis)* of the Magdeburg Lutherans. The *Apology* had been issued in 1550 to justify Magdeburg's resistance to Charles V on the grounds that he was persecuting true religion rather than defending it. Resistance was therefore justified by princes and magistrates. In effect this was an extension of the orthodox Protestant position, and was endorsed, for example, by Beza.[47] Luther eventually taught a doctrine of active resistance, but normally vested the right of such resistance only in the princes. In 1539, however, Luther, Melanchthon, Bucer, and Justas Jonas (the German humanist turned Lutheran theologian) agreed that subjects could defend themselves and resist if the state sought to compel them to worship idolatrously.[48] The Magdeburg Lutherans, led by Niclas von Amssdorff, were of a similar mind. Because a ruler who suppresses true religion represents the devil rather than God, mere passive resistance is insufficient to satisfy God. Subjects must therefore actively resist. The princes were called upon to aid the people of Magdeburg on the grounds that they derived their authority directly from God and were responsible to maintain right worship for their subjects. During Knox's sojourn in Germany he may have seen a copy of the *Apology*; at the very least he discussed its contents prior to 1564.[49]

During the 1564 debate John Craig, Knox's colleague, advocated the contractual relationship between sovereign and subjects. Craig testified that he had heard a debate on this topic in 1554 in Bologna, where Thomas de Finola, Rector of the University, contended that rulers had to be reformed or were to be deposed by those who chose, confirmed, or admitted them to office,

> as oft as they break that promise made by the oath to their subjects: Because that their Prince is no less bound by oath to the subjects, than are the subjects to their Prince, and therefore ought to be kept and reformed equally, according to the law and condition of the oath that is made of either party.[50]

Craig perhaps discussed this disputation with Knox in the course of their work in Edinburgh during the preceding three years, yet Knox's position had already been formulated. At the most, Craig confirmed his views.

Near the end of his life Knox continued to protest that he rendered nothing but lawful obedience in the course of his career. In the meeting of the General Assembly in March 1571 he replied to those who resented his attacks on Mary Stewart. Because they professed obedience to her, they were traitors. She was not his sovereign, nor, because of her impiety, was she God's subject. As for himself, "I have liued as a subject, and obeyed as a subject, to all lauchfull ordinance of God within this realme."[51]

Determining the sources of Knox's ideas on disobedience and resistance is a complex affair. In addition to the ideological sources there were obvious practical considerations. If Scottish policy had followed that of the early years of the Earl of Arran's regency, there would have been no need for a Protestant rebellion in Scotland. But the repressive policies of Beaton in the mid-1540s created a condition conducive to rebellion. The revolt of the Castilians, in which Knox openly defied the Scottish government, was a major outcome of Beaton's policies, and a lesson for Knox in the practice of resistance. Subsequently, against a background of intolerance in Scotland, the repressive policies of Mary Tudor were instrumental in Knox's urging a course of active resistance.[52]

In view of Knox's active resistance at St. Andrews in 1547, he was probably influenced by his earlier readings in the church fathers, by the views of John Major and the medieval intellectual tradition he reflected, and perhaps by the doctrine of obedience in the *First Helvetic Confession*. Among the fathers, Augustine, one of Knox's favorites, took a distinctly conservative position. Subjects must obey their rulers in matters which are not immoral, and if the state orders something that contravenes divine precepts, passive but not active disobedience is the correct course of action. Christians are given a government that is best for them, even if it is unjust. They are to obey the commands of their rulers as the commands of Christ unless the former conflict with the latter, in which case redress must be had to verbal protest and passive resistance.[53] This position is in accord with Knox's views in Edwardian England, except that he was then concerned with a Protestant government whereas Augustine's principles apply clearly to non-Christian governments as well as Christian ones.

The views of Ambrose on obedience are basically akin to those of Augustine. Passive resistance to monarchs commanding things contrary to divine Law is proper, but armed attacks on the sovereign are not. A conscientious man must die before he obeys a command he knows is wrong. Kings are not subject to temporal law, but are accountable only to divine Law. Knox was sharply opposed to such a conception.[54] Although he read Ambrose, he did not learn his concept of active disobedience from him, as has been asserted.[55]

Chrysostom, who was another of Knox's favorite church fathers, took a similar position on the question of disobedience. Because it amounts to anarchy, disobedience to rulers is an evil, yet it is worse than anarchy to be led by an iniquitous ruler. In such a case the Christian is not to obey but "flee and avoid him" if his commands contradict a matter of faith. Subjects indeed must be obedient in all other matters, but so ought rulers to be watchful and sober.[56] Of the church fathers he read, with the exception of Origen, Knox was probably closer to Chrysostom than to the others on the matter of obedience, for he at least followed Chrysostom's advice and fled England rather than suffer persecution under Mary. Tertullian, on the other hand, despite his sharp separation between Athens and Jerusalem, would seemingly have urged martyrdom rather than flight.[57] Knox also read Origen, who clearly distinguished between the natural law created by God and the written law formulated by man. Whereas the latter must be obeyed as long as it does not contradict natural law, Christians have an obligation to govern their lives in accordance with natural law even if it means violating the laws of the state. It is even reasonable for Christians to form associations in opposition to state laws if this is done to further the truth.[58] There are various points of kinship between the views of Origen and Knox, one of the more interesting being the notion of natural law. There is no way to ascertain precisely how much Knox was influenced by Origen and perhaps Chrysostom on these general issues, but such influence was probably less than that originating from the medieval political tradition and contemporary thinkers.

There is ample precedent in medieval political theory for Knox's views. Kingship as a contractual bond between rulers and governed based on a preexisting system of legal rights which, if violated, justified revolt, was a feudal heritage. Writing in the context of the investiture controversy, the eleventh-century author Manegold of Lautenbach distinguished (as Knox essentially did later) between the office of the king, which was sacred, and an individual sovereign who could justly forfeit his authority. A king does this when he becomes a tyrant, that is, when he destroys justice, overthrows the peace, and breaks faith. Subjects are not bound to obey a tyrannical ruler. Manegold also foreshadowed Knox in propounding the idea of a contract *(pactum)* between king and people which was equally binding on both parties.[59] In the following century John of Salisbury stated a doctrine of tyrannicide on the grounds that tyranny abused the power granted to man by God. He cited biblical and classical precedents, though he was aware that he was running counter to the patristic tradition. The essence of his position was virtually the same as that enunciated by Knox in 1558: the unjust ruler who violates the laws and customs of his land no longer can claim the obedience of his subjects, who may justly resist him and, if necessary, depose and execute him. Although John, unlike Knox, regarded kings as responsible to God alone, he and Knox were one in seeing tyrannicide as the agent of an avenging God.[60] In the thirteenth century Thomas Aquinas opposed tyrannicide, but nevertheless favored active resistance against a tyrannical ruler, aimed at abolishing his tyranny in a manner that would not do more harm than the tyranny itself. Consequently, in a manner akin to Knox, Aquinas cautioned that "action against a tyrant should not be taken by the private presumption of individuals but rather by public authority." Because the contract between king and people is no longer binding if the king acts in a tyrannical fashion, public authority, "the multitude," may depose him.[61]

William of Ockham stressed the necessity of obedience to temporal authority, but qualified this by asserting that the emperor (as well as the pope) has no plenitude of power in spiritual and temporal affairs. Imperial authority is derived from God, but through the medium of the people. The community, though usually inferior to a temporal ruler, can correct, imprison, or depose him in cases of necessity. Such cases arise when temporal commands or positive laws (which were supposed to be established only for the public good) threaten the general welfare of society in either a spiritual or a material sense. At that point natural law enjoins that extraordinary measures outside of positive law be taken. It is of utmost interest to note that Ockham claimed for theologians (as Knox for a time did) the right to determine when exceptional situations arose. *In casu necessitatis* legitimate violence may be used to resist criminal violence, with the sanction of natural law, to the point of the deposition of the ruler.[62]

The republican political views of William's contemporary, Marsilius of Padua, are based on the principle that laws are made by the people, and the ruler must govern in accord with them. Because the ruler is elected by the people, if he infringes the laws he can be corrected, deposed, and punished by the people. The authority to judge the ruler may be exercised by delegated persons, but ultimately it belongs to the people as legislator alone. Three factors are to be used in considering correction of a ruler. First, any grave excess must be punished, lest the outrage of the people destroy the state. Second, if possible the excess should be dealt with by law, but if the law does not determine the penalty, the people as legislator must specifically determine the punishment. Third, a slight excess by the ruler should be overlooked to preserve the stability of the state and the respect for the ruler. Nevertheless, if slight excesses are frequently committed, they must be punished as determined by law. The most crucial difference between the views of Marsilius and those of his predecessors is "the antecedent tradition's emphasis upon final causes, . . . [which] had the result that the criteria rendering the ruler corrigible were formulated in terms of 'injustice' or 'tyranny,' but these in turn referred not to explicit provisions of positive law but rather to a 'higher law.' " Marsilius, however, did not define law and government so that moral and theological criteria were the determining factors (as they were for Knox). Rather, he relied upon purely political definitions. The practical result is that his system allows for corrective action against a tyrant in the context of the positive legal and governmental framework of the state. He is not faced with the choice of submission or tyrannicide or revolution.[63]

The political views of Wyclif differ in certain respects from those of his contemporaries. Like them, he believes temporal authority originates with God, but is devolved on the ruler through the election of the community. He differs, however, in stressing the necessity of obedience to the king as the vicar of God. Whether the sovereign is just or unjust, the subject must obey. Nevertheless, if the ruler acts to injure God as distinct from an act which injures the subject personally, resistance is required, but "in patience and submission," not "by force or fraud." Apart from this exception, obedience is required, even if the ruler is a perverse king or tyrant, for both possess power (as distinct from dominion) to rule from God. Wyclif, of course, believes sovereigns should govern justly and in accordance with the law, but he does not posit any legal right in the community to act against an unjust ruler.[64]

Pierre d'Ailly, Jean Gerson's teacher, accepted the patristic idea that a tyrant might be divinely sanctioned as punishment for sin, but he did not use this as the basis for a theory of passive obedience. Neither, however, would he justify tyrannicide, which he deemed an illegal and arbitrary act. Similarly, he condemned Wyclif's contention that the *populares* could act of its own accord to correct a delinquent lord. What d'Ailly would approve was active disobedience channeled through the legal action of the community (the origin and source of political authority) against the tyrant. The latter could be forced to reform or be deposed. "D'Ailly's rejection of any arbitrary, individual right to kill a tyrannical ruler or to revolt against him should, therefore, be seen in the context of his other conclusion that the whole community possessed the right to protect itself by legal, institutional means, against the depredations of such a ruler."[65]

Gerson reiterated the distinction between office and office-holder—a distinction that existed in Roman juristic thought as well as earlier medieval writings. "Gerson's main objective," in the words of Zofia Rueger, "was to prove the fundamental lawfulness of conciliar action taken against the Pope, not the ecclesiastical monarchy. . . ." Yet Gerson also argued that an unjust ruler could lawfully be resisted according to natural law principles. Positive laws not conforming to divine and natural law (terms that at times appear to be interchangeable in Gerson's writings) do not have to be obeyed. Gerson went so far as to renew the justification of tyrannicide, though in carefully qualified circumstances. It was a last resort and could be used only if the tyranny was intolerable, could not be reformed or removed by legal means, would be worse than the tyrannicide, and could be removed by means which were not evil and were used by men with impeccable motives.[66]

Knox's mentor, John Major, followed in the tradition of d'Ailly and Gerson at the University of Paris. There are numerous parallels between the political views of Knox and Major which indicate the likelihood of influence. Most striking is the similarity between their doctrines of resistance, though Major obviously did not equate Catholic sovereigns with idolatrous tyrants, as Knox certainly did. Both men also critically viewed the masses. Major, foreshadowing Knox, taught the primary sovereignty of the people, though recognizing as a general rule the supremacy of the monarchy. Knox did not specifically distinguish between general rule *(regulariter)* and certain cases *(casualiter)* in so many words, but the whole tenor of his thought runs in this direction. He would have agreed with Major's belief that kings are given their right to rule by God through the people, and that tyrannical monarchs could therefore be deposed.[67] Knox's belief that nations must be governed by their own laws and not the laws of foreign states may be due to Major's influence, but when, in 1558, Knox appealed to the commonalty of Scotland to resist the government actively, he parted ideological company with Major. Although the latter wrote of the right of the people to rebel against a tyrannical monarch, his conception of the people was that of the nobility acting in behalf of the masses. Knox accepted such a position before 1558, but thereafter when he talked of the people assembled together in one commonwealth engaging in active resistance, he meant literally that. While there is substantial likelihood that Knox was influenced by Major, caution must be exercised lest too much be credited to Major. The two men differed not only in character and intellect, but also in important ideological matters. Certainly both favored reform of the church, but the nature of that reform differed considerably. Politically, Major's views were worked out in a constitutional framework, but while Knox too used constitutional ideas, his framework was fundamentally religious.[68] Perhaps Major's most important contribution to Knox was his conveyance to his student of that aspect of the medieval tradition which developed notions of limited, contractual government and the legitimacy of active resistance in appropriate circumstances.

The concept of resistance in high and later medieval thought was usually based in part on Roman law, the key being the *lex regia* by which the Roman Senate and people traditionally bestowed power to the emperor at the commencement of each reign. Many medieval commentators believed this grant was revocable for due cause, especially after Aquinas supported this view. The Aristotelian revival of the twelfth and thirteenth centuries was influential in shifting support from absolutism to this position. A group of Roman lawyers and publicists emerged "who used the similarities between Aristotle and Roman law to justify a conception of the ruler as a mere delegate of the popular will, who could always in the long run be held responsible to it."[69] It was this concept of accountability that led writers, especially beginning in the fourteenth century, to develop doctrines of the legitimacy of resistance. Subsequently, opponents of absolutism in the sixteenth century sometimes availed themselves of the *Corpus Juris Civilis*, among them being Marius Salamonius and Andrea Alciati.[70] When sixteenth-century Protestant writers began advocating resistance, appeals for support were sometimes made to Roman law as well as to feudal and canon law. Beza, for example, cites Roman civil law in his *Du droit des magistrats* (1574), but cautions that "I use these arguments not to suggest that [Roman] civil law or the opinion of this or that philosopher should be taken as a rule of conscience, but only to show the manifest unreason of that opinion which allows no lawful way to halt flagrant tyranny, no matter how iniquitous or cruel."[71] Philippe de Duplessis-Mornay uses numerous analogies from Roman civil law in his *Vindiciae contra tyrannos* (1579).[72] Knox was, in one form or another, acquainted with the Roman law, notably the *Corpus Juris Civilis*, as well as the writings of Cicero and the canon law, as reflected in *The First Blast* and *The Appellation*.[73] It is therefore tempting to suspect Roman law as a possible source of his views on resistance. The fact remains, however, that his citations of Roman law relate to the status of women, not the question of resistance. As a consequence one can only speculate about the possibility that his studies of Roman law aided his formulation of resistance theory.

With respect to the possible influence on Knox's ideas of resistance by early Protestant thought in Scotland, very little can be said. Patrick Hamilton did not leave a record of his views, nor did Wishart. There is, however, a hint of Wishart's views in the record of his trial, at which he was charged with refusing to obey the Lord Governor's command to desist preaching. He retorted that Christians were commanded to obey God rather than men, and "that it is not lawful for the threats and menacings of man to desist from the preaching of the Evangel." Thus Wishart favored some kind of disobedience. His translation of the *First Helvetic Confession* stipulates only that magistrates are to be obeyed as long as their commands do not repugn divine precepts. The nature of disobedience is not specified.[74] Thus any possible influence from Hamilton, Wishart, or the *First Helvetic Confession*, barring the example of defiance and martyrdom, was negligible.

As a minister of the Church of England, Knox probably

learned of the views of Tyndale and his followers on obedience. Tyndale believed rulers were appointed by God and subject to his Law alone. They were not to be actively resisted, and rebellion and tyrannicide were forbidden. Yet Christians were not to obey commands contrary to divine Law, though this meant suffering the consequences and tarrying patiently until divine judgment was executed against the tyrannical ruler. Although monarchs were conceived of as being in a contractual relationship, their violation of the contract did not justify active resistance by their subjects. In practice Tyndale was not quite so conservative, for he issued an unsanctioned edition of various books of Scripture, went abroad without permission, and disseminated prohibited books in England. His practice as much as his theory influenced such men as Hooper, Coverdale, and John Bale, Bishop of Ossory.[75] While in England Knox blended with this tradition. The difficulty of applying its principles was manifested at Edward's death. Whereas Cranmer, Ridley, and Edwin Sandys, the Vice-Chancellor of Cambridge, openly supported Lady Jane Grey, Bale and Hooper backed Mary Tudor. Knox, having actively rebelled once, cast his lot with Lady Jane, though not in a totally overt manner.[76] England was warned by Knox not to enter into a league with an idolatrous ruler and to beware the dangers of a foreign marriage.[77] Knox was willing to abide by Tyndale's theories on obedience as long as the sovereign was Protestant, but as soon as the threat of a Catholic monarch appeared he resumed his thoughts on active resistance.

Once on the Continent he contacted Calvin, Bullinger, and others. When he eventually settled down in Geneva he associated with the men responsible for the Geneva Bible, in which the annotations indicate a doctrine of obedience akin to that expressed by Tyndale. Christians are to be obedient to civil authority in all things except those contrary to divine precepts. The note to 1 Kings 21:11 indicates the importance of obeying the Laws of God rather than the wicked commands of princes, and the note to Acts 5:29 expresses the same idea. It is specifically stated in the note to Matthew 26:52 that "the exercising of the sworde is forbide to private persones." Thus at the time when Knox, Goodman, and Ponet were thinking in terms of active resistance, the annotators were taking a more conservative position.[78] There was therefore no influence on Knox's doctrine of resistance from this quarter.

Neither was there any influence from his fellow exile John Foxe, whose *Ad inclytos praepotantes Angliae proceres, ordines, & status, totamque eius gentis nobilitatem, pro afflictis fratribus svpplicatio* was published at Basle in 1557. The theme was an appeal to the English nobility to persuade Mary Tudor to cease persecuting Protestants. Although he did not advocate tyrannicide or urge rebellion, he openly favored a working alliance of the nobility and monarchy to prevent tyranny and sedition. Absolutism was rejected, and Foxe warned of disturbances in the state if the monarch became tyrannical. Laws had to be administered with moderation and virtue. Yet even if the sovereign were ungodly, Foxe refused active resistance, for governments and their policies were allotted to men by God. Similar views were subsequently expressed by Laurence Humphrey in his *Optimates, sive de nobilitate*, published at Basle in 1560, and the English version, *The Nobles or of Nobilitye*, published at London in 1563.[79]

On the Continent one of the more likely sources of influence on Knox's thought was Bishop John Ponet's *A Shorte Treatise of Politike Power* (1556). There is, however, no direct evidence to indicate that Knox relied on or even read Ponet's work. It has generally been thought that the possibility of influence is extremely unlikely because of Ponet's strong interest in constitutionalism, popularly conferred responsibility, and natural law.[80] Yet a reexamination of the views of both men brings out various marked similarities. Both men, for example, protested against Mary's rule because it violated divine Law as revealed in Scripture, and both men blasted not only her idolatry but also her marriage to Philip as a betrayal of England into foreign hands. Like Knox's, "Ponet's protest was that of a prophet who recognized divine standards located in Edwardian legal practice and hence remained unaware of any tension between his prophecy and his patriotism." Both men also used empirical criteria in their arguments, and the social compact is included in their writings. Knox stressed the commission to resist as something which was divinely bestowed, but, unlike Ponet, he also made the contract between ruler and ruled part of his argument. In any case, for Ponet the *vox populi* should be the *vox Dei*. Both men sanctioned tyrannicide, including, in certain circumstances, tyrannicide by private persons.[81] Thus it is quite likely that Knox was aware of Ponet's views. If not, the two men arrived at similar conclusions by drawing in part upon the same sources: the Bible, the medieval political tradition, John Major, and the *Apology of Magdeburg*.[82]

Knox almost certainly discussed his views on resistance and female sovereignty with Goodman, whose *How Superior Powers Oght to be Obeyd* was dated January 1, 1558, from Geneva. Before writing their respective works, both men had records of active resistance against established governments. Goodman asserted that magistrates and nobles have a duty to "bridle" their sovereigns, and that all men are responsible to disobey commands from their rulers which are contrary to divine precepts. To obey an ungodly ruler is to rebel against God. Deposition and execution of an idolatrous or tyrannical monarch were sanctioned by Goodman as duties of all persons. A monarch who blasphemes God and oppresses his subjects forfeits his right to govern, hence Goodman called for the deposition and execution of Mary Tudor. Like Knox, he spoke of mutual obligations between ruler and ruled, and in consequence if one party ceases to fulfill its responsibilities the other is no longer bound by the agreement. Yet Goodman cautioned against rash action, advising patience, penitence, and prayer. Goodman completed his treatise before Knox concluded his 1558 tracts. In view of the close friendship between the two men, their cowork at Geneva, and the fact that they reached the same conclusions on the same political problems at virtually the same time, Knox almost certainly was influenced by Goodman, as Goodman was very likely influenced by Knox.[83]

Knox may also have been influenced by Theodore Beza, whose ideas might also be reflected in the works of Goodman and Ponet. Beza's *De haereticis a civili magistratu puniendis* appeared in 1554 as a defense of Calvin's willingness to burn a heretic.[84] In the work Beza argued that governments are established by social consent, which is likewise the source of human law. Magistrates in Christian states are representatives of God and are bound by the Word of God in spiritual matters. In turn subjects must obey them in all temporal things, but princes who abuse their authority cannot be trusted with the power to punish heresy. Under evil princes, lesser magistrates must endeavor to preserve true religion. While they can lead resistance to evil princes, they must be under the church's supervision. A course of resistance cannot be adopted until prayer is first tried, which was exactly Knox's practice in the mid-1550s. Magdeburg is cited as an example of approved resistance, so that the *Apology of Magdeburg* probably influenced Beza. Beza's views resemble those of Bucer, and the source of this apparent influence may have been the second edition of Bucer's *In Evangelium Matthei Enarrationes* (1530).[85] If so, Bucer's impact on Scotland may be felt not only in the doctrine of the Lord's Supper but also in the doctrine of active resistance.

One further source of potential influence on Knox remains to be noted: John Willock. Knox and Willock probably met in 1551 when Willock was preaching in the Border areas and Knox was ministering at Berwick and Newcastle. They met again at Erskine of Dun's house in 1555. Like Knox, Willock had been involved in active resistance before their meeting in 1555, for he had been embroiled in the rising against Mary Tudor which resulted in the execution of his patron, Henry, Duke of Suffolk, in 1554. Conceivably Willock discussed this affair with Knox in 1555. The similarity of their views by 1559 is definitely known, for in October of that year Willock and Knox testified before an assembly of nobility, barons, and burghers in the Tolbooth on the question of suspending the Queen Regent for her tyrannical policies. Willock argued that magistrates are divinely ordained, though their power is limited by God, and that they have a duty to their subjects. They may be deposed for just causes, but God does not always remove such rulers directly but through appointed means. Therefore the Queen Regent could be deposed because she failed to minister justice to her subjects impartially, preserve them from the invasion of strangers, and permit the open preaching of the divine message. She was also, charged Willock, an idolatress who despised the counsel and requests of the nobility. Expressing agreement, Knox made several further points, including the admonition that the iniquity and misgovernment of the Queen Regent "ought in nowise to withdraw neither our hearts, neither yet the hearts of other subjects, from the obedience due unto our Sovereigns." She must be deposed for the preservation of the commonwealth, not because of malice and envy, and if she should openly repent and submit to the nobility, she must be restored to the regency. Knox's view was slightly more cautious and conservative, but he and Willock agreed on the fundamental issue of the right to resist actively and to depose a tyrannical ruler.[86]

A variety of intellectual sources appears to have influenced Knox in his development of the appropriate form of disobedience. Apart from the practical political exigencies which were present, he may well have drawn from Origen and possibly Chrysostom among the fathers; medieval political thought as channeled primarily through John Major; the Magdeburg *Bekenntnis*; and John Ponet, Christopher Goodman, Theodore Beza, and John Willock. The influence of George Wishart, the *First Helvetic Confession*, and John Calvin appear to have been minimal. Bullinger cautioned Knox but did not deter him from developing and expressing his views more fully, and Viret may have openly encouraged him, in which case he was of tremendous influence in Knox's intellectual development. Henry Balnaves probably had no impact on Knox's political views at all. Knox is known to have read Aristotle, on whom his mentor, John Major, was an authority. Thus it may be that an early interest in tyrants came directly or indirectly at least partially from the ancient Greek philosopher. Certainly there is no justification for arguing either that Knox "adopted" the teaching of Calvin on rebellion, or that his "ideas, even the idea that Christians may bear the sword against tyrants, were all his own, were anti-Genevan. . . ."[87]

Although Knox cannot be divorced from dependence on the thoughts of these men, a substantial place must be given to the Bible as a source of influence for his political thought.[88] To be sure, he came to the Bible with preconceived notions of what he expected to find, but Scripture did not disappoint him. Given his conception of his prophetic vocation, his basic temperament and existing religious and political conditions in Scotland and England, he would very likely have reached the decision to resist actively if Scripture had been silent on the issue. But the Old Testament provided ample examples of the deposition of rulers. Following biblical precepts as he understood them, he extended the right of rebellion against idolatrous and tyrannical sovereigns from the magistrates and nobility to the elect. Although not well received initially, his view was subsequently influential. Beza and later Huguenot writers were among those influenced, as perhaps was Calvin.[89] It has even been suggested — and not altogether without merit — that Knox was a key link in the development of political ideology that culminated in the American Revolution. "The line of succession runs from Martin Luther to John Calvin, from John Calvin to Philippe de Duplessis-Mornay, from Philippe de Duplessis-Mornay to John Knox, from John Knox to John Milton, from John Milton to John Locke, and from John Locke to Alexander Hamilton."[90] Although the line of succession is more complex than this, and should have the Magdeburg *Bekenntnis*, Pierre Viret, and others as influences on Knox, it is fitting to recognize the significant contribution of the great Scottish reformer, particularly in the context of the Bicentennial celebration of the American Revolution a few years ago. Indeed, Knox's role is symbolic of the significant Scottish contribution to the growth of the American nation.

THE GYNECOCRACY
CONTROVERSY

John Knox has gained a certain degree of notoriety in the popular mind as an antifeminist because of his attack on female sovereigns in *The First Blast of the Trumpet against the Monstrous Regiment of Women* (1558). Yet his attack was by no means original, for similar views were propounded in the sixteenth century by diverse writers. In 1523 the Spanish humanist Juan Vives argued (in *De institutione foeminae Christinae*) that women lacked strength, intelligence, and discretion to govern; after 1540 English readers could study these ideas in their native tongue. In 1553 Sir David Lyndsay, an early acquaintance of Knox, had completed *Ane Dialogue betuix Experience and ane Courteour, off the Miserabyll Estait of the Warld*, in which he reaffirmed the traditional notion that men were divinely ordained to have preeminence over women. On this basis women could not rule.

> Ladyis no way I can commend
> Presumptuouslye quhilk doith pretend
> Tyll vse the office of ane kyng,
> Or Realmes tak in gouernyng. . . .[1]

In the aftermath of Knox's *First Blast*, Laurence Humphrey, who had spent the Marian exile at Basle, Zürich, and finally Geneva, wrote his *De religionis conseruatione & reformatione uera* (Basle, 1559), in which he repeated the familiar belief that women were weaker vessels than men, but acknowledged that God called women to rule in special cases. Jean Bodin (in *Les Six Liures de la République*, 1576) repeated most of the traditional arguments against gynecocracy, and Knox's fellow Scot, George Buchanan, expressed similar views in the late 1560s, and again in his *History of Scotland* (1582). In *The Faerie Queene* Edmund Spenser used the figure of Radigund to express the unnatural government and base humility of women, though admitting that on occasion God granted women lawful sovereignty. Spenser was aware of the controversy stirred up by Knox and his fellow exiles, Christopher Goodman and Anthony Gilby, over gynecocracy. Among others who expressed such views were the Huguenot Francois Hotman and the essayist Montaigne, yet it is Knox who continues to be depicted as the arch hater of women.

There is some truth in Professor John E. Neale's observation that sixteenth-century statesmen believed government was "a mystery revealed only to men. They had less faith in Deborah than John Knox, and were more dangerous for being more reasonable."[2] Yet there was already evidence of a more liberal and enlightened outlook. Various Renaissance Englishmen were praising and defending women, noting their intellect, virtue, and physical prowess. In 1542 David Clapham translated Cornelius Agrippa's *De nobilitate & praecellentia foeminei sexus* (1529) into English; it praised the ability of women to govern realms. Thomas Elyot's *The Defence of Good Women* (1540) contended that females had all the prerequisites necessary to rule successfully. A more enlightened attitude on the part of Knox would not therefore have required originality on his part.

The question of women rulers first assumed importance for Knox in 1554 when he asked the Swiss reformer Heinrich Bullinger if a female could rule by divine right and transfer the right of sovereignty to her husband. In reply Bullinger asserted that according to divine law women were to be subject to men. He cautioned Knox, however, that women who ruled in compliance with the laws of a realm and hereditary rights did not wholly lack biblical sanction, "as the gospel does not seem to unsettle or abrogate heredity rights, and the political laws of kingdoms. . . ." If, however, the monarch was not a Deborah but an ungodly and tyrannical ruler, Christians were to take note of the example of Athaliah (2 Kings 11). At the appropriate time God would destroy such a government by his own people, supplying them with the proper qualifications. Bullinger would not answer Knox's query about the transfer of sovereignty, but referred him to those acquainted with the laws and customs of the realm involved.[3]

John Calvin's position, which Knox also ascertained, was virtually the same. He was willing to tolerate female sovereigns, but only as a punishment or an exception, not as a rule. His response to Knox, which he substantially reiterated in a letter to Bullinger, asserted that female sovereignty was contrary to natural law and was to be regarded as a visitation of divine anger. Yet on occasion God bestowed sovereignty on women "with a certain heroic spirit," such as Deborah, as a reproach to the sloth of men.

> Yet though absolute anarchy should be the result of such rule, I laid it down, that to the private citizen I would give no further liberty than to express his sorrow, since the government of a woman badly adjusted to the country is like the government of a tyrant, which has to be borne till God put an end to it.[4]

Despite such advice, Knox subsequently wrote and secretly published his *First Blast*, provoking the strong displeasure of Queen Elizabeth not only toward Knox but also toward Geneva in general. Early in 1559 Calvin wrote to Sir William Cecil to state his position concerning female sovereigns after Elizabeth had cooly received his commentaries on Isaiah. Elizabeth's attitude is understandable, though Knox had not intended to attack her, but rather her half-sister, Mary Tudor. Calvin explained to Cecil that female government was a deviation from the original and proper order of nature, and was to be regarded, like slavery, as a punishment of man due to the fall. Yet God sometimes selected women (Deborah being the standard example) to govern. Such divine exceptions could be determined by the "singular good qualities" which they demonstrated. On such occasions women might better reveal divine glory than men.

> I came at length to this conclusion, that since both by custom and public consent and long practice it has been established, that realms and principalities may descend to females by hereditary right, it did not appear to me necessary to move the question, not only because the thing would be invidious, but because . . . it would not be lawful to unsettle the governments which are ordained by the peculiar providence of God.

Knox, Calvin charged, had exhibited "thoughtless arrogance."[5]

Despite popular opinion, Knox did not have a natural dislike for women. He married twice, and there is no indication that he had anything more than the normal difficulties experienced by marital partners. He corresponded frequently with women in his role as a spiritual counselor. There is no reason to believe that he was troubled by feelings of social inferiority with respect to his dealings with women, though "women's approbation and submission were one of his deepest needs all through his life...."[6] Some women doted over him, and Mrs. Elizabeth Bowes and Mrs. Anne Locke even followed him abroad. To those who sought his advice as a casuist, he was a "father in God." Nevertheless, during most of his career he experienced substantial difficulties because of female rulers. Mary Tudor had driven him out of England, and Mary of Lorraine's temperamental treatment of Protestants made his work in Scotland extremely difficult. Elizabeth had a personal antipathy toward him, and justifiably so. Mary Stewart's refusal to renounce Catholicism and a moderately gay court life infuriated him, especially since her winsomeness — which can still be enchanting four centuries later, as evidenced by Lady Antonia Fraser's biography — periodically swayed the lords on whom he relied to support his cause. A fourth Mary was always lurking in the background when not immediately present — the Virgin Mary of Catholicism. In the period leading to the antifeminist outburst in *The First Blast*, Knox had an anti-Marian fixation. Psychologically Mary was the demon that troubled his mind. Throwing an icon of Mary overboard as a galley slave[7] had not been enough to purge his mind.

The identification of Mary Tudor and the Virgin Mary of Catholicism was explicitly made by Knox in *A Faithful Admonition* (1554). It was not enough to call the Tudor Queen a Jezebel and a cursed idolatress; he had to identify her as "your Mary the virgine, . . . an open traitoresse to the Imperiall Crown of England. . . ." He taunted the English Catholics to "let her be your virgine, and a goddes mete to maintaine such idolatrers. . . ."[8] Knox was probably alluding to John Harpsfield's Convocation sermon of October 1553, in which Mary Tudor was eulogized as Mary the Virgin.[9] Knox had a violent hatred of both Roman Catholicism and Mary Tudor, for Mary had forced him to leave his pastoral work in England and the girl he loved, and was creating grave spiritual difficulties for the flock he had left behind. He was an emotional man, and much of that emotion focused on hatred of Mary — the Catholic Queen and the Catholic Virgin.

The explosion of this hatred resulted in the writing of *The First Blast*. It was not written simply because Knox sought to pander to popular prejudices which he did not share.[10] *The First Blast* is, in a special sense, a personal tract, revealing his passionate but usually controlled temperament. The explosive passion which gave birth to the tract seethes just below the surface. The passion is a confused mixture of righteous indignation, personal bitterness, animosity, and frustration. All of this is focused not only on Mary Tudor, but also on Mary of Lorraine and Mary the Virgin, who together formed a trinity of evil in his mind.

The thesis of *The First Blast* is that rule by a woman is contrary to natural and divine law.

> To promote a Woman to beare rule, superioritie, domin-
> ion, or empire above any Realme, Nation, or Citie, is repugnant
> to Nature; contumelie to God, a thing most contrarious to his
> reveled will and approved ordinance; and finallie, it is the sub-
> version of good Order, of all equitie and justice.[11]

Knox was so incensed that he regarded female rule as the most detestable and damnable thing on the face of the earth. To substantiate his thesis he urged a simple empirical test. Women, he observed, were blind when it came to matters of civil government, demonstrating only foolish frenzy in place of judgment and wise counsel. Their political abilities are grossly inferior to those of men, and experience reveals their tendency toward cruelty and inconsistency. Any man who simply observes women can determine for himself why they should not be allowed to govern.[12] As Nietzsche would subsequently and more eloquently argue, the inferiority of females is self-evident. The selective bias of Knox's approach is patently obvious. Most authors writing in response to *The First Blast* repudiate the results of his empirical test by the use of historical examples of able female sovereigns.

Knox himself was forced to admit that not all women rulers were disasters. Like Calvin and others, he believed that God sometimes made exceptions to his law, though normally female rulers were forbidden. Knox cited the order of creation (man before woman) and the curse pronounced upon woman at the fall as evidence. Woman was made to serve and obey man and to rear his children. For man to alter this order is to lower himself to a subbeastly level, since even the animals recognize male superiority. The sovereignty of the male is part of the divine moral law as well as natural law. It is expressed in Deuteronomy 17, and is, Knox argued, as binding in the sixteenth century as it was in the days of the Hebrews, for the divine moral law is constant and unchangeable. Knox advocated the right of the English and Scottish people to obey the moral law as it was obeyed by the Hebrews, that is, by electing a new king if a deceased ruler died without a male heir. Refusal to obey this law would bring destruction to the state, hence the nobility must refuse to serve as officers of a queen who rules in rebellion against God. They are to repress her tyranny with all means at their disposal, sharing this duty with the estates and people. A tyrannical woman sovereign must be deposed *and executed*, for to protect her is rebellion against God. Knox left no doubt as to the primary target of his demand for vengeance — the Jezebel of England.[13]

The sources of Knox's concept of gynecocracy are amply noted in the pages of *The First Blast*. After receiving the replies of Calvin and Bullinger to his queries, he apparently devoted considerable attention to the patristic fathers with an eye to their views on female sovereigns. The results are impressive. There are citations from or references to the works of Tertullian, Augustine, Origen, Ambrose, Chrysostom, and Basil the Great. "Divers others" were also consulted but not mentioned. The views of Aristotle as expressed in his *Politics* are discussed, and there is a marginal reference to Cicero. Knox also read historical works for empirical evidence of female inability to rule. As a result of his historical studies he was convinced "that men illuminated onlie by the light of nature, have seen and have determined, that it is a thing moste repugnant to nature, that women rule and governe over men."[14] Scripture of course, was assiduously mined for supporting evidence. The Hebrew prophets and the Pauline corpus provided the bulk of the biblical support. For good measure, citations from classical law were also added.[15]

Contemporary authorities are not noted, but there is a possibility that Knox's use of empirical criteria and natural law may have been influenced at least in part by John Ponet, another Marian exile. Ponet's *Shorte Treatise of Politike Power* made much of such arguments, though there is no evidence that Knox read Ponet's treatise. Undoubtedly, however, Knox discussed his views with Christopher Goodman in Geneva, and the two men very likely influenced one another.[16] A major thesis of Goodman's *How Superior Powers Oght to be Obeyd* (Geneva, 1558) was that government by a woman contravened nature, was conducive to civil disorder, and was prohibited by divine law.

Similar views were expressed by another exile, possibly Thomas Becon, in *An Humble Supplicacion vnto God* (Strasbourg, 1554). After lavishing praise on Henry VIII and Edward VI, the author bemoans Mary's reign as an evident token of divine displeasure. Selectively using his evidence he cites Jezebel, Athaliah, and Herodias as examples of the usual type of female ruler, namely, wicked, superstitious, and idolatrous. Although most of the tract is concerned with the contrast between Protestantism and Catholicism, it parallels *The First Blast* in its regard for woman as one "whom nature hath formed to be in subieccio vnto ma/& who thou be thyne holy Apostle comaundest to kepe silece/& not to speake in the cogregacio."[17]

The First Blast backfired. It had barely been published when Mary Tudor died and was succeeded by Elizabeth. In spite of their common interest in a Protestant Scotland, relations between the new queen and Knox were always cool. Knox had offended her by his defense of the right of rebellion and by his antifeminist attack. Although he refused to retract his position, he attempted to conciliate Elizabeth. In a letter written to Sir William Cecil from Dieppe on April 10, 1559, he condescendingly agreed to maintain Elizabeth's lawful authority if she would confess that she ruled by a special dispensation of divine mercy, and not according to natural or divine law. If she refused, Knox prophesied punishment, warning that her throne would not be stable unless she exemplified humility and personal dejection before God. In a letter to Cecil from Edinburgh, written on July 19, 1559, he followed this up by warning that yf the most part of Wemen be such as willingly we wold not thei should reing over us; and yf the most godlie, and such es have rare giftes and graces, be yitt mortall, we aught to tak head, least that we in establissing one judged godlie and profitable to hir countrey, mack enteress and titill to many, by whom not only shall the treutht be impugned, but also shall the countrey be brought to bondaige and slavery.[18]

The following day, on July 20, 1559, Knox wrote to Elizabeth directly. He freely admitted his authorship of *The First Blast* (which had appeared anonymously), but refused to retract any principal point until proven wrong. He naively urged that Elizabeth not take offense at what he had written, pointing out that the tract had not been meant to apply to her. In fact, he was grateful to God for her reign. He warned her, however, that she must recognize that she governed by a special divine dispensation or she would experience a reign that would be both troublesome and brief.[19] Elizabeth naturally did no such thing. She supported the Protestant cause in Scotland, but basically for reasons of state, not religion. She represented the new order, Knox the old. The difference was not merely one centering on the position of women. Knox, though not without modest feelings of nationalism, typified the old era that culminated in the Wars of Religion; whereas Elizabeth, though not without personal religious convictions, typified the new era that placed the welfare of the state above all else. Yet Knox, though arguing in essentially religious terms, helped contribute to the new world a doctrine of lawful rebellion against unjust sovereigns, which was one of the greatest contributions of the old order to the new.

Knox did not stress his views on female rulers in his dealings with Mary of Lorraine. During his visit to Scotland in 1555–56, the regent had quashed an attempt by the Catholic prelates to try him for heresy, probably to preserve peace and retain the allegiance of the Protestant nobles. Several of the latter persuaded Knox to write a letter to her encouraging the regent to embrace Protestant ideals. Tactfully, Knox chose not to discuss the issue of female rulers in the letter; yet Mary received it derisively.[20] When, therefore, he expanded on the letter in the months following the writing of *The First Blast*, he informed her that he considered her "power...but borowed, extraordinarie, and unstable, for ye have it but by permission of others; and seldom it is that Women do long reigne with felicitie and joy. For as nature hath denyed to them a constant spirit of good government; so hath God pronounced, that they are never geven to reigne over men, but in his wrath and indignation." This time he overlooked Deborah, pressing ahead to use Mary's personal experiences as evidence of divine wrath. She had lost her sons and her husband, James V, "the memoriall of his name, succession, and royall dignitie perishing with him selfe. For albeit the usurped abuse, or rather tyrannie of some realmes, have permitted Women to succede to the honour of their fathers, yet must their glorie be transferred to the house of a strangier."[21] Relations between Knox and Mary never improved, and Knox took apparent pleasure in the unpleasant nature of her death from dropsy on June 11, 1560, which he attributed to divine judgment.[22]

The issue of gynecocracy played a somewhat greater role in Knox's relationship with Mary Stewart. In his first interview with her Knox was attacked for the views he had expressed in *The First Blast*. Although he refused to retract them, he did agree to live under her rule in peace, as long as she refrained from persecuting Protestants. He compared himself to Paul in the reign of Nero. In any case, he claimed, the real object of his attack in *The First Blast* had been the Jezebel of England, Mary Tudor. To Mary, Queen of Scots, however, it appeared quite plainly that he had not restricted his remarks to the English queen, but had discussed the general question of female rulers. Knox sidetracked further discussion of the issue by encouraging her not "to raise trouble for that which to this day hath not troubled your Majesty, neither in person nor yet in authority."[23] In his subsequent discussions with the queen, Knox seems to have followed his own advice, for the subject of female rulers was not debated. Instead Knox concentrated his attacks on Mary's Catholicism and defended his own activities on behalf of Protestantism.

Mary Stewart, Elizabeth, and Cecil were not alone in their dislike of the views expressed in *The First Blast*. Matthew Parker, Archbishop of Canterbury, and his Anglican colleagues found Knox's views irritating and offensive, especially since some Englishmen seriously doubted whether they should obey Elizabeth.[24] John Jewel, Bishop of Salisbury, felt constrained to repudiate a

Catholic charge that imputed Knox's views to all the Marian exiles.[25] Other exiles were likewise unhappy. John Foxe, the martyrologist, for example, appears to have gently admonished Knox, judging from the latter's letter to Foxe, dated May 18, 1558.[26] Foxe, moreover, was on friendly terms in Basle with John Aylmer, who attacked Knox in print. Calvin and Beza reacted by banning the sale in Geneva of Knox's *First Blast* and Goodman's *How Superior Powers Oght to be Obeyd*. In a letter to Bullinger dated September 3, 1566, Beza explained: "As soon as we learned the contents of each, we were much displeased, and their sale was forbidden in consequence. . . ."[27]

John Aylmer, former tutor of Lady Jane Grey and a Marian exile, attacked Knox in *An Harborowe for Faithfvll and Trewe Svbiectes, agaynst the Late Blowne Blaste, concerninge the Gouernmēt of Women* (Strasbourg, 1559). Aylmer used Scripture, law, history, and logic to refute Knox, accusing him of confusing the particular question with the general. Because of Mary Tudor's faults one could not conclude that all female sovereignty violated "nature, Reason, Right, and Lawe. . . ."[28] Women generally had a right to rule, though in ecclesiastical functions they were decidedly inferior to men. Aylmer explained that this was because ecclesiastical matters were of greater moment than matters of state, in that the former involved the soul, the latter the body. He did not deny Elizabeth's right to oversee the affairs of the church, but he refused to allow her to exercise ministerial functions.[29] Moreover any drawbacks associated with female sovereignty in England could be countered by the limited nature of the monarchy.

> Thou seest it euydently proued, that it standeth well inoughe with nature and all good order, with iustice and equitie, with lawe and reason, with Gods and mans ordinaunce, with custome and antiquitie: that a woman leafte by hir progenitors, true heire of a realme, hauing the consent of hir people, the stablishment of lawe, auncient custome, and Gods callyng, to confyrme the same: may vndoubtedly, succede her auncestors lawfully reignyng, in lawful succession, both to enheritance and regiment.[30]

Elsewhere, a retort to Knox was issued by John Leslie, Bishop of Ross, with the explanatory title, *A Defence of the Honour of the Right Highe, Mightye and Noble Princesse Marie Quene of Scotlande and Dowager of France, with a Declaration aswell of Her*

*Right, Title & Intereste to the Succession of the Crowne of Englande,
as that the Regimente of Women ys Conformable to the Lawe of God
and Nature* (1569). Leslie considered Knox one of the "newe
vpstarte Doctours,"[31] and devoted the third book of his treatise
to refuting Knox's thesis that the rule of women is repugnant to
natural and divine law. The first two books had been devoted to
a defense of Mary Stewart from charges that she was involved in
the murder of Henry, Lord Darnley, and to an espousal of her
right to the English throne. So the issue of gynecocracy survived
to play a role in the struggle over the succession to Elizabeth's
throne. Only Mary Stewart's execution in 1587 and the accession
of James in 1603 allowed the issue to fade from men's minds.

On the Continent, the Catholic author Peter Frarin of Louvain wrote perhaps the most perceptive remarks about Knox's
motivation. Initially he wondered if Knox wrote *The First Blast*
"for hatred and malice he bare againste women . . . ," something
Frarin believed most men would quickly reject. On reflection, it
seemed more likely to Frarin that Knox was merely using the
attack against women rulers as a pretense to encourage the English
to rebel against Mary Tudor.[32] This, of course, was essentially
what Knox himself implied in his first interview with Mary Stewart, though he never repudiated his 1558 views on women rulers.

Knox retained his views on gynecocracy to the end of his life.
In February 1568 he wrote to John Wood, a diplomatic friend,
noting that men "yitt storme" against *The First Blast*. Nevertheless
he was still convinced that his views were correct, having seen
neither law nor Scripture to indicate otherwise. Goodman, however, recanted his views.[33] In 1571 some of Knox's detractors in
the General Assembly criticized him for praying for Elizabeth
and not Mary Stewart, thinking that this contradicted the views
he had expounded in *The First Blast*. Knox reacted with his cus-
tomary vehemence: his *First Blast* was "groundit upoun guid rea-
sone, upoun Godis plaine treuth, and upon maist plaine and just
lawes. . . ."[34] To the end he steadfastly defended the old order
with respect to female rulers. Yet the real object of his dislike was
not merely female sovereigns *per se*, let alone women in general,
but *Catholic* monarchs, especially female Catholic rulers.

In the immediate context of 1558 it is hardly surprising that
he failed to make this distinction clear. The female rulers with

whom he had had experience were Catholics — Mary Tudor, Mary of Lorraine, Mary Stewart, and Catherine de Medici. Elizabeth was yet a princess with an uncertain future. That she would later become, in Knox's eyes, a modern Deborah, was no certainty in 1558, though many must have cherished this hope. Although Knox never recanted in the manner of Christopher Goodman, in practice he virtually ignored his inflammatory theses on female rulers from 1559 to his death in 1572. Mary Stewart, not Knox, raised the issue in their first interview, and the latter showed no inclination to pursue it. His incessant attacks on Mary focused on her Catholicism, not her femininity. Refusing to the end to be converted to the new order, he appears at least to have realized, from 1559 on, the futility of further attacks on female rulers on grounds of the inferiority of their sex. Yet his views have survived him, and indeed have found acceptance in that very nation which was ultimately founded in the context of the new order, the United States.

CHAPTER
‡ NINE ‡

CALVINISM, DEMOCRACY, AND KNOX'S POLITICAL THOUGHT

In the course of the long-standing debate on the possibility of democratic tendencies in the thought and practice of John Calvin and his followers, recent attention has focused on limited case studies. Certain of these studies have a direct relevance to understanding the role of John Knox in the history of Calvinism. It is the purpose of this chapter to reexamine Knox's position, in part by the use of these studies, in order to clarify that position and to add a further dimension to the broader debate. It is not, however, the purpose of this chapter to engage in an exercise of comparative government to determine whether or not Knox's Scotland was more or less democratic than its sister states. Nor will an endeavor be undertaken to shift the focus of this historic and worthwhile debate from its principal question: Are the sources of modern democracy to be found in the thought and practice of Calvin and his disciples? Although the essence of modern democracy is debatable, for the purpose of this essay it is used in the sense of a society governed directly or indirectly by the people, with power originating in a broadly based citizenry whose rights as individuals are guaranteed through constitutional or legal means. Modern democracy obviously did not exist anywhere in sixteenth-century Europe, but there is a clear relevance in understanding how and where it developed.

At the outset it must be remembered that Knox, like Calvin, had a great deal to say about politics, but not about the ideal form of government. According to Knox, government was divinely instituted for man because of his inability to live in peace without it. To the secular authorities God entrusted two basic powers, that is, the punishment of vice and the maintenance of virtue. This authority of the secular rulers was not without limit, but was to be exercised for the profit and comfort of the governed, not the benefit of the governors.[1] The authority of rulers was conceived by Knox to be strictly limited by the precepts of divine law, which meant especially that they "should admitte into their kingdomes no worshipping of God, except that which is commanded in the Scriptures."[2] Knox was totally committed to the divine Law as expressed in the Bible, which led him on occasion to urge violations of temporal law. Overall, however, his actions manifest a deep respect for the rule of law in society, as exemplified, for example, by his adherence in England to the *Book of Common Prayer* (despite his strong criticisms of it), his compliance with the Frankfurt magistrates after he lost his quarrel with the Coxians,[3] and his concern for the work of the Scottish Parliament. Consequently, although Knox did not set forth an exposition of the ideal form of government, it is clear that any form which would be acceptable to him would have to rest on the basic principles of the divine origin of sovereignty, the limited powers of secular authority, and the primacy of law — especially divine Law as revealed in Scripture.

These principles are not incompatible with monarchy, aristocracy, or democracy (i.e., polity). They are principles which Calvin also accepted, although John T. McNeill has argued that the repeated criticism of kings throughout Calvin's writings logically resulted in a depreciation of monarchical government.[4] Certainly in the last chapter of the *Institutes of the Christian Religion* Calvin states a clear preference for a government which is an aristocracy or an aristocracy tempered by a democracy (polity).[5] Yet Calvin's experience of royalty in his formative years was in many respects different from Knox's. Calvin's initial difficulties occurred with Francis I, a strong Renaissance prince often regarded as one of the "new monarchs." The controversy surrounding Nicholas Copp's inaugural address (which Calvin helped compose) at the University of Paris and the persecution which followed the affair of the placards forced Calvin's flight to Basel and ultimately Geneva, where his contacts were with aristocratic governments tempered with democratic elements. Knox, in his formative years, experienced weak sovereigns whose authority was exercised by prominent nobles, namely, the Earl of Arran, the Duke of Somerset, and the Duke of Northumberland. Not until Mary Tudor ascended the throne did Knox encounter a reasonably strong monarch who ruled personally and imposed a policy of persecuting Protestants. The conjunction of Mary's rule in England with the repressive policy in Scotland of the regent Mary of Lorraine drove Knox to his most extreme criticism of monarchs in his 1558 tracts, but the accession of Elizabeth I the same year and subsequent weakening of the French position in Scotland may have been responsible for his not adopting a critical position on monarchical government akin to Calvin's.

No matter how attractive the government of a city-state such as Geneva might have been to Knox—and there is no hard evidence that it was—such a government would clearly have been inapplicable to the much larger and less urbanized Scotland of the sixteenth century. He did not, therefore, criticize monarchy itself, though he had some definite things to say regarding its nature. Sovereigns did not receive their right to govern from lineal descent, popular sovereignty, or military force, but from God.[6] Any attempt by a monarch to impose commands which contravened divine precepts could legitimately be disobeyed. Although Knox believed that sovereigns had perverted the institution of monarchy by failing to fulfill their divinely appointed obligations, at no time does he conclude that monarchy itself must be abolished, or even that another form of government is preferable to monarchy. Nor does he advocate either an elective or a constitutional monarchy, either of which would have had obviously democratic implications.

One of the most potentially democratic principles in Knox's political thought is his developed doctrine of resistance by the people against tyrannical rulers. His earlier writings do not explicitly embrace this position, though they rest on the principle that obedience to rulers is required in all things except those contrary to divine precepts. In his *Admonition or Warning*, written in December and January 1553–54, Knox contends that it is the duty of every "Civill Magistrate" to "slay all ydolateris."[7] The Scottish scholar J. H. Burns takes Knox's phrase "Civill Magistrate" to mean only the sovereign, in which case Knox was not thinking of active resistance.[8] Knox, however, may be using the phrase in a broader sense, since the same work refers to the defense of Jeremiah (albeit from "pestilent preistis," not a king) by princes and nobles.[9] In any case, by May 31, 1554 he was willing to encourage his English friends that God would "styr up one Jehu or other to execute hys vengeaunce uppon these bloudde-thyrsty tyrauntes and obstinate idolators."[10] The following July he called to God to provide a Phinehas, Elijah, or Jehu to topple Mary Tudor, and praised Jeremiah's exhortation to cease obedience to one's princes and obey the enemies of one's state.[11] In July 1558, in his *Appellation* to the Scottish nobles and estates, Knox set forth the responsibilities of the inferior magistrates to remove a tyrannical sovereign. The same responsibility had been asserted in *The First Blast of the Trumpet*, which was published in Geneva in the spring of 1558.

Before 1558 Knox had not explicitly gone beyond what Calvin himself had written in the last chapter of the *Institutes*. *The First Blast*, however, made it the duty of the people as well as the magistrates to see that a tyrannical monarch (such as Athaliah) was overthrown and executed.[12] The *Appellation* made the punishment of idolaters and blasphemers, regardless of status, the concern of every person in the state in accordance with his Christian vocation and the possibility afforded to him by God to wreak vengeance.[13] Knox's letter to the commonalty of Scotland, which accompanied the *Appellation*, asserted that subjects could lawfully require from their temporal rulers the provision of godly ministers and the expulsion of false prophets. If the rulers declined, the commonalty could provide for and defend such clergy against government persecution. Yet Knox also made it clear that the people ought to work with the estates and nobility rather than against them.[14] There is thus no demand for the creation of a democratic state in these works, but a clarion call for religious reform in the context of the existing social and political structures of England and Scotland. Simultaneously, however, the assertion of individual responsibility in the context of limited government has democratic implications, even if Knox did not intend this to be the case.

The question then arises as to whether or not Knox's development of resistance theory is a logical working out of Calvin's political principles. The answer to this question is partially suggested by the research of Helmut Koenigsberger, whose studies of the Huguenots, the Catholic Leagues, and the Dutch Beggars led him to the conclusion that "religion was the binding force that held together the divergent interests of the different classes and provided them with an organization and a propaganda machine capable of creating the first genuinely national and international parties in modern European history. . . ."[15] The crucial point which Koenigsberger so effectively demonstrates is that the French Catholic Leagues manifested many of the organizational and propagandistic characteristics of the Calvinist-inspired Huguenot and Beggar movements. Consequently these organizations are the response of religious minorities, willing to use force as a tactic, to the growing power of the state. The source of rebellion is essentially external, not an ideological outgrowth of Calvin's political principles.

If Koenigsberger's thesis is applied to Scotland, certain difficulties immediately appear. The relative remoteness of the region, the absence of a powerful regent backed by effective military forces, and the largely independent ways of the Scottish nobility cannot be ignored. Nevertheless, the Scottish Protestants, like their counterparts in France and the Netherlands, represented the social spectrum. The role of the Lords of the Congregation is too well known to need recounting, and W. Stanford Reid has recently demonstrated the role of the burgesses in the coming of the Reformation to Edinburgh.[16] It was lords such as the Earl of Glencairn, Lord Lorne, Erskine of Dun, and Mary Stewart's half-brother, Lord James Stewart, who led the reform movement while Knox was in exile in Geneva, though he had been in Scotland in 1555 and communicated with Scottish leaders from Geneva in the next three years. It was the burgesses of Edinburgh who took the lead in July 1559 in denying the authority of the regent, Mary of Lorraine, by calling Knox to become minister of St. Giles' Kirk.[17] As on the Continent, the moving force behind the activities of the lords and burgesses appears in large measure to have been a response to external political conditions, in particular Mary's recent crackdown on Protestantism in the aftermath of the Peace of Cateau-Cambrésis.[18] In both cases, however, Calvin and Knox respectively contributed advice and encouragement to the rebel forces.

Behind the revolutionary activities, particularly of the nobles, was another factor; that is, Knox's insistent demands that the Scottish Protestants fulfill their covenant responsibilities. It was in the covenant context that Knox developed and urged his doctrine of resistance to tyrants. In *An Admonition or Warning* (1554), where Knox called on civil magistrates to slay idolaters, "the league betuixt God and us" is set forth as the basis for this demand. "The league betuixt God and us requyreth avoyding of all ydolatrie," but "the slaying of ydolateris appertenis not to everie particular man."[19] Four years later, however, the "covenante" obligations were delineated in such a manner as specifically to require the commonalty to wield

> the sworde in their own hand to remove such enormities from amongest them. . . . If any go about to erect and set up idolatrie, or to teach defection from God, after the veritie hath bene receaved and approved, that then, not only the Magistrates, to whom the sword is committed, but also the People, are bound, by that othe which they have made to God, to revenge to the uttermost of their power the injurie done against his Majestie.[20]

Because the extension of tyrannicide to the common people has democratic implications,[21] it would bolster the arguments of those who find democratic tendencies in Calvin's thought, if it could be demonstrated that Knox derived his covenant principles from the Geneva reformer. But this is not the case, at least in terms of their theological writings. As has been shown elsewhere,[22] Calvin's concept of the covenant is essentially promissory in nature, though it is possible to see a more reciprocal covenant notion at work in his efforts to persuade the Genevans to accept *Les Ordonnances Ecclesiastiques*. Theologically Knox treated the covenant as a conditional promise calling for man's reciprocal obedience. Apart from the Old Testament, the possible theological sources for Knox's concept of the covenant include the writings of William Tyndale, Oecolampadius, and Heinrich Bullinger (through John Hooper), all of whom stressed the conditional nature of the covenant. But a more important source was the ancient Scottish custom of banding, which originated in the feudal era in conjunction with the oath of fealty and the clan-family relationship. Scotland had a long tradition of men banding together by sworn pledges of fidelity, despite prohibitory royal legislation.[23] In 1556 the gentlemen of the Mearns entered into such a band for the purpose of maintaining Protestant preaching. At the time Knox was visiting the laird of Dun. The following year Knox urged the reform-minded lords and lairds to get on with the task, with the result that such men as the Earls of Argyll, Glencairn, and Morton, the Lord of Lorne, and John Erskine of Dun signed a Protestant covenant on December 3, 1557.[24] Thus Knox's concept of the covenant, which provided the foundation for his doctrine of resistance, had its origins in the world of Scottish feudal politics, but was thereafter developed in altered political circumstances into the basis for a revolutionary party akin to the kind described by Koenigsberger in France and the Netherlands.

Having been freshly reminded of the Scottish rite of banding by the gentlemen of the Mearns, Knox returned to Geneva in September 1556. Within the next two years he completed the development of his doctrine of resistance, with its democratic implications. One cannot discount the influence on this development of his discussions early in 1554 with Calvin, Bullinger, and Pierre Viret. Hans Baron has demonstrated the importance of the civic experience of Strasbourg in Martin Bucer's exposition of the legitimacy of resistance by *magistratus inferiores*, that is, the Strasbourg magistrates.[25] Calvin, of course, almost certainly was influenced by Bucer in this regard. Bucer's influence on Knox's doctrine of the Lord's Supper (through the medium of the *First Helvetic Confession*) has been demonstrated.[26] It also appears that Bucer may have influenced Knox's development of resistance theory through the agency of Pierre Viret.

The advice Knox received in 1554 from Calvin and Bullinger would not have encouraged him to undertake a more democratic enunciation of resistance doctrine.[27] There is no record of what Viret told Knox, but the recent research of Robert Linder makes possible a reasonable reconstruction. Viret justified armed resistance against tyrants if two preconditions were fulfilled, the first of which was the trying of other means, including prayer and patience. The second condition was that armed resistance must be led by legitimate lesser magistrates whose authority derived from the people. Viret never sanctioned Christians to resist actively as

175

individuals, such as Knox subsequently did, but he linked liberty and religion by asserting that "once the people somehow had gained a measure of political and religious freedom, they possessed the authority to resist any tyrannical encroachments upon it."[28] The advice, therefore, that Knox received from Viret in 1554 may have been an additional factor in motivating Knox to express a more democratic resistance theory.

Attempts have been made to find democratic implications in the theological doctrines of Calvin. Since Knox shared many of these doctrines, one can reasonably expect to find the same democratic implications, if they exist. The evidence, however, distinctly indicates that Knox did not develop any political implications that may be inherent in his (or Calvin's) theology. In his long treatise on predestination,[29] Knox does not take occasion to argue either that the special role of the elect should mean an aristocratic government of the chosen, or that the universal depravity of all men (hence their spiritual equality) should lead to a democratic state. Because Knox is openly critical of the masses in the pages of his *History of the Reformation in Scotland*, it seems quite apparent that he was unsympathetic to democracy. This is also clearly reflected in his predestination treatise when he recounts Calvin's attempts to impose discipline in Geneva:

> The Consistoire called for justice to be executed, and for penalties to be appointed, for the inobedient and open contemners. But nothing coulde prevaile; for the multitude of the wicked was so great, that in votes and voices they did prevaile. And so was the iniquitie of the wicked mainteined for a long ceason.[30]

Clearly a democratic government determined by "votes and voices" could be prejudicial to the establishment of a godly commonwealth. Even when considering the democratic implications of Knox's doctrine of resistance, one must remember that it is the godly individuals who share the responsibility of tyrannicide, not the reprobate. When equality is mentioned, it occurs in a spiritual, not a political, context. The *Book of Discipline*, of which Knox was a coauthor, stipulates, for example, that there is to be no respect of persons, since all are equal in God's sight. This position is elsewhere stated: "In the hope of the life to come he hath made all equall."[31] The priesthood of all believers and the perspicuity of Scripture, making it available to all (illumined) men, similarly deal with equality in the spiritual realm in Knox's writings, but are not given any political connotations. This does not rule out the possibility that a later disciple of Knox might read democratic political principles into these doctrines, but there is nothing inherent within them that would make such a reading either logical or compelling.

Attempts have also been made to show that Calvin's ecclesiastical polity, with its elements of popular participation, was conducive to the development of political democracy. Robert M. Kingdon has already analyzed the debate between two Calvinists — Jean Morely, who advocated a form of Congregational polity, and Theodore Beza, who defended a Presbyterian position. Morely specifically made an analogy between Congregational polity and political democracy, in which he defended a democracy dominated by law as the best type of civil government. Morely's supporters were largely obliterated in the Huguenot wars, but a similar debate subsequently developed in England between the Presbyterians and the Independents.[32] In Scotland during Knox's lifetime debate over polity ranged between presbyterian and episcopalian poles,[33] bypassing the question of congregational polity. Nevertheless, the type of church government established for the reformed Kirk of Scotland by Knox and his colleagues included a good deal of popular participation — perhaps more than in Calvin's Geneva.

The coauthored *Book of Discipline* gave the primary responsibility for the selection of a minister to the local congregation, which had forty days to choose a candidate. If it failed to do so, the superintendent and his council were empowered to intervene. In Geneva, on the other hand, primary responsibility rested with the Venerable Company of Pastors and the Little Council, with the local congregation having essentially the right of ratification. The Scottish candidate did, of course, have to undergo an examination of his doctrine, personal life, and ability by the ministers and elders of the Kirk as well as the congregation. If his life, doctrine, and abilities were found acceptable by the ministers, elders, and local congregation, the latter was normally obligated to accept him as its minister. In practice the differences between Scotland and Geneva were probably minimal.[34]

There was fairly broad participation in the procedures laid down for the selection of superintendents, though in practice there were only five, and these were appointed by the Council. According to the *Book of Discipline* subsequent superintendents were to be selected in a more representative manner. When a vacancy occurred, the ministers, elders, deacons, and magistrates or council of the principal town in the district were to nominate two or three suitable candidates. The latter were to be examined by the ministers of the province and the neighboring superintendents, with the final selection being determined by election.[35] Because these provisions were not carried out, it is difficult to imagine that anyone derived democratic ideas from them.

The laity were given an even more direct role in the governing of the church through the institution of elders and deacons. Elders were to be elected annually by the congregation, with no limit on the successive number of terms as long as the freedom of the annual election was maintained. Elders had the responsibility of assisting the minister in the governance of the church, especially in the supervision of both the ministers and the members. Deacons also were elected annually, though they could not be reelected until a three-year period had elapsed. Their responsibility was to handle the church's financial affairs, including the distribution of alms to the needy.[36] All male members of the congregation could participate in the church's decisions at the local level, and under Melville Scottish Presbyterianism operated democratically through elected representatives. Moreover, the General Assembly of the church which Knox helped establish included clergy and laity, and functioned in a democratic manner. Later in the century it played a major role in battling the absolutist tendencies of James VI.

Certainly the polity established by Knox and his colleagues for the selection of elders and deacons was more democratic than that in Geneva, where these officers were chosen by the Little Council, with the advice of the ministers and subject to the approval of the Council of Two Hundred. Of the twelve elders, two had to be members of the Little Council, four of the Council of Sixty, and six of the Council of Two Hundred. With Calvin himself participating in the work of constitutional revision, these councils had come to be selected in a more aristocratic manner, further underscoring the differences in the mode of selecting elders and deacons in Geneva and Scotland. It must be remembered, of course, that Calvin's concept of aristocracy was one of worth, not heredity.

If there is any merit in considering popular participation in church government as a school for preparing men for civil democracy, then the polity of the Kirk of Scotland was more effective than Calvin's church in Geneva. It is, however, essential to bear in mind that the reformed Kirk had to struggle desperately for survival during its early years. Not only did Mary Stewart and her followers oppose it, but the Protestant lords and lairds themselves refused to enact the *Book of Discipline* into law and provide the reformed Kirk with the financial support it required. The Kirk retained marked elements of the earlier revolutionary character, because it faced the hostility of a Catholic sovereign and a nobility determined to retain its hold over ecclesiastical lands. The democratic elements in the polity must be seen as at least in part a reflection of the continuing revolutionary nature of the Reformed churches, and not as a conscious preparation for the creation of democracy in the state.

Knox's position on the relationship of church and state is also relevant to the question of democratic tendencies. His comments sometimes have an Erastian tone, but such comments occur in the context of discussions in which the godly character of the state is asserted or assumed. Given a godly state, Knox's preference was that it support and protect the church, but not directly control it. This is reflected in the *Scots Confession*, which asserts that rulers and magistrates are obligated to maintain true religion and suppress idolatry and superstition. By 1567 it had been long apparent to Knox and his colleagues that the state was less than godly. The *Book of Discipline* had not received governmental sanction, nor had the queen's mass been abolished. Three years earlier the General Assembly had apointed a committee to look into the matter of ecclesiastical jurisdiction. In 1567 Parliament appointed a committee, which included Knox and his colleague, John Craig, "to searche more speciallie, and consider what other speciall points or causes could apperteane to the jurisdictioun, priviledge, and authoritie of the said kirk...." Parliament already recognized ecclesiastical jurisdiction with respect to preaching, the administration of the sacraments, and the correction of manners. The General Assembly agreed with the purpose of the committee, but appointed its own, again with Knox and Craig among its members. It is obvious that Knox and his friends were interested in establishing a more independent jurisdiction from the state.[37]

Knox favored less involvement of the state in church affairs than did Zwingli, Bullinger, and possibly Calvin. All sought a harmonious relationship between church and state based on the ideal of a godly magistracy. Knox preferred to restrict the state's function in religion to certain specific areas. First, the state was to support the true faith and suppress idolatry and atheism. Secondly, the state was to serve as a higher court of appeal from judgments rendered by a corrupt church, provided always that the members of a godly church had the right to disobey the state if the latter contravened divine precepts. Thirdly, the state was to collect tithes and dispense the appropriate portion to the church. Fourthly, the state was to punish vices repugnant to God as well as traditional crimes. In effect, the state was to create and maintain an environment in which Protestantism could flourish.

The church for its part was to refrain from the participation of its ministers in the government, though all members of the church had a responsibility to scrutinize critically the affairs of the government in the light of biblical principles. Knox made this point manifest in his debate with Sir William Maitland of Lethington at the meeting of the General Assembly in June 1564: "The servants of God mark the vice of kings and queens, even as well as of other offenders, and that because their sins be more noisome to the Commonwealth than are the sins of inferior persons." Knox freely acknowledged that the secular power was divinely ordained, but he distinguished between the power and the ordinance upon which it was based on the one hand, and the recipient of the power on the other. The ordinance was holy and perpetual, but the "men clad with the authority, are commonly profane and unjust; yea, they are mutable and transitory, and subject to corruption. . . ." On this basis Christians could judge the behavior of their ruler and, if it violated biblical precepts, resist his authority without defying that power which was divinely ordained.[38] It was then a possible step — though Knox did not take it — to move from the right of the people to judge the religious policy of the government and intervene in it if necessary to the right of the people to participate in government. This implicit conclusion plus Knox's explicit principle of limited monarchical authority helped lay the foundation for the eventual establishment of a constitutional monarchy.

A final area which is relevant to the question of democratic sources is the educational reform proposed in the *Book of Discipline*, of which Knox was a coauthor. Calvin was an active educational reformer whose principal contribution was founding the Geneva Academy, in part to enable citizens to serve the commonwealth. Although the Academy was not established until 1559, Knox was influenced by Calvin's work with the educational system in Geneva. When he returned to Scotland he helped chart a course of reform characterized by a universal education at the basic level, aid for poor students, and a revised curriculum. Certainly such a system is necessary, if there is to be a functioning political democracy; and the advocacy of universal schooling is significant in this regard. Likewise the proposal to provide education based on ability rather than wealth or social status is a democratizing principle. Nevertheless, it is apparent that Knox had no democratic political principles in mind. The educational system was to be infused with religious ideals and governed by the church, which was responsible for schools and schoolmasters. Students who were not certified by the church as godly could not attend the universities, and teachers and administrators had to undergo theological examinations. In the long run this system, which was not enacted for financial reasons, would probably have created intellectual dissent and corroded ecclesiastical authority, but its proposers obviously did not have this in mind.[39]

In conclusion, it is reasonable to accept the fact that there are democratic implications in Knox's thought, though these are definitely not intended to suggest the establishment of a political democracy in the state. Secular authorities have limited power and must govern in accord with divine law. Monarchs who become tyrannical can be actively resisted by individuals, but the individuals must be godly and engage in such action as part of their covenant obligations. These individuals also play important roles in the churches to which they belong, both in the selection of ministers, elders, and deacons, and in their participation in the government of the church through the latter offices. To the extent to which these practices reveal democratic tendencies, the credit must go less to Calvin than to other, primarily external sources. Chief among these is the revolutionary nature of the Reformed party in Scotland, with its strong ties to the feudal custom of banding. Some influence also comes from Knox's associations on the Continent with such men as Viret and Calvin. On the whole this examination of John Knox does not lend much support to those scholars who have argued that Calvinism fostered the growth of democracy, but neither does it repudiate the fundamental thesis that certain seeds are present in the Reformed tradition out of which democracy slowly developed.

THE CHRISTIAN COMMUNITY:
Social and Ecumenical Considerations

Knox's chosen participation in the prophetic tradition did not blot out all other concerns, leaving him transfixed with nothing but the tasks of legitimate rulers and religious reformation. His attack on the idolatrous Catholic tyrants did not leave him, as Michael Walzer has argued, "with virtually no social connections or sympathies, and with but one political passion: to drive fallen man 'up the Lord's hill'."[1] That passion was dominant in Knox's order of priorities, but he did not neglect other concerns. Mary Tudor was denounced not only for her idolatrous beliefs but also for endangering English independence by her marriage to Philip of Spain. Knox also had a marked concern for the rights and liberties of Englishmen, and called upon "the auncient lawes and actes of Parliamentes before established in Englande" to judge the rightness of his cause.[2] In his 1558 *Appellation* to the nobility and estates of Scotland he appealed his case in part on the basis of Scottish legal precedent, indicating a concern for Scottish rights and liberties.[3]

Once he returned to Scotland he continued to fulfill the role of the prophet even while expressing concern for such social needs as education and poor relief. There can be no question that the prophetic task dominated his work, but it did not keep him from extensive participation in formulating the *Scots Confession* and the

Book of Discipline, where he gave attention to social concerns. Traditionally this was in keeping with the Hebrew prophetic tradition, for the prophets had denounced social injustice and called for "the infusion of the Israel they knew with a new spirit which they demanded."[4] This was precisely what Knox did, and it involved him in much more than the single-minded and vehement denunciation of idolatry. In fact, his social ideas mark him as one of the most progressive reformers of the sixteenth century.

As in the case of theology and polity, so in the areas of education and poor relief Knox borrowed from the Reformation heritage. He had no sense of Scotland as the elect nation in the manner in which Thomas Brightman subsequently saw England, but instead shared John Foxe's conception of the universality of the church and the applicability of the apocalyptic tradition to the entire congregation of the elect.[5] Consequently he sought to give the Kirk of Scotland a modest ecumenical outlook, a sense of being a vital part of the Christian *oikoumene*. Just as he respected the political traditions of other states, particularly England, so he had due esteem for the ways of other Protestant churches, with the exception of the Anabaptist and Separatist traditions. Such esteem is reflected in the eclectic theology and polity which he bequeathed to the Scottish Kirk, which in turn provided it with natural links to the broader Christian community.

KNOX'S SOCIAL AWARENESS:
The Problems of Poverty and Educational Reform

In his excellent biography of John Knox, Professor W. Stanford Reid remarks that the Scottish reformer helped to enable the Kirk of Scotland "through its care of the poor and control of education to exert a powerful influence upon society as a whole."[1] In accurately recognizing Knox's contribution in these areas, Reid has poignantly reminded his readers that Knox deserves to be remembered for more than his advocacy of popular rebellion against tyrannical sovereigns (important as that is) and his opposition to female rule. It is the purpose of this chapter to explore further Knox's social awareness with respect to poverty and education, and additionally to suggest several sources of possible influence on Knox's proposals for poor relief and his educational ideas.

I. RESPONSIBILITY FOR THE POOR

Christians, according to Knox, have basic social obligations, including a responsibility to care for the poor. He was sympathetic toward the needs of the lower classes, though it is a mistake to see this as evidence of a naturally democratic spirit.[2] Care for the poor has ample biblical sanction, and has consequently been advocated by men of all types in the history of Christianity. Exercising one's responsibility to help the lower classes is as compatible with the aristocratic spirit of *noblesse oblige* as with the democratic spirit. Knox was concerned about the poor because Scripture demanded it and because his God embodied justice and mercy, which believers were to manifest toward the less fortunate in society. Although he conceived of social obligations primarily in religious rather than political terms, he had to have been aware of the dangers of uncontrolled poverty for social order and a reformed society.

The poor had been an object of concern in Scotland, as elsewhere,[3] before the Reformation. The provincial council of 1549, for example, had expressed alarm concerning misappropriation of endowments for the poor. Sir David Lyndsay, an early acquaintance of Knox, blamed the crown for allowing oppression of the poor. He was particularly sympathetic toward the commons, with their burden of high rents, church exactions, and unjust judicial decisions. Knox's probable mentor, John Major, urged that princes or communities decree that there would no longer be any beggars and provide for the impotent. Prior to the Reformation, "sturdy beggars," who had no credentials and roamed the country demanding assistance, were banned. A 1552 edict prohibited a beggar from pursuing his trade outside his own parish. It is thus not surprising that Knox and his colleagues gave some attention to the poor, though with the pressing business of ecclesiastical reformation, the enigma of poverty might well have been relegated to a minor concern. Certainly the change of landlords from Catholic to Protestant did little if anything to alleviate the burdens imposed on tenants. Increasing a sense of responsibility for the poor was perhaps more difficult for the Protestant reformers than procuring desired changes in theology and worship.[4]

In an epistle to the congregation at Berwick, Knox had urged his fellow Christians to continue and even increase their care for the poor. Those able to work but preferring idleness were not to receive help, regardless of their poverty. Orphans, widows, and others unable to work were to receive aid. Knox promised rewards for those who helped the poor, going so far as to promise eternal life for those who were liberal with their funds. Liberality toward the poor was, Knox argued, a sign that the elect were grateful for the benefits God had provided them.[5] In 1556, as an exile, he continued to manifest his concern for the poor. "The poore, we sie altogidder neglectit by the Bischopis, proud Prelatis, and filthie Clargie, who upon thair awn bellies, licens, and vanitie, consume whatsoever was commandit to be bestowit upon the poore." The remedy which Knox proposed was to take the tithes from the Catholic clergy and bestow them on the Protestant churches, where they could be used to sustain a godly clergy and provide necessary relief for the poor, widows, orphans, and strangers, "for whais releif, all sic rentis and dewteis wer cheiflie apoyntit to the Kirk."[6] He pursued this theme in 1558 when he appealed to the Scottish nobles and estates to remove and punish the Catholic clergy, "togyther also with all idle bellies, which do robbe and oppresse the flock. . . ." The bishops especially were singled out and charged with "the neglecting of their office, for the substance of the poore, which unjustly they usurpe and prodigally they do spend. . . ."[7]

Knox and his fellow authors of the *Book of Discipline* likewise dealt with the problem of poverty. Each kirk was assigned the task of providing for its own poor, with aid going to widows, orphans, elderly, lame, impotent, and honest persons who had fallen into penury. Beggars were excepted, being recommended for punishment to the civil magistrate, who was to compel able-bodied men to labor. All persons unable to work were to return to their places of birth or long-time residence and seek assistance from the churches in those localities. Not all who were unemployed were responsible for their plight, and it is these whom the church must help. One method of assistance was relief from the payment of teinds. The deacons were specifically assigned the responsibility of collecting funds to disperse quarterly to the needy. In this manner Knox and his fellow framers of the *Book of Discipline* believed that begging could be abolished, all able-bodied men put to work, and all needy cared for by the kirk.[8]

In the ensuing years there are various examples of action taken by the Scottish Kirk to care for the poor. In 1562, for example, Knox persuaded the Edinburgh authorities to petition the queen to grant them the former Dominican property in Edinburgh as a site to erect a hospital for the poor. Mary agreed in 1563, stipulating that the work be completed in ten years. In the same year the kirk session of Aberdeen ordered compilation of a poor roll; all native-born poor were to be enrolled to "conform to other godly reformed towns." The following year the General

Assembly expressed concern with the burial of the poor in the rural areas of Scotland. The session of the Assembly held in June 1565, enacted "for sustentation of the poor, that all lands founded to hospitalitie of old be restored agane to this same use, and that all lands, annualrents, or any other emoluments pertaining any ways to the friers of whatsumever ordour, or annualrents, altarages pertaining to Priests, be applyed to the sustentatione of the poor, and uphald of Schooles. . . ." Sometimes the action of the church was less ambitious. In 1572, for example, the session of Methlick approved the purchase of bedclothes for a bedridden lady on the condition that the clothes be returned at her death for further distribution to the needy. In the same year the minister at Aberdeen worked with the town council in distributing money to the poor that had been collected by designated representatives who passed through the burgh collecting alms on a weekly basis.[9] These examples would seem to indicate that the encouragements to care for the poor which Knox and his colleagues included in the *Book of Discipline* were being heeded as the Reformation spread.

Knox manifested a general concern for the basic social obligations of the Christians in *The Order and Doctrine of the General Fast*. The winters of 1563 – 64 and 1564 – 65 had been unusually harsh. Although numerous Protestant ministers were in financial difficulty, Knox appealed to them in December 1565 to continue their work. He also asked the brethren of the congregation to provide voluntary support for the ministers. The General Assembly ordered a general fast for the last Sunday of February 1566 and the first Sunday of March. The document explaining the fast is largely from Knox's hand, and includes an exhortation to the respective classes to fulfill their social obligations. Christians are reminded that they cannot expect spiritual relief from God if they refuse to provide relief from the unjust burdens imposed on their fellow man. Evoking the concept of *noblesse oblige*, Knox called especially upon earls, lords, barons, burgesses, and artisans to consider the means by which they gained their wealth. Deceit, unjust dealing, avarice, and unmercifulness to the poor were classed by Knox with murder, adultery, and pride. He appealed to a higher law than civil statutes as the standard for men's conduct. Despite the fact that earls, lords, barons, gentlemen, merchants, and artisans might legally be making their excessive profits and inflicting undue obligations upon the poor, divine law did not countenance such actions. A specific appeal was made for goods to be sold for reasonable prices, recalling the just price concept of the medieval world. Knox asked the upper classes to apply the Golden Rule to their dealings: If they were husbandmen would they be content being treated as they were now treating laborers? Knox would exempt no group or class for unjust dealings: judges, lawyers, merchants, artisans, and laborers were to deal justly and mercifully with their fellow man.[10]

Knox's appeal for social justice was certainly not revolutionary, nor was it a placid defense of the *status quo*. With respect especially to Knox it simply is not true that "the drive of the Reformers against riches and privilege [was] a radical move comparable to that of the Diggers and Levellers after the English Civil War. . . ."[11] Knox was no spokesman for lower class interests. He wanted the poor to be cared for, but he advocated nothing like the later economic communism of Gerrard Winstanley. More so than most other Protestant reformers, he successfully appealed to all classes to conduct themselves in accordance with the dictates of the higher law. He was most critical of the social abuses of the landed nobility, lairds, and burgesses, yet within these classes he found the source of his strongest support. To be sure, the Catholic nobles and lairds were subjected to more criticism than their Protestant counterparts, but even his Protestant supporters did not escape criticism entirely. He called for justice for the poor, but he provoked no Peasants' Revolt which would have forced him, as it did Luther, to take sides in a divisive class conflict. He had strong supporters in the west of Scotland as well as in the east and they came from every important social class. With his outspoken prophetic manner he offended all equally, but permanently affronted no major class because of reactionary or revolutionary views. His offense was the offense of the Hebrew prophets — calling for justice and warning of judgment. In his own time and in his own way he echoed the demand of Amos: "Let justice roll down like waters, and righteousness like an everflowing stream."

The key principles in Knox's plan for poor relief — assistance for the impotent but not the sturdy beggar, the administration of aid by the local parishes, and the compulsion of able-bodied persons to work by the magistrate — reflect Knox's experience with the Edwardian system of poor relief. When he landed in England in March 1549, the Act of 1536 was in effect. Parish and municipal authorities had the responsibility of collecting voluntary donations in the churches to aid the impotent, but no provisions had been made to establish a program of public works to assist the able unemployed. A man or woman without visible means of support who was unemployed for a minimum of three days was liable to branding, enslavement, or imprisonment—harsh terms which Knox did not want imitated in Scotland. The English themselves were repelled by the provisions calling for the mutilation of beggars, the whipping of children, and the enslavement of people, hence the Act was repealed in 1550 and the Act of 1531 revived. Under the latter act the impotent could be licensed and allowed to beg in their local communities. The able-bodied unemployed were whipped and returned to their homes, and those who begged without license were fined. Both acts recognized the distinction between sturdy beggars and impotent poor, the responsibility of the magistrate to repress begging by the able, and the importance of voluntary giving in the local parishes to assist the needy, all of which were principles subsequently advocated by Knox and his colleagues.

During his sojourn in Geneva Knox appears to have been influenced more by the ideal than the administrative details of poor relief. In Geneva too the distinction was made between the impotent poor and the sturdy beggar. The *Ordinances* of 1541 prohibited begging and charged the deacons with administration of the system of poor relief. The focus of the latter was the Hôpital-Général, which provided facilities for orphans and the elderly, shelter and food for visitors unable to afford lodging, and food for distribution each week to poor households. One of the most striking features of this system is the degree of lay control, vested in the four *procureurs*, who administered the Hôpital, and one *hospitallier*, who supervised the actual care of the poor. There is no evidence that Knox proposed a similar establishment for Edinburgh, though he favored a strong degree of lay involvement in administering the system of poor relief. What must especially have impressed Knox was the strong sense of responsibility to aid the impotent poor which prevailed in Calvin's Geneva.[12]

II. Educational Reform

Apart from his contribution to the *Book of Discipline*, Knox has relatively little to say in his extant writings on the subject of education. In his treatise on predestination (published in 1560) he argued that a man educated in languages and the writings of godly men was better able to avoid error and more apt to teach the truth effectively than a man without such knowledge. Yet in a meeting of the General Assembly in 1564 he asserted that "worldy wisdom" played a role in the maintenance of idolatry and the betrayal of truth. Education was important, but it had to be the right kind of education — one governed by biblical precepts. In his *Brief Exhortation to England* in 1559 Knox had pointed out the necessity of education for the preservation of Protestantism, urging the founding of schools in all English cities and major towns. He insisted, however, that the oversight of these schools be committed to the magistrates and godly learned men. He clearly believed in the danger of allowing men not devoted to the Protestant cause to teach in the educational system.[13]

The difficulties posed by education to Knox's cause were made manifest to him in 1572. The regent Moray had been assassinated in 1570 by a Hamilton, and Knox had subsequently criticized all the Hamiltons from his pulpit in St. Andrews. Archibald Hamilton thereupon refused to attend Knox's sermons. When threatened with ecclesiastical discipline, Hamilton appealed, as an undergraduate, to the University of St. Andrews for protection. Archbishop John Douglas, Rector of the University, and others approached Knox to resolve the conflict. Knox protested in July 1572, contending that no school or university had the right to judge the church. Alluding to the medieval universities, he warned that universities had a record of opposing the church in the past. Within a month he wrote to the General Assembly at Perth, urging them above all else to "preserve the Kirk from the bondage of the Universities." The universities were to govern themselves in accord with Christian standards, and the church was to keep them within its jurisdiction to guarantee that those standards were maintained.[14] Any assessment of Knox's contribution to education must keep this in mind. Like nearly all the reformers, he was definitely not a champion of intellectual inquiry. The universities and schools were to be ecclesiastically censured, as on the Continent, in order to preserve the integrity of the faith and propagate Christian truth as seen through the eyes of Knox and his colleagues.

The section on education in the *Book of Discipline*[15] is one of the more substantial achievements of the Reformation period. Knox and his associates attempted to set forth in some detail a plan for Scotland that manifested the educational aims he had outlined in his *Brief Exhortation to England*. The educational system the Scottish reformers envisaged was thoroughly religious in its philosophy and aims: education was to train youth to be godly and virtuous. The churches in the Scottish towns were to have the responsibility of appointing schoolmasters. The churches in the countryside, following tradition, were to entrust the education of their children to ministers or readers, who were now to be responsible for basic education and the Calvinist catechism. Every major town was to have a college or grammar school for instruction in the arts, especially logic, rhetoric, and languages. Sufficient teachers and stipends were to be provided for these colleges. Scholarships were to be furnished for poor students, with the church playing the key role in supplying funds.

All children were to be given an education, regardless of their socio-economic status. Parents were not to be allowed to prevent their children from receiving an education in order to employ them in the fields or shops. Students who demonstrated special aptitude were to be charged to continue their studies in order to benefit the commonwealth. Ministers and elders would be responsible for conducting quarterly examinations of students to ascertain their progress and decide which students were to continue to a higher level. Those judged unfit to continue were trained in a craft. No student could graduate without possessing sufficient knowledge of Christianity.

A student who pursued the maximum course of education would spend several years learning to read, to understand Calvin's catechism, and to grasp the rudiments of Latin grammar. An additional three or four years would be devoted to the mastery of Latin, with logic, rhetoric, and Greek also receiving four years of study. The remainder of one's schooling (to the age of twenty-four) was to be spent studying law, medicine, or divinity. The cessation of study in divinity at the age of twenty-four is interesting in view of the medieval universities' practice of not granting the doctorate in divinity before the age of thirty-five. In fact, the shorter periods of study in law, medicine, and divinity indicate the need for these people in Scotland as well as a belief that the traditionally long periods of study were unneccessary.

Scotland would continue to have its three universities at St. Andrews, Glasgow, and Aberdeen. No new ones were proposed, despite previous signs of interest in higher education at Edinburgh. In 1556 Mary of Guise's administration had appointed two noted scholars, Edward Henderson and Alexander Sym, to give public lectures on civil and canon law, Greek, and other subjects in Edinburgh. Two years later, part of the legacy left by Robert Reid, Bishop of Orkney, was intended to establish a college of law in that city. Yet Knox and his colleagues would have done no more than establish a college at Edinburgh for instruction in the arts, which was also their intention for the other major towns of Scotland. They rightly recognized that what higher education in Scotland needed was not a new university but reform of the existing ones. After all, Scotland already had one more university than England, where the educational system was markedly superior. Scottish students, including Knox's own sons, often studied in English or Continental universities, whereas the reputation of the Scottish universities did not attract foreign scholars. The position of Knox and his colleagues on the number of the universities was in keeping with the earlier views of John Major, who "look[ed] with no favour on this multitude of universities; . . . in consideration of the physical features of the country, this number of universities is not to be condemned."[16]

Some indication of the poor state of affairs in the Scottish universities in 1560 is indicated in the number of students attending. At St. Andrews there were thirty-one entrants in 1557, indicating a total enrollment of some one hundred and fifty students. The following year, however, there were only three entrants. After 1560 the number of entrants averaged thirty, indicating that at St. Andrews the major reason for the sharp decline in enrollment just prior to 1560 was due to the upheavals in religion. The situation at Glasgow was worse. The average number of annual entrants in the century preceding 1550 was ten, with none recorded between 1509 and 1535. In the aftermath of the Reformation a 1563 letter of Mary Stewart observes "rather the decay of ane Universitie nor ony wyse to be reknit ane establisst foundatioun." Aberdeen also experienced difficulty, having, for example, virtually no arts students in 1549. By 1562, according to the English ambassador to Scotland, there were only fifteen or sixteen scholars at the university. Recognition of the need for reform in the universities was not new with Knox and his colleagues, for the Catholics had been aware of the problem, as evidenced, for example, by the legislation of the provincial council of 1549.[17]

Subjects of instruction in the universities were to include dialectic, mathematics, physics, medicine, moral philosophy, law, Greek, Hebrew, divinity, economics, politics, cosmography, astrology, and natural philosophy. Unlike the medieval universities, the reformed Scottish universities were not to include Latin grammar and literature. This does not, however, indicate a lack of classical or linguistic interest on the part of the reformers, for Latin was to be mastered prior to university entrance. In this respect the program of the reformers was more rigid than that of the Catholic reformers in 1549.[18] The inclusion of Greek, which Knox learned (with Hebrew) at Geneva, is noteworthy. Only Aberdeen apparently taught Greek before the 1550s, though a smattering of the language may have been available in the grammar schools. In any case, though Greek was not unknown to all Scotsmen in the fifteenth century, there is no evidence to indicate that it was taught in Scotland until the sixteenth century, and even then not on a wide basis.[19] The oft-cited statutes of the Aberdeen Grammar School are of late date (1553), and are hardly contributory evidence to the mistaken notion that the Scots had fully assimilated the classical scholarship of the Renaissance before 1560.[20] There is, however, no reason to go to the opposite extreme and refer to the deprecation of all classical studies in the projected reformed universities.[21] The study of Greek was included; indeed, Knox's colleague, John Row, taught Greek at Perth in 1560; John Willock also knew Greek, and it was taught at Montrose. Although the major interest of the drafters in Greek was for biblical studies, Knox at least is known not to have been antipathetic to humanism.

The formulators of the *Book of Discipline* also devoted some attention to regulations for other matters pertaining to the universities. To be admitted, students had to have recommendations from their schoolmasters and ministers testifying of their learning, docility, age, and family background. Provisions were also made for the government of the universities. Knox's contribution to this section was probably slight, and it may be more reflective of the legal minds of Row and John Winram, a veteran of several Catholic reforming councils. With their assistance, John Douglas, Rector of St. Andrews University, was very likely the drafter of the section on the universities, though Knox was certainly called upon to approve their proposals.

Several characteristics of the educational scheme proposed by Knox and his associates are particularly significant. First, the scheme provided for universal education at the basic level. Possibly the educational program (because of its religious premises) was meant to include girls, as was increasingly the English practice at the pre-grammar-school level, though girls certainly would not have been admitted to the universities. Nevertheless, Scotland, one of the most backward states in Western Europe, would have had the first universal compulsory program of education. The notion of universal education was basically new to Scotland with the reformers. The masters of the Elgin Cathedral schools had been required to teach any who came to them for instruction, but this is quite different from universal education at the state level. More problematical is the act of Parliament in 1496, according to which all barons and freeholders of substance were to send their eldest sons and heirs to school commencing at the age of eight or nine. They were to remain in grammar school until they had mastered Latin, whereupon they were "to remane thre yeris at the Schulis of Art and Jure sua that thai may have knawlege and understanding of the lawis Throw the quhilkis Justice may reigne universalie. . . ." Yet this act was never put into operation, was only concerned with providing Scotland with competent administrators of justice, and involved only eldest sons and heirs of the nobility and freeholders of substance. The provisions of the *Book of Discipline* were potentially more extensive. If girls were meant to be included in the lower level of the educational process, this was revolutionary, for there is no evidence that such was contemplated by the Scots in the medieval period. The admonition to expand the number of schools was not, however, revolutionary, but in keeping with recent practice. Before 1560 there were grammar schools connected with most cathedrals, collegiate kirks, and major burghs. New grammar schools had recently been founded at Crail (1542) and Kirkwall (1544). Yet more schools were needed, as indicated, for example, by the subsequent unsuccessful attempts of the General Assembly to establish new schools in Moray, Banff, Inverness, and other northern shires.[22]

Secondly, attention was paid to the needs of poor students, so that the opportunity to receive a comprehensive education would depend on ability, not wealth or social background. This was clearly a democratizing principle. Yet this was not new, for the church had earlier provided for the maintenance of poor scholars. The reformed Kirk continued in this tradition. In June 1563, for example, the General Assembly urged adequate provision for poor scholars.[23] Moreover, such students were frequently aided by funds derived from fines levied by kirk sessions.

Thirdly, the educational program was moderately liberal in its curriculum, de-emphasizing the Scholastic theology that had been a major factor in medieval higher education. Knox and his colleagues advocated the kind of university program that was generally favored by the English Puritans in the seventeenth century, but did not go nearly as far as the more radical English reformers, such as John Webster and John Hall, later proposed. Although some attention was paid to Greek and, at the grammar-school level, to Latin language and literature, the weakest element in the curriculum was probably the insufficient attention given to classical and humanistic studies. One of the strongest aspects of the curriculum was the inclusion of instruction in the crafts, so that Knox and his friends preceded the Elizabethan Statute of Apprentices (1563) in their concern for utilitarian training. The advantages here can best be appreciated when one recalls the reactionary practices of the Scottish guilds, where crafts heretofore had to be learned.

Fourthly, the entire educational program was pervaded by a religious philosophy that aimed to train young people to be godly in whatever occupation they served. The universities would not accept students who could not demonstrate a godly character. Knox and his associates wanted a change in the type of student who received a higher education. Not only must the students be godly, but they must also be docile, that is, capable of undergoing instruction, particularly from the Protestant point of view. The religious emphasis in education was, of course, quite in keeping with medieval and contemporary educational practice. There had been no notion of a purely secular education, and Knox and his colleagues were far from introducing one. Religion was no less important in the Reformed schools than in the older Catholic ones. If anything, the Scottish reformers increased the religious emphasis by calling for the application of rigid religious requirements to entering university students.

Fifthly, overall supervision of the educational system rested in the hands of the church, which had the responsibility to provide the schools and schoolmasters. In 1563 the General Assembly expressed its intent that all education be entrusted only to those professing the Protestant faith; all others were to be removed from their teaching positions. Two years later the Assembly stipulated that superintendents or visitors of the Kirk had to examine the doctrine of teachers and those in charge of schools, colleges, and universities before admission to their positions. This was reenacted two years later.[24] Ministers and elders also determined who continued in the educational process, and ministers had to provide prospective university students with recommendations. Knox himself sought for stricter control of the universities by the church. It is interesting to note that Knox and his colleagues were pressing for ecclesiastical control of education during that period in Scottish history when the existing grammar schools were passing from the control and patronage of the church into the jurisdiction of the town councils.[25] Although the burghs sought no innovations in the traditional curriculum and were interested only in matters of patronage and prestige, Knox and his colleagues were not willing to tolerate even this infringement of the burghs in the Kirk's sphere.[26] In this regard they were, like nearly all contemporary Christian leaders, educational conservatives.

The educational scheme was not utopian, and in various respects did not depart radically from the medieval system. The *sine qua non* for its success was money and personnel. Knox intended that the educational funds be taken from the monies used by the Catholic church for education, and from the incomes of suppressed abbeys and chantries, but the rapacity of the nobles wrecked the scheme.[27] Because the Scots were not willing to provide the funds, the shortage of qualified instructors was not a limiting factor. Certainly the latter problem could have been rectified in reasonable time if the money had been forthcoming. The most serious defect of the proposed system from the modern standpoint is the very reason given for its existence — the training of godly youth. The system sought to produce young people who accepted the Calvinist catechism as a prerequisite for graduation or higher studies. Freedom of intellectual inquiry would not have been tolerated in key areas of the curriculum. The docility sought by the reformers in university students was not merely the ability to learn; it included acceptance of the church's teachings. In 1565 the Kirk of Scotland, as was noted, actually moved to ensure its control over Scottish education by requiring that teachers and those in charge of schools, colleges, and universities be examined by the church. The Kirk's decree was upheld by Parliament in 1567. Knox recognized the potential "bondage" of the church to the universities, but he failed to recognize the equally dangerous "bondage" of the universities to the church. Just as he had no concept of freedom in the religious sphere, and because he had no such concept, so he was unable to conceive of freedom in the educational and intellectual world. In fairness, of course, it must be remembered that ecclesiastical control of education was a common practice in sixteenth-century Europe, whether in Catholic, Lutheran, or Reformed territories. The system favored by Knox was certainly less rigid than that advocated by Ignatius Loyola and developed by the Society of Jesus.

The system as the Scottish reformers envisaged it would proabably have been self-defeating. Ultimately universal education coupled with a moderately liberal curriculum would have created intelligent dissent and eroded authoritarian ecclesiastical intellectualism. In spite of the religious restrictions and the fact that the program was not adopted by the state, therefore, the advocacy of the program and the pattern it provided was a landmark in the history of education. In numerous ways it foreshadowed modern education, notably in its comprehensiveness and its egalitarian and practical spirit. But the *Book of Discipline* would never provide the precise pattern for modern educational development, which is commonly based on secular ideals rather different from Knox's religious principles.

Knox's views on educational reform were influenced by John Calvin and probably Martin Bucer. There is also a possibility that he derived some general ideas on reform from the earlier Scottish interest in improving education, including the ideas of John Major. The modest interest of the provincial councils in reform has been noted. There had also been concern among the Lollards, in whose Ayrshire region Knox had preached. As early as the first part of the fifteenth century the Lollard Quintin Folkerde had exhorted the Bishop of Glasgow and his clergy to take an interest in religious education. Concern for educational improvement may not have been widespread in Scotland, but examples appear in various circles. There is an example in the royal petition of 1495 calling for the founding of a university at Aberdeen. The petition observed that certain places in Scotland were geographically isolated, so that some men were "rude and ignorant of letters, and almost barbarous, who . . . cannot have leisure for the study of letters, nay, are so ignorant of these letters that, not only for preaching the word of God to the people of those parts but also for administering the sacraments of the church, proper men cannot be found." Interest in furthering, if not necessarily reforming, education was regularly manifested in the decades before 1560. In 1512, for example, St. Leonard's College, St. Andrews, was granted a charter of foundation by Alexander Stewart, Archbishop of St. Andrews and a pupil of Erasmus. In 1525 the vicar of Lathrisk, Sir W. Myrton, founded grammar and song schools in the town. In 1538 James Beaton, Archbishop of St. Andrews, founded St. Mary's College to promote the study of divinity, civil and canon law, natural philosophy, medicine, and other subjects. Between 1532 and 1545 Bishop William Stewart of Aberdeen built and furnished the library and other buildings at Aberdeen. Knox's own probable mentor, John Major, was concerned about the state of the Scottish universities, and may have conveyed this concern to his pupil. He complained of the lack of major gifts to St. Andrews and of the poorness of Glasgow in endowment and scholars. These are just some of the indications of native Scottish interest in educational improvement.[28] Knox may well have been influenced by the general concern common to such endeavors, but he was also influenced by Continental ideas.[29]

Geneva was probably the most important source of influence for Knox's educational views. Calvin continued the medieval emphasis on the religious nature of education. During his stay in Geneva Knox had sufficient time to observe the educational system, with its particular emphasis on training the young. Calvin's new college at Geneva was not, however, founded until 1559. Unless he discussed the proposal with Calvin it is therefore very unlikely that Knox was influenced by it, as has been claimed.

That such a discussion occurred is a distinct possibility, given Calvin's long-standing interest in educational reform. As early as 1536 it was decided to establish a public school for children in Geneva, with Antoine Saunier as rector. The following year Calvin brought the humanist and educational reformer Maturin Cordier, under whom he had studied at the Collège de la Marche in Paris, to Geneva to help reorganize the college. The *Ordinances* of 1541 stress the importance of an adequate educational system, particularly to prepare youth for the ministry and civil government. Cordier, however, did not return with Calvin from exile, and his place was taken by Castellio (from 1541 to 1544), who had taught at the Collège de la Rive, begun by Saunier in 1536. The lower schools in Geneva needed reforming, hence Calvin contacted Claude Baduel of Nimes, who visited Geneva in 1550. Calvin's continuing interest in educational reform was again manifested in 1557, when he visited Strasbourg and examined the academy of Jacob Sturm.[30] It is difficult to conceive that Knox could have been unimpressed by this vibrant movement of educational reform.

There is a distinct possibility that Knox may also have been influenced by Bucer, whose educational ideas were known on the Continent and also in Edwardian England. Bucer's *De Regno Christi* had been presented to Edward VI in 1551. In it the author called for the reformation of the English universities because they were remiss in producing religious teachers. Like Knox, Bucer's major concern with education was religious rather than humanistic. He urged Edward to open more schools at the preuniversity level and provide for poor scholars, so that the deserving poor could receive their education free. As Knox later stated, education was not only for the furtherance of the faith but also for the welfare of the commonwealth. As early as 1543 Bucer had joined with Melanchthon and others to draft a set of regulations on church government for Cologne. Included in the regulations were directions for schools. They specified that every town was to have a properly supported Latin school with pious and learned instructors, and a curriculum which included grammar, dialectic, Greek, music, and religion. Advanced schools were also stipulated, with a curriculum of religion, dialectic, Greek, grammar, mathematics, physics (including astronomy and cosmography), and law. Attention was also given to the support of poor students. While the program set forth by Knox and his associates in the *Book of Discipline* does not fully correspond to the views of Bucer, the ample parallels underscore the likelihood that Knox knew of Bucer's views (or perhaps the similar views of Jacob Sturm, a magistrate and rector of the Strasbourg Gymnasium).[31]

There is also a slight possibility that Knox, during the course of his travels, learned (indirectly) of plans for educational reform by leading Lutherans. Philip Melanchthon published recommendations for the schools and churches of Thuringia in 1528, which have been likened to the *Book of Discipline*. He stressed the need to educate children in sound doctrine in order that they could ultimately be of service to church and state. His ideal was learned piety, a happy blending of humanism and evangelical faith. "On earth," he wrote, "there is nothing next to the Gospel more glorious than humanistic learning, that wonderful gift of God." Language and grammar were stressed as the basis of a liberal education.[32] Luther and Melanchthon, like Knox, sought to have schools in every parish and secondary schools in every sizeable town. Luther's views on education are set forth in his 1524 treatise *To the Councilmen of all Cities in Germany That They Establish and Maintain Schools*. It has been suggested that this book influenced Knox as well as Calvin,[33] but there is no evidence to indicate that Knox knew the work, though he may have heard of some of its ideas indirectly. Unlike Knox, Luther placed considerable emphasis on the importance of linguistic study and libraries. He also explicitly called for the education of girls, a notion for which Knox may ultimately be indebted to him. Both men called for increased expenditure of funds for education, proposing that some of the money come from sources previously committed to Catholicism. Both men likewise called for provisions to ensure that exceptional pupils were able to continue their studies for a longer time than others.[34] Thus Knox's concepts of education appear to be derived from a varied background, though any estimate of the sources which influenced him cannot be made with absolute certainty.

Knox's proposals for educational reform, developed in conjunction with his Scottish colleagues, surely stand comparison with the educational views of other Protestant leaders. In matters of education as in poor relief, the influence of Knox casts a long shadow over future centuries. It is therefore appropriate that Professor Reid, in concluding his biography, should recognize that Knox's "concept of the responsibility of the church for the care of the poor was maintained down into the nineteenth century," and that the emphasis he and his colleagues gave to education "became a basic characteristic of the Scot both at home and abroad. . . ."[35] John Knox's social awareness in fact gave to Scottish Protestantism a strong sense of social responsibility.

CHAPTER
‡ ELEVEN ‡

THE KNOXIAN PARADOX:
Ecumenism and Nationalism
in the Scottish Reformation

One might expect that the effect of John Knox's reforming activity in Scotland would be the intensification of Scottish nationalism and a corresponding withering of whatever sense of *oikoumene* had previously existed. Certain aspects of his work do indeed point in this direction, but Knox tempered the growing spirit of Scottish nationalism in religion. As a consequence of his work the Scottish Kirk in the later sixteenth century had a modest but real ecumenical outlook. Knox was no ecumenist in the sense that he promoted major conferences for unity and harmony, though he did urge the holding of conferences between the faithful of England and Scotland. Nor is he the equal of Martin Bucer in the task of reconciliation. Temperamentally his partisan spirit was unsuited for such a role. He may, however, be compared in his ecumenical spirit with Thomas Cranmer, who welcomed Continental theologians and "kept constantly in mind the idea of a common Christian council and of some league of Protestant Churches."[1] Despite disagreement between the two men on matters of worship (which did not prevent them from belonging to the same communion), both looked to Continental Protestants for fellowship and intellectual inspiration. Knox's ecumenical spirit did not keep him from experiencing sharp confrontations with differing beliefs, but it did enable him (as it does ecumenical leaders of the twentieth century) to "recognize the inadequacy of any one tradition," and to combine its insights with his own, bringing the respective churches closer together in their opportunity for Christian fellowship.[2]

Knox was instrumental in providing the reformed Kirk of Scotland with an unusually eclectic theology and polity that were conducive to the Kirk's active participation in the Christian *oikoumene*, the universal fellowship of Christians (which, for Knox, excluded the Catholics and the Anabaptists). Simultaneously, however, the distinctiveness of the eclectic theology and polity, coupled with Knox's incipient development of the covenant concept, paved the way for a nationalistic Kirk. This is the Knoxian paradox. Yet Knox's governing principle was never conceived in either nationalist or ecumenical terms. That principle, narrowly conceived and reflecting an intolerance born out of strong convictions, was stringent adherence to divine precepts. Stated simply, it required that "in the religion of God onlie oght his owne Word to be considered. . . ." "Vaine religion and idolatrie I call whatsoever is done in Goddes service or honour, without the expresse commaundement of his own Worde."[3] The subject of this chapter concerns the relationship of this principle, which was Knox's deepest motivation, to the national and ecumenical orientation of the Scottish Kirk in the Reformation.

The Scottish Kirk in the fifteenth century was not only influenced by the emergence of nationalist feelings, but also contributed to the growth of those sentiments. It did so in a variety of ways. First, in keeping with the spirit of nationalism, liturgical reform was undertaken to give new emphasis to the Scottish saints in the liturgy. Secondly, national pilgrimage centers were popularized by the Kirk. The effectiveness of the Kirk's efforts appears in the interest shown by James III, James IV, and James V in undertaking pilgrimages to the shrines of Scottish saints, sometimes annually. Thirdly, Scottish nationalism was one of the motives for the foundation of Scotland's three oldest universities in the fifteenth century. King's College, Aberdeen, was founded explicitly *ad patriae ornamentum*. Finally, there is evidence to indicate that the more elaborate churches being built were erected at least in part to rival those of other lands, a fact noted by foreign dignitaries.[4]

During the sixteenth century Scottish Catholics continued to think in terms of the national character of their Kirk. A striking illustration of this is in the work of the reforming councils held between 1549 and 1559. Much of the councils' work involved reaffirmation of universal Catholic practices and dogma, but there is a striking lack of reference to the papacy. The articles enacted by the 1549 council on which inquisitors were to found their inquiries refer to the authority of general councils but not the papacy. The 1552 council decreed that Archbishop John Hamilton's *Catechism* be read in the kirks despite its silence on papal authority. The *Compendius Tractive* (1558) by Quintin Kennedy, Abbot of Crossraguel, who was present at the 1549 council, dealt substantially with the question of ecclesiastical authority, but omitted any discussion of the papacy. Once more, the 1559 council discussed the right of the Kirk or of a general council to define matters of the faith, but ignored the papacy.[5]

This implicit criticism of papal authority in Scotland had its roots in conciliarism, nationalism, and the practical issue of the control of the Scottish Kirk and its wealth. In the fifteenth century criticism was manifest in antipapal legislation and Scottish participation in the conciliar movement. In the sixteenth century, interest in conciliarism waned and Scottish Catholics began to go their own way on several doctrinal matters as they increased control of the Kirk. Hamilton's *Catechism*, for example, is closer to the teaching of Luther than of Trent on the matter of justification, and from the Catholic standpoint the treatment accorded to the mass is unsatisfactory. The 1552 council also accepted the suggestion of the temporal lords that the sacraments be not administered until the people had been given an explanation of the rites in the vernacular — a practice that may reflect the Protestant insistence on the conjunction of the Word and sacraments. To be sure, the vast bulk of Catholic dogma was retained, but in the years before 1560, Scottish Catholics were obviously thinking more in terms of *Scottish* Catholicism than *Roman* Catholicism.[6]

Reform-minded leaders of Scottish Catholicism in the mid-sixteenth century failed to effect what they desired, making the task of Knox and his colleagues simpler. Had the Catholics been able to produce effective leadership and a dedicated, educated clergy, and had they not been so heavily encumbered by their meddling French allies, it is conceivable that they could have relied on nationalist sentiment to repudiate the program advocated by the Protestants. Certainly they had already been fusing Scottish Catholicism and nationalism for more than a century. There were even Catholic leaders, including Knox's probable mentor, John Major, who had advocated an Anglo-Scottish alliance on nationalist grounds, as Major did in his *History* of 1521.

Knox, however, made little use of nationalist sentiment. On the contrary, he was actually accused of preferring England's cause to that of Scotland. In 1571, a year before his death, he answered such charges thus: "What I haue bene to my cuntrie, albeit this vnthankful aige will not knowe, yet the aiges to come wilbe compelled to beir witnes to the truth."[7] The phrase is nebulous, but what in fact he had been to his country was a man whose transcending principle was steadfast loyalty to the Word of God, not Scotland.

The charges of his accusers are not altogether ungrounded. Knox had a pronounced liking for England. His first wife was English, and three of the four women whom he loved most deeply — Mrs. Bowes, her daughter, and Mrs. Anne Locke — were English.[8] His language was English, and even after he permanently returned to Scotland he made no effort to revive his Scots dialect.[9] Those whom he selected as the godfathers of his sons were the Englishmen William Whittingham and Miles Coverdale. The boys went to Cambridge University, not to one of the Scottish universities, and the younger became a vicar in the Church of England. In January 1554 Knox explicitly affirmed his concern for England over Scotland: "Somtyme I have thought that impossible it had bene, so to have removed my affection from the Realme of Scotland, that eny Realme or Nation coulde have bene equall deare unto me. But God I take to recorde in my conscience, that the troubles present (and appearing to be) in the Realme of England, are double more dolorous unto my hert, then ever were the troubles of Scotland."[10] Knox's concern for England during his exile makes it evident that this was no idle statement. His attacks against Mary Tudor embodied more than accusations of idolatry, for their gravamen is that she endangered English independence and the general welfare of the English commonwealth, that she violated English laws and trampled upon English liberties. The tenor of Knox's writing is indeed such that a modern scholar can refer, not without reason, to "Knox's English nationalism," noting that his political writings during the Marian exile "were more those of an ordinary [English] patriot than of a prophet. . . ."[11]

Knox's continual desire for amity with England during the course of the Scottish Reformation was thus due to more than the political necessity to use England as a counter to France. His deep-rooted respect for England and its church, established while he was in England during the Edwardian period, make it most unlikely that his friendship for England after 1558 was merely that of the politique. He loved England and respected English Protestantism, "seeing that in principalls we all agree."[12] Although he was undoubtedly disappointed that the Elizabethan church had stagnated rather than pressed for further reforms of the kind he envisaged, he maintained an ecumenical outlook toward it. When queried in 1568 about the advisability of separating from the Church of England, he counseled against such action on the grounds that it would wrongly condemn the ministry of that church.[13] In this connection it should be noted that although there are grounds for regarding Knox as one of the fathers of English Puritanism, there is nothing in his thought that would support the later *jure divino* Presbyterianism of Thomas Cartwright and his colleagues. Knox would have reformed, not abolished, episcopacy. This was, of course, in keeping with the position of English Puritans before Cartwright.[14] Where Knox most strongly influenced the Puritan tradition was on the matter of authority, namely, stringent adherence to express biblical principles in religious matters.[15]

The concern of Knox and his Scottish colleagues for the Church of England is manifest in the action taken by the General Assembly on December 27, 1566. A letter was sent from the General Assembly to the bishops and pastors of the Church of England urging a more tolerant policy toward the use of surplices and other vestments. The letter bears evidence of Knox's authorship: civil authority is to be resisted if it burdens "the consciences of the faithful further than God chargeth them in his own word." Knox's favorite target — idolatry — is attacked once more: "If surplice, corner-cap and tippet have been the badges of idolaters in the very act of their idolatry, what hath the preachers of Christian liberty, and the rebukers of superstition to do with the dregs of that Romish Beast?"[16] The letter manifests not only Knox's ecumenical concern, but also the subordination of that concern to his governing principle — fidelity to the divine commands. Tact was not allowed to temper prophetic proclamation. Certainly a closer unity would have existed if he had been willing to accept the *Book of Common Prayer*, but unity was subordinate to obedience to the Word.[17] This incident underscores the fact that although men of ecumenical spirit continue to have sharp confrontations on matters of consequence, they do not allow such confrontations to disrupt the sense of fellowship and concern. Knox clearly did not succumb to the national or insular isolationism that threatened the Church of England.[18]

Knox's ecumenical outlook extended to various continental Protestant churches. His early desire to visit the German Lutherans never materialized, but he remained indebted to early Lutheran influence on his thought. The possibility for greater contact with the Lutherans was actually ruled out by the Lutherans themselves, not Knox, for they were markedly hostile to the Marian exiles for political reasons and differences about the nature of the Real Presence.[19] Knox's connections with the Reformed churches in Switzerland, France, and Germany are well known, as are his dealings with Reformed leaders such as Calvin, Heinrich Bullinger, Pierre Viret of Lausanne, and Theodore Beza. These contacts continued after the Reformation in Scotland was under way. There was, for example, the submission of the *Second Helvetic Confession of Faith* from "the Churches of Geneva, Berne, and Basle, with other Reformed Churches of Germany and France"[20] to the Scottish Protestants in 1566. The *Confession* was enclosed with a letter from Beza to Knox — not to one of the superintendents — underscoring Knox's ecumenical leadership in Scotland. Beza's letter attested to Knox's ecumenical spirit when he wrote that "there has always existed, and . . . there will exist to the last between us, that complete union of mind which is confirmed by the bond of one and the same spirit and faith."[21] Additional evidence of the continuing ties exists in extant letters between Calvin and Knox (1559, 1561) and from Beza to Knox (1569, 1572). The correspondence is very candid, though Calvin urges Knox to be more moderate and Beza warns him of the dangers of episcopacy (an opinion Knox did not fully share).[22]

Geneva was clearly aware of differences with Scotland on various matters, but this did not hinder relations between the churches. During the same period (c. 1565–66) Knox's correspondence also manifests his continued interest in the affairs of the Huguenots.[23]

An open letter from Knox and the superintendents John Spottiswoode, John Winram, and John Erskine of Dun, dated December 26, 1565, provides an interesting illustration of an informal ecumenical outlook. The letter was written on behalf of Robert Hamilton, Christopher Goodman's successor at St. Andrews, and Robert Campbell of Kinzeancleuch, a friend of Knox. The letter is addressed to the churches in England, France, Germany (including perhaps the Lutherans?), and elsewhere, requesting that they receive the two men warmly.[24] All details of their journey, if taken, are apparently unknown.

The possibility for ecumenical fellowship was enhanced by the eclectic theology of the reformed Kirk of Scotland, molded substantially but not exclusively by Knox. To read the works of Knox or the *Scots Confession* of 1560 and find nothing more than unadulterated Calvinism betrays a preconceived judgment of their contents. It also necessitates overlooking a pertinent statement by Knox himself. Following the debate with William Maitland of Lethington at the General Assembly of June 1564, Knox was ordered to write to Calvin "and to the learned in other Kirks" to ascertain their judgment on the general question of the obedience of subjects to their sovereigns. Knox refused, saying, "I myself am not only fully resolved in conscience, but also I have heard the judgments in this, and *all other things* that I have affirmed within this Realm, of the most godly and most learned that be known in Europe. I came not to this Realm without their resolution; and for my assurance I have the handwritings of *many*. . . ."[25] There is no question that Knox admired Calvin, but he did not blindly and slavishly follow the Geneva reformer.

With respect to Knox's theology, several points may be noted. First, the doctrine of predestination, so important to Calvin, receives little treatment in the writings of Knox and the *Scots Confession* (where the chapter on election is devoted to the work of Christ). A major place is given to predestination in the controversial tract published by Knox in 1559 against an anonymous opponent whom Knox loosely calls an Anabaptist, but the circumstances in which it was written are significant. Its composition came on the heels of the publication of Knox's *First Blast of the Trumpet*, a treatise which severely displeased Calvin. Knox was close to being *persona non grata* in Geneva, and needed to atone to Calvin and the Genevan authorities for the publication of this work. He obviously remembered being forced to leave Frankfurt by its magistrates for the political views he had uttered in his *Admonition to England*. Moreover, Knox's treatise was written in the aftermath of Calvin's controversies with Sebastian Castellio and Jerome Bôlsec. In the ensuing intellectual climate in Geneva it became something of a shibboleth to defend Calvin's doctrine. Beza made it the subject of his *Summa totius Christianismi* (1555). Knox's colleague William Whittingham translated it into English as *A Briefe Declaration of the Chiefe Points of the Christian Religion* and published it in Geneva (1556). Anthony Gilby contributed *A Briefe Treatise of Election and Reprobation* (1556). Thus in writing about predestination Knox was undertaking an exercise designed to preserve his Geneva base of operations and perhaps restore his damaged reputation in England. Surely if the doctrine had meant so much to him, it would have received a more significant place in his other writings. Where it does appear in other works, it is essentially a paraphrase of biblical material.[26] In any case, the doctrine of predestination was not Calvin's peculiar preserve. As early as February 1553, probably more than a year before he began reading Calvin, Knox was thinking in terms of predestination.[27] He subsequently developed this concept in Geneva, but once he returned to Scotland his interest in the doctrine quickly waned.

Secondly, one of the early sources of Protestant influence on Knox was Lutheranism. Knox warmly commended Henry Balnaves' compendium of Christianity with its theme of justification by faith and its marked reliance on Luther's commentary on Galatians. His précis of Balnaves' work was undertaken "to give my Confession of the article of Justification therein conteined."[28] Knox went on, however, to blend Luther's doctrine of justification with Calvin's view of the role of the law in the Christian life. Lutheran influence is also likely on Knox's doctrine of the atonement (through *Patrick's Places*) and his conception of the Christian family (through

Balnaves), and possibly his educational views (through the proposals of Luther and Melanchthon).

Thirdly, Scottish scholars have commented on the special emphasis given by Knox to the Lord's Supper. James S. McEwen has contended of Knox that "it was precisely in his teaching on the sacraments that he departed significantly from Calvin," both in emphasis and practice.[29] A major difference between Calvin and Knox on the Lord's Supper was Knox's willingness to administer the sacrament before the establishment of an organized visible church, as he did in Scotland in 1555 – 56.[30] Knox's doctrine and practice of the Lord's Supper are drawn largely from Martin Bucer and Heinrich Bullinger, the major figures in the formulation of the article on the Lord's Supper in the *First Helvetic Confession* (1536). That article was designed to reconcile the Lutherans and the Swiss, and thus had ecumenical intent.[31] Knox learned of Bucer's and Bullinger's views through George Wishart, and affirmed in the 1560s that he was practicing the Lord's Supper exactly as he had in 1547 at St. Andrews.[32] Knox's statement has long puzzled historians, who have concluded either that Knox was mistaken or that he was a Calvinist in 1547. He was neither. He accepted Bucer's general doctrine and practice in 1547, which later harmonized with Calvin's views because Calvin also was indebted to Bucer for his general concept of the Lord's Supper.[33] Indeed, the influence of Bucer (and Bullinger) on the Scottish Reformation has never been adequately recognized.

Knox was stricter than Calvin in excluding everything from the sacrament that was not expressly sanctioned by Scripture. Calvin, in fact, wrote to Knox in April 1561, pleading that Knox use discretion and be more tolerant on the matter of ceremonies. "The mysteries of God [must] be not polluted by absurd or unmeaning mixtures. With this exception, you know well that certain things, though not positively approved, must be tolerated."[34] The incident reveals a difference between the two men on the fundamental question of authority as well as the Lord's Supper. Knox's stricter concept of authority is more akin to that of Wishart, Balnaves, and the Zwinglian John Hooper, one of Knox's colleagues in Edwardian England, than to that of Calvin. If Knox's position on authority had been more lenient, of course, the possibilities for greater ecumenical fellowship would have been improved. Yet for him the key to such fellowship was strict adherence to Scripture. An intensive analysis of other aspects of Knox's thought reveals further evidence of its eclecticism.

The eclectic theology was paralleled by an eclectic system of kirk government, as demonstrated by Janet MacGregor and Gordon Donaldson. The office of superintendent, for example, combined elements from the Lutheran superintendents of Germany and Denmark, the Edwardian bishops, the Swiss Reformed visitors, John à Lasco's superintendents, and the views expressed by Bucer in *De Regno Christi*. The eldership was akin to that in the Genevan church, but Knox may also have learned of the eldership through the work of Wishart. The office of reader was probably borrowed from Zürich and Basle. In other respects the polity of the Scottish Reformed Kirk reveals the influence of Valérand Pullain and the Hessian polity of 1526 developed by Francois Lambert. To say, as one of Knox's biographers does, that "Knox took his ideas of Church organisation . . . from Calvin . . ."[35] is inaccurate.

More significant is the fact that Knox's position on the ministry was mediatory. On the vital question of episcopacy he was not opposed to bishops; in fact he urged an increase in their number in England in 1559.[36] Yet he did not accept the often concomitant doctrine of apostolic succession, nor did he repudiate the underlying equality of all ministers, including bishops, whose only superiority was the exercise of delegated supervisory powers (as were given to the superintendents of the reformed Kirk of Scotland). As late as the year of his death (1572) Knox criticized the abuses associated with episcopacy in Scotland, but not episcopacy *per se*. What he sought was a reformed episcopacy — a position advocated or approved by a host of other writers, including Calvin, John à Lasco, Rudolph Gualter, Bucer, and the formulators of the *Second Helvetic Confession*. The ecumenical possibilities of Knox's mediatory position have been overlooked by later writers seeking to tie him to the more conservative Anglican position or the Presbyterian polity that developed after his death.[37]

The eclectic polity and theology enhanced the likelihood for *oikoumene*. One aspect of Knox's thought that *initially* mitigated against a strongly nationalist Kirk was his concept of the covenant.

An authority on the Scottish Reformation recently stated that Knox did not make use of the term "covenant" or of the covenant conception in his thought. This is erroneous. The best illustration of Knox's use of the covenant idea occurs in his 1554 tract, *An Admonition or Warning that the Faithful Christians in London, Newcastle, Berwick, and Others, May Avoid God's Vengeance*. Here Knox makes it abundantly clear that there is a covenant, and that the fundamental covenant obligation is to serve God and avoid idolatry. "In making whilk league, solemnedlie we sweir never to haif fellowschip with ony religioun, except with that whilk God hath confirmit be his manifest Word."[38]

Knox's concept of the covenant in this work was not patterned after Calvin's thought. Calvin depicted the covenant as God's promise to man, which had been fulfilled in the Incarnation, death, and resurrection of Christ. Although Calvin did not ignore man's obligations, he treated them as of less importance than the promissory aspect. Apart from his 1556 tract on baptism, Knox, on the other hand, dealt with the covenant essentially as a conditional promise calling for man's reciprocal obedience. This emphasis on the covenant as contract was made by Zwingli and Bullinger (among others) on the Continent, and by William Tyndale, John Hooper, and others in England. It is also found in Oecolampadius' writings, which were circulating in Scotland as early as 1540. There was also a native Scottish tradition upon which Knox may have drawn: the custom of private "banding" or "bonding," usually undertaken for the defense of lives and property. This band evolved into a "semi-legal baronial pressure group," of which there are the well-known examples of 1556–72. Knox used the idea of band or covenant in this sense in his *History*, but he also developed concepts of the covenant more akin to those found in the Zwingli-Bullinger and Tyndale traditions. Knox's earliest concept of the covenant was that of an individual engaging in a reciprocal contract with God. Yet the individual is not isolated; he is one of a number of believers acting in concert, though not as a nation. An example will illustrate the point: "It is necessarie," Knox wrote in 1554, "that we avoyd ydolatrie, because . . . otherwise we declair oure selves little to regard the league and covenant of God; for that league requyreis that we declair oure selves enemyis to all sortis of ydolatrie."[39]

It is significant that the idea of being in covenant, bond, or league with God is initially developed in a work written to English Protestants. The covenant notion would lend itself well to a nationalist cause, but Knox did not initially use it in that sense. He recognized that the covenant had had nationalist meaning in the past, and he used this notion in one of his subsequent works. His conception of the covenant in *An Admonition* has distinct ecumenical implications: "All that be in this league ar one bodie, as Moses doth witness [Deut. 29], recompting men, wemen, childrene, servandis, princes, preastis, reularis, officeris, and strangeris within the Covenant of the Lord: Then plaine it is, that of one bodie thair must be one law; sa that whatever God requyreth of one, in that behalf, he requyreis the same of all."[40] This is the foundation of Knox's concept of *oikoumene*, or universal Christian fellowship.

The one law to which Knox referred had to do with service to God and the extirpation of idolatry. In later writings he developed this obligation against the background of a covenant or bond between God and his people. Two other types of covenant also appear in his works. In his *Faithful Admonition to the Professors of God's Truth in England* (1554), he implies the existence of a covenant between monarch and people based on national law and custom — a concept which developed in the late medieval period. Mary Tudor is castigated by Knox as a traitor to the English crown and people because, contrary to Parliamentary law, she had "made a proude Spaniarde kynge. . . ." She had violated her oath to the English people. Along the same lines, the Scots were later encouraged to emulate the "solemned othe and convenante" made between Asa and his people to serve God and punish idolaters (2 Chron. 15). Mary Stewart was subsequently reminded of her "mutual contract" with the Scottish people.[41]

Beginning in 1558 Knox discussed a covenant between the temporal powers and God. In his *Appellation* to the nobility and estates of Scotland, he argued that the reformation of religion and the punishment of idolatry was the duty of the civil magistrate. As proof he cited the covenant made by Josiah with God on behalf of the people (2 Kings 23),[42] but he never relinquished the idea of a direct covenant between God and his people. In his 1564 debate with Maitland of Lethington he contended that the people of a commonwealth were given sufficient force by God to resist and suppress open idolatry because they were bound by God to keep their land unpolluted.[43]

In his development of these covenant concepts Knox avoids the possible implications for Scottish nationalism. His concern is to stress the duty of believers to obey the higher Law, not the unity of the Scottish people in a national covenant with God. His conception of a united people is fundamentally one of united believers opposed to pagans and idolaters; the element of nationalism, when it is present, is thoroughly subordinate. A key biblical example used by Knox is Exodus 34, where the Hebrews are reminded of the covenant with God not to worship false gods and idols. Referring to this covenant Knox wrote to the Scottish nobility and estates that "the Gentiles (I mean everie citie, realme, province, or nation amongest the Gentiles, embrasing Christ Jesus and his true religion) be bound to the same leage and covenant that God made with his people Israel. . . ."[44] Knox never came closer than this to stating that the Scots are a covenanted nation.

He obviously conceived of the possibility of a covenanted nation, but he makes virtually nothing of the idea, and certainly does not use it to benefit significantly from the spirit of Scottish nationalism. He clearly does not think of Scotland as the elect nation of God, as did the Scottish Covenanters. Moreover, he is not so loyal to a Scottish monarch that he will countenance obedience if the sovereign is idolatrous. Luther's theory of obedience is much more conducive to the growth of nationalism than Knox's. The overt nationalism which characterizes Luther's appeal to the German princes finds no counterpart in Knox's *Appellation* to the Scottish nobility, where the emphasis is on active resistance to idolaters as a divine command. Even the common people, because of their covenant with God, must actively resist an idolatrous ruler, even a Scottish one. Yet Knox's doctrine of active resistance, while not conducive to nationalism, hardly furthered ecumenical relations, especially with the Church of England and the Lutheran churches.[45]

The key to Knox's actions and beliefs is thus his adherence to the divine will above all else. This principle transcended any concerns whether ecumenical or nationalist in nature. His devotion to truth as he saw it prompted him to help to develop in Scotland a Kirk with an eclectic foundation and a modestly ecumenical outlook. It so happened that that Kirk was well-suited to the growing spirit of Scottish nationalism. No longer was there even a nominal relationship to a foreign head. The eclectic theology and polity of the Kirk made it a distinctively Scottish Kirk, even while enhancing the opportunity for ecumenical fellowship. Knox's statements about the covenant obligations of a commonwealth to God helped lay the foundation for the later development of the notion of Scotland as a covenanted nation. Paradoxically the eclectic foundation of theology and polity which Knox contributed to the Kirk of Scotland made it *sui generis*, and thus a suitable vehicle for the expression of Scottish national consciousness.

EPILOGUE

As a theologian Knox displayed virtually no ability to develop dramatically fresh interpretations, nor will he ever be accorded a place among the theologians of the first rank in Western civilization. Yet he was a man of no mean ability, and as the principal formulator of the theology, liturgy, and polity of the reformed Kirk of Scotland, he drew upon a wide variety of sources, ranging from native Scottish elements to the Lutheran, Reformed, and English traditions. Although he was not original, neither was he a slavish imitator. As a knowledgeable and perceptive man with a marked inclination to be servile to no one but his God, he was instrumental in the fashioning of a Kirk with a broadly eclectic heritage. His governing principle was a professed adherence to the express precepts of Scripture — Old Testament as well as New. Those ideas, institutions, and patterns of worship which he borrowed had to be faithful to biblical principles as he understood them. While he did not have the whole array of possibilities before him at any given moment, as he was exposed to new ideas and subjected to varying influences he developed patterns of thought and action that were much indebted to those men and institutions with whom he had come in contact. The result was a Kirk that was not quite like any other in Christendom, but yet owed virtually all its constituent elements to others.

There has been a tendency to think along the lines that Knox was scarcely an original thinker who borrowed almost literally everything he knew and taught directly from Calvin.[1] Such a conclusion misunderstands the development of Knox's views and their relation to Protestant thought and its antecedents in the sixteenth century. Some writers have attributed significant influence on Knox to thinkers other than Calvin, notably Major (for political thought), Wishart, and Luther and his Scottish followers.[2] There has been no satisfactory attempt to deal fully with the impact on Knox's thought of such men as Bucer, Bullinger, Hooper, and, to a lesser degree, Beza,[3] Zwingli, Tyndale, and perhaps Willock and Coverdale. A few writers have done some exploring of possible influence by such men as Ponet, Goodman, the Magdeburg Lutherans, and the church fathers.[4] The studies in this volume have endeavored not only to analyze aspects of Knox's thought but also to suggest areas of probable influence on his writing. That Knox has not simply followed the Genevan pattern in polity has been recognized for some time, especially in the research of Janet MacGregor and Gordon Donaldson.[5] The present studies have questioned the common notion that Knox's theology is nothing more than transplanted Calvinism, though Calvin's influence in numerous areas must be recognized; the pendulum must not swing too far in the opposite direction by ignoring Calvin's impact on Knox.

In reflecting on these studies it may be well to bring together the conclusions with respect to Knox's debt to others. The heavy indebtedness to Scripture is obvious throughout his writings, which reveal a special affinity for the Pentateuch (especially Deuteronomy), the Psalms, the prophets (notably Isaiah and Jeremiah), the Gospels (particularly John), Acts, and the Pauline corpus (especially Romans and 1 Corinthians). The prophetic tradition was particularly meaningful for Knox, who conceived of himself as part of that tradition. Apart from Hebrew influence, his motivation in this regard probably came from Wishart and was fortified by the example of such Edwardian "preacher-prophets" as Hooper, Grindal, Lever, and Bradford. Calvin apparently had little if anything to do with this important aspect of Knox's outlook.

Knox's concepts of Scripture and authority reflect his reading of the church fathers, including Tertullian, Athanasius, and Augustine, his favorite father. His professed adherence to express scriptural precepts likely reflects the influence of Wishart and

Balnaves as well perhaps as Tertullian. This conception was likely fortified in England by contact with the Zwinglian views of John Hooper, who on this matter was more rigid than his master Bullinger. Likewise Knox was stricter in this regard than Calvin, who urged the Scot to be more temperate. In the matter of interpreting Scripture, Knox gave more emphasis to the recorded words than to Calvin's notion of an inner spiritual testimony of their validity and meaning. With respect to the basic task of interpreting Scripture, Knox aided in establishing the weekly exercise in Scotland, having apparently learned of this institution from Wishart or in Edwardian England before witnessing a somewhat similar institution in Geneva.

Knox's treatise on predestination reflects the marked influence of Calvin, but this treatise is atypical and seems to have been largely a pedantic exercise undertaken to smooth Calvin's ruffled feathers after the unauthorized publication of *The First Blast of the Trumpet*. Moreover, Knox approved the *Scots Confession* the same year the predestinarian treatise was published, despite the fact that the former contained no specific chapter on predestination. To the extent that predestination is treated in the *Confession*, the influence of Willock is probable. Yet Knox did not find Calvin's doctrine of predestination disagreeable, though he opted to give the subject relatively little treatment in his writings (apart from the predestinarian treatise).

With respect to Knox's view of the church, heavy reliance on Scripture is evident. The remnant discussed by the Hebrew prophets was likened by Knox to the contemporary church, and the persecuted elect of old were linked by a common band to the persecuted Christians in his own day. He repudiated the Separatist position. The influence of the Reformed tradition on Knox may be seen in his repeated stress on the true church as comprised of the elect. He was impressed early by the value of discipline in the church, which appears to reflect the influence of à Lasco, Pullain, the discussions surrounding the *Reformatio Legum Ecclesiasticarum* of 1552, and the *First Helvetic Confession*. Calvin, however, appears to have exercised the key influence on Knox's view of the sabbath.

Knox left little indication of his views on baptism before 1556 (when he was in Geneva), which makes it difficult to trace the antecedents of his ideas on this doctrine. Yet it appears likely that at the outset of his reforming career his views on baptism were influenced by Wishart and the *First Helvetic Confession*, and perhaps even by the *Shorter Catechism* of Leo Jud. Knox's view of the relationship of the league or covenant and baptism may be due to several sources, including the thought of Bullinger, Calvin, and the Tyndale tradition, including Coverdale. There is also the possibility of influence in this area from Hooper and à Lasco. Unfortunately there is insufficient evidence to be more precise, but it is virtually certain from what is known that much of Knox's thought on baptism was developed before he came into contact with Calvin.

The evidence is considerably better for tracing the antecedents of his doctrine of the Lord's Supper. The dominant doctrinal influence is definitely that of Bucer and to a lesser degree Bullinger, whose views were first transmitted to Knox via the *First Helvetic Confession* as translated by Wishart. Knox followed Hooper and à Lasco in opposing the practice of kneeling during the Lord's Supper, though this had been his position from the outset of his reforming career. He differed from most of the reformers, including Calvin, in his belief about the administration of the Lord's Supper before the establishment of an organized visible church. He was also more extreme than the major reformers in his feelings on the frequency of the sacrament. Possibly he borrowed the idea of a Saturday sermon as preparation for the Lord's Supper from Archbishop Hamilton's *Ane Godlie Exhortatioun*. Once on the Continent Knox helped draft and used the *Order of Geneva*, based largely on Calvin's *La Forme*, which the latter had taken from Bucer, and Bucer from Diebold Schwarz. Finally, Knox personally affirmed his debt for his concept of this sacrament to Augustine, Jerome, Origen, Fulgentius, and Vigilius. Above all, however, the key to Knox's concept of the Lord's Supper is Bucer, not Calvin. To the extent that Knox's views on the Supper are akin to those of Calvin, the primary reason is that both men are disciples of Bucer on this subject.

Knox's views on the ministry are derived from a variety of sources. The selection of ministers in the Kirk of Scotland is based on the precedures favored by Calvin, Pullain, à Lasco, and Lambert, whereas the office of reader was probably discovered by

Knox on visits to Zürich and Basle. Precedent for the office of superintendent in the Kirk may be the Lutheran churches of Denmark and Germany, but the office also appears in à Lasco's church order, sent to Knox by Calvin. One of the earliest sources of influence on Knox may have been Bucer's *De Regno Christi*, which has a description of a superintendent much like that later instituted in Scotland. Of course the English bishoprics could also have provided a model, particularly the preaching emphasis attached to them in the Edwardian period. Moreover, the selection of superintendents in the Scottish Kirk reflected the practice of the English and German Protestants. The Scottish eldership is akin to that of Geneva, but Knox may have first been exposed to the eldership through the work of Wishart, who seems to have instituted elders in the Dundee area. The election of deacons in the Scottish Kirk follows the pattern established in Pullain's congregation, and the duties of deacons are akin to those of the French Protestants, perhaps reflecting Knox's travels among them. The bulk of this material comes, of course, from the coauthored *Book of Discipline*, so that the influence from these sources could have come through others in addition to Knox.

Knox's views on gynecocracy were tentatively formed before his meeting with Calvin, but the commonness of his view makes it nearly impossible to trace the origins of influence. One possibility is Sir David Lyndsay, assuming he held the position in 1547 that he published in 1553, and another is the church fathers. Perhaps before but certainly after the receipt of his answers from Calvin, Bullinger, and Viret, Knox immersed himself in Tertullian, Augustine, Origen, Ambrose, Chrysostom, Basil the Great, and others. Aristotle, Cicero, and various historical works were also consulted, as well as the Hebrew prophets, the Pauline corpus, and classical and canon law. Possibly Knox also learned of the views of John Ponet, and finally discussed his ideas with Christopher Goodman.

Knox likewise derived his concept of the league, band, or covenant from various sources, including the notion of the covenant in the Old Testament and the ancient Scottish custom of banding. Knox began to write about the league at the outset of Mary Tudor's reign, indicating the likelihood of English influence on him as well. The views of Tyndale may have influenced him directly or indirectly; his friend Coverdale is known to have been influenced by Tyndale. Influence may well have come from John Hooper, who had accepted Bullinger's concept of the covenant. Comparable views were propounded by Oecolampadius, whose writings were circulating in Scotland as early as 1540. By 1554 Knox had read Calvin's commentary on Jeremiah, but Knox's views on the covenant in 1554 were different from those of Calvin. Two years later, Knox broadened his notion of the covenant in a baptismal context as the result of Calvin's influence through the medium of the *Order of Baptism*.

Knox's views on disobedience and rebellion are even more complex to trace. Because of his manifestation of active resistance at St. Andrews as early as 1547, the earliest sources of influence appear to be the writings of Origen and possibly Chrysostom, elements of the medieval political tradition as mediated particularly through John Major, and perhaps the views of George Wishart and the *First Helvetic Confession*. Among these sources Major and Origen are probably the most important, the former for notions of limited, contractual government and the legitimacy of active resistance in particular circumstances. In England Knox tempered his views along the line of Tyndale and his disciples. Once on the Continent he sought the advice of Calvin, Bullinger, and Viret. Bullinger urged caution but did nothing to dissuade Knox from thinking along the lines of active resistance, and Viret may actually have encouraged him. Knox may subsequently have been influenced by the views of Ponet, for there is considerable common ground between the two men. Knox definitely knew of the *Apology of Magdeburg*, and was aware of Beza's position on the acceptability of active resistance. Beza in turn appears to have been influenced by Bucer. Finally, it is almost certain that Knox discussed his views on this subject with Goodman. Any influence by Calvin in this sphere would at best be modest; in fact there is reason to believe that Calvin was influenced by Knox on the acceptability of active resistance by the common people.

With respect to education Knox was influenced by Calvin and very likely by Bucer. Perhaps he knew of the views of Sturm, Luther, and Melanchthon, and he must have been cognizant of the earlier interest in Scotland in educational reform, including some opinions on the subject by John Major. Knox clearly sanctioned the proposals for educational reform of some of his co-drafters of the *Book of Discipline*, especially Douglas and possibly Row and Winram.

In theology as well as polity Knox was not merely a disciple of Calvin, though he admired him. Knox was instrumental in securing the use of Calvin's *Catechism* in the Kirk of Scotland, but the *Catechism* was not comprehensive and contained statements acceptable to a broad spectrum of sixteenth-century Protestants. He thought highly of Geneva, but largely because of its emphasis on law and order in a Protestant context and its welcome of British exiles.[6] In liturgy, however, Knox had a marked preference for the Genevan way.

Knox's theology contains elements traceable to a variety of major sources, notably Lutheranism, the Reformed tradition (the strongest influence apart from Scripture), Edwardian Anglican-ism, Scottish Christianity, and the church fathers. Without careful qualification no label except "Reformed" accurately indicates his theological and ecclesiastical position. While recognizing his debt to others, it must be emphasized that he consciously selected views from these sources and discarded others. He was not a truly orig-inal thinker, but neither was Calvin. Even Luther and Zwingli, who developed some original insights, were heavily indebted to others. Like Calvin, Knox learned from various sources before formulating his own theology. His views are colored by his ex-perience, for he was not simply writing about something he aca-demically inherited; he wrote of his religious experience, drawing upon the thoughts of others to help him communicate that expe-rience to others. The theology he developed reflects not only the views of others but also his own experience, mind, integrity, and conviction of the need for reformation.

It must also be emphasized that Knox did not lack influence. To be sure, he was not a theologian of the first rank noted for his systematic ability or dramatically new interpretations. Like Calvin he was an eclectic thinker, but unlike Calvin he was not a system-atic theologian. Yet in the manner of Calvin he was a man of action who left his imprint on the international scene. Apart from his impact on Scottish history, his influence extended in particular to English Puritanism. His views were influential enough in En-gland to merit an attack by no less a scholar than Richard Bancroft more than two decades after Knox's death. The latter's influence also extended to Reformed Protestantism on the Continent through such men as Theodore Beza, the Huguenot Pierre Bayle, and probably Calvin himself. Ultimately Knox's theory of active resistance contributed to the ideological tradition that culminated in the American Revolution.[7] In terms of both his life and his thought, he was one of the most influential men of his age.

NOTES

INTRODUCTION TO SECTION ONE

1. *The Autobiography and Diary of Mr James Melvill*, ed. Robert Pitcairn (Edinburgh: Wodrow Society, 1842), p. 26. Melvill became minister of Kilrenny, Fife.

2. Randolph's letter is printed in *The Works of John Knox*, ed. David Laing, 6 vols. (1846–64; New York: AMS Press, 1966), 6:146 (hereafter cited as *Works*).

3. Knox, *Works*, 6:592. Yet five years earlier, on August 19, 1565, he had preached at St. Giles', Edinburgh, in the presence of Queen Mary and Lord Darnley, asserting that God had in fact revealed secrets unknown to the world to him and had made his "tong a trumpet" (*Works*, 6:229–30).

4. *Calendar of the State Papers, Relating to Scotland*, ed. Markham John Thorpe, 2 vols. (London: Longman, Brown, Green, Longmans, & Roberts, 1858), 1:192. Cf. Alexander R. MacEwen, *A History of the Church in Scotland*, 2d ed., 2 vols. (London: Hodder and Stoughton, 1915, 1918), 2:100.

5. Knox, *Works*, 6:558.

6. *The Zürich Letters*, trans. and ed. Hastings Robinson (Cambridge: The Parker Society, 1842), p. 150.

7. Melvill, *Autobiography*, p. 26.

8. Knox, *Works*, 3:13–28.

9. Ibid., 3:185–86.

10. Ibid., 4:502–3, 519.

11. Ibid., 6:244.

12. Richard Bannatyne, *Memoriales of Transactions in Scotland, MDLXIX–MDLXXIII* (Edinburgh: Bannatyne Club, 1836), p. 285.

CHAPTER ONE

1. *John Knox's History of the Reformation in Scotland*, ed. William Croft Dickinson, 2 vols. (London: Thomas Nelson and Sons, 1949), 1:87 (hereafter cited as *Knox's History*).

2. Ibid., 1:91.

3. Knox, *Works*, 3:34, 35; Jasper Ridley, *John Knox* (Oxford: Oxford University Press, 1968), pp. 93–95.

4. Ridley, *John Knox*, pp. 113–14; Ridley, *Thomas Cranmer* (Oxford: Clarendon Press, 1962), p. 338.

5. Knox, *Works*, 4:43–44.

6. Ibid., 4:231.

7. Ibid., 4:446, 468.

8. Patrick Collinson, *The Elizabethan Puritan Movement* (Berkeley and Los Angeles: University of California Press, 1967), p. 172; Ronald J. Vander Molen, "Anglican against Puritan: Ideological Origins during the Marian Exile," *Church History* 42 (March 1973): 45–57. For the Frankfurt controversy see Knox, *Works*, 4:3–68; Collinson,"The Authorship of *A Brief Discours off the Troubles Begonne at Franckford*," *Journal of Ecclesiastical History* 9 (October 1958):188–208; Ridley, *John Knox*, Chapter Eleven.

9. *Knox's History*, 2:283.

10. Ibid., 2:258, 267, 281.

11. *Reformed Confessions of the Sixteenth Century*, ed. Arthur C. Cochrane (Philadelphia: Westminster Press, 1966), pp. 291–92; *The Zürich Letters* (Second Series), trans. and ed. Hastings Robinson (Cambridge: The Parker Society, 1845), p. 364.

12. Bannatyne, *Memoriales*, p. 99.

13. *Knox's History*, 2:280–81 (italics mine). Cf. Gordon Donaldson, *The Scottish Reformation* (Cambridge: Cambridge University Press, 1960), pp. 62, 78.

14. *Knox's History*, 2:268.

15. The letter is in Knox, *Works*, 6:123–24.

16. *Knox's History*, 2:84.

17. Ibid., 2:97.

18. Ibid., 2:18.

19. Ibid.

20. Knox, *Works*, 6:194.

21. Ninian Winzet, *Certain Tractates*, ed. James K. Hewison, 2 vols. (Edinburgh: The Scottish Text Society, 1888, 1890), 1:32.

22. Knox, *Works*, 5:166. Cf. *Knox's History*, 1:92.

23. Hugh Watt, *John Knox in Controversy* (London: Thomas Nelson and Sons, 1950), pp. 37–38, 41–42.

24. Reprinted in Knox, *Works*, 4:165.

25. Ibid., 4:162 (italics mine).

26. Ibid., 4:518–19.

27. Ibid., 4:446–47.

28. Ibid., 6:194.

29. *Knox's History*, 2:267.

30. Ibid., 2:267–68.

31. Knox, *Works*, 5:331–32.

32. Ibid., 6:501.

33. Ibid., 6:194.

34. For examples of Knox's use of the church fathers see *Works*; for Augustine, 3:75; 4:383–84, 389–90, 492–94, 519; 5:32–33, 39, 62, 77, 170–71, 180, 326, 332–33, 344, 419; 6:194, 196, 505; for Chrysostom, 3:351; 4:386–89, 392–93, 511; 6:202; for Tertullian, 4:307ff., 381–83, 446, 524; for Ambrose, 4:384–86; 6:505; for Origen, 3:75; 4:383; 5:88; for Jerome, 3:75; 6:194, 505; for Basil the Great, 4:389; 5:32; for Athanasius, 6:287–88; for Cyprian, 4:524; for Lactantius, 4:524; for Firmian, 4:524; for Symmachus, 4:512; for Fulgentius, 3:75; for Vigilius, 3:75. Bernard of Clairvaux is cited too: 6:505.

35. For a full statement of this argument see Chapter Eight.

36. Athanasius, *Select Writings and Letters*, ed. Archibald Robertson, *A Select Library of Nicene and Post-Nicene Fathers of the Christian Church* (Second Series), ed. Philip Schaff and Henry Wace, 14 vols. (Grand Rapids: Eerdmans, 1953), 4:453; G. D. Henderson, "John Knox and the Bible," *Records of the Scottish Church History Society* 9 (1946):108.

37. Augustine, *Anti-Pelagian Writings*, ed. Philip Schaff, *Select Library* (First Series), 14 vols. (Grand Rapids: Eerdmans, 1956) 5:330.

38. Heiko A. Oberman, *The Harvest of Medieval Theology*, rev. ed. (Grand Rapids: Eerdmans, 1967), pp. 361–412; Oberman, *Forerunners of the Reformation* (New York: Holt, Rinehart and Winston, 1966), pp. 53–65.

39. *Knox's History*, 2:241.

40. Ibid., 2:242.

41. *The Miscellany of the Wodrow Society*, ed. David Laing (Edinburgh: Wodrow Society, 1844), 1:11–12, 21. For the issue of *adiaphora* see Bernard J. Verkamp, "Zwinglians and Adiaphorism," *Church History* 42 (December 1973):486–504. For the influence of the *First Helvetic Confession* on Knox's sacramental thought, see Chapter Five.

42. Reprinted in Knox, *Works*, 3:528, 531; Watt, "Henry Balnaves and the Scottish Reformation," *Records of the Scottish Church History Society 5* (1935):37.

43. Luther, *A Commentary on St. Paul's Epistle to the Galatians*, ed. Philip S. Watson (London: James Clarke & Co., 1953), pp. 518–19.

44. *Original Letters Relative to the English Reformation*, ed. Hastings Robinson, 2 vols. (Cambridge: The Parker Society, 1846–47), 1:95; *Early Writings of John Hooper*, ed. Samuel Carr (Cambridge: Cambridge University Press, 1843), p. 105; W. M. S. West, "John Hooper and the Origins of Puritanism," *The Baptist Quarterly* 15 (October 1954): 346–56. For Hooper's possible influence on Knox's covenant views, see Chapter Six.

45. *Reformed Confessions*, p. 96.

46. *Knox's History*, 2:258.

47. George Yule, "Continental Patterns and the Reformation in En-

gland and Scotland," *Scottish Journal of Theology* 22 (September 1969): 307–9; Zwingli, cited in Charles Garside, Jr., *Zwingli and the Arts* (New Haven: Yale University Press, 1966), p. 54.

48. Yule, "Continental Patterns and the Reformation," p. 309.

49. Calvin, *Institutes of the Christian Religion*, IV, x, 14; IV, viii, 9; IV, x, 23–24; IV, xviii, 12, compared with his letter to Knox, *Works*, 6:124.

50. Reprinted in Peter Lorimer, *John Knox and the Church of England* (London: H. S. King & Co., 1875), pp. 259, 261.

51. Ibid., pp. 298–300.

52. Yule, "Continental Patterns and the Reformation," p. 311.

53. See Chapter Five.

54. W. Stanford Reid, *Trumpeter of God: A Biography of John Knox* (New York: Charles Scribner's Sons, 1974), p. 120. This is the best biography of Knox and the proper starting point for all study of him.

55. Knox, *Works*, 3:301; Lewis W. Spitz, Sr., "Luther's Sola Scriptura," *Concordia Theological Monthly* 31 (December 1960):741; Wilhelm Niesel, *The Theology of Calvin*, trans. Harold Knight (Philadelphia: Westminster Press, 1956), pp. 27, 30, 33.

56. Knox, *Works*, 3:310–13. For Knox's prophetic role see Paul M. Little, "John Knox and English Social Prophecy," *Journal of the Presbyterian Historical Society of England* 14 (May 1970):117–27.

57. Knox, *Works*, 4:133, 5:385.

58. Ibid., 4:135–36.

59. *Knox's History*, 1:352.

60. Ibid., 2:280–81.

61. *Catechisms of the Scottish Reformation*, ed. Horatius Bonar (London: Nisbet, 1866), p. 71.

62. *Miscellany of the Wodrow Society*, 1:11.

63. *Knox's History*, 2:234–43.

64. In Knox, *Works*, 3:440, 448, 450–54.

65. Ibid., 3:166.

66. Ibid., 3:64. Cf. 3:154, 197, 356; 4:519.

67. James S. McEwen, *The Faith of John Knox* (Richmond, VA: John Knox Press, 1961), p. 39; Henderson, "John Knox and the Bible," p. 104.

68. Calvin, *Institutes*, IV, viii, 9.

69. H. Jackson Forstman, *Word and Spirit* (Stanford: Stanford University Press, 1962), p. 65 (cf. chap. IV).

70. Paul Althaus, *The Theology of Martin Luther*, trans. Robert Schultz (Philadelphia: Westminster Press, 1966), pp. 50–51; *A Compend of Luther's Theology*, ed. Hugh T. Kerr (Philadelphia: Westminster Press, 1943), p. 11; Spitz, "Luther's Sola Scriptura," pp. 743–44.

71. Knox, *Works*, 5:102.

72. Ibid., 3:46–47; George Johnston, "Scripture in the Scottish Reformation: II. Scripture in the Public and Private Life of Church and Nation," *Canadian Journal of Theology* 9 (1963):48.

73. *Knox's History*, 2:18.

74. Ibid., 2:266–67; Augustine, *On Christian Doctrine*, ed. Philip Schaff, *Select Library* (First Series), 2:539; *The Confessions of St. Augustine*, VI, v, 2.

75. Michael Walzer, *The Revolution of the Saints* (Cambridge: Harvard University Press, 1965), p. 101.

76. Knox, *Works*, 3:204; 4:137ff., 379.

77. Henderson, "John Knox and the Bible," pp. 104–5.

78. Knox, *Works*, 4:502, 506–7.

79. Contrary to John R. Gray, "The Political Theory of John Knox," *Church History* 8 (June 1939):146.

80. Ridley, *Knox*, pp. 446–48; Reid, *Trumpeter of God*, p. 243.

81. Henderson, "John Knox and the Bible," p. 103; James Denney, "John Knox: His Religious Life and Theological Position," *Hartford Seminary Record* 15 (August 1905):289; Forstman, *Word and Spirit*, p. 110; Henderson, *Church and Ministry* (London: Hodder and Stoughton, 1951), p. 16.

82. *Knox's History*, 2:266–67.

83. See Chapter Eight; V. E. D'Assonville, *John Knox and the Institutes of Calvin* (Durban: Drakensberg Press, [1969]), chap. VII.

84. Contrary to McEwen, *Faith of Knox*, p. 38.

85. Calvin, *Institutes*, I, vii, 4–5. See T. H. L. Parker, *Calvin's Doctrine of the Knowledge of God*, 2d ed. (Edinburgh: Oliver & Boyd, 1969), p. 74; Forstman, *Word and Spirit*, pp. 70ff.; Edward A. Dowey, *The Knowledge of God in Calvin's Theology* (New York: Columbia University Press, 1952), pp. 106–11.

86. *Knox's History*, 2:266–67.

87. Knox, *Works*, 5:166.

88. *Miscellany of the Wodrow Society*, 1:11.

89. Knox, *Works*, 5:88.

90. *Knox's History*, 2:18.

91. Knox, *Works*, 3:366–67.

92. Roland H. Bainton, *Studies on the Reformation* (Boston: Beacon Press, 1963), p. 220.

93. Watt, *Knox in Controversy*, p. 99.

94. *Catechisms*, ed. Bonar, p. 72.

95. Agnes M. MacKenzie, *The Scotland of Queen Mary and the Religious Wars, 1513–1638* (Edinburgh: A. Maclehose & Co., 1936), p. 88.

96. John Strype, *Memorials of . . . Thomas Cranmer*, new ed. (Oxford: Oxford University Press, 1812), p. 420; Watt, *Knox in Controversy*, p. 101.

97. Bannatyne, *Memoriales*, p. 283.

CHAPTER TWO

1. Knox, *Works*, 5:189; the propositions are on pp. 184–89.

2. Eustace Percy, *John Knox* (Richmond, VA: John Knox Press, 1965), p. 203.

3. McEwen, *Faith of Knox*, p. 64.

4. Champlin Burrage, *The Early English Dissenters in the Light of Recent Research (1550–1641)*, 2 vols. (Cambridge: Cambridge University Press, 1912), 1:62.

5. Knox, *Works*, 5:221–22, 224, 226–31.

6. Cited in Sebastian Castellio, *Concerning Heretics*, ed. with intro. by Roland Bainton (New York: Columbia University Press, 1935), p. 110. On the matter of the authorship of *De Haereticus* see Bainton, "Sebastian Castellio, Champion of Religious Liberty," *Castellioniana: Quatre Études sur Sébastien Castellion et l'Idee de la Tolérance*, by Bainton, Bruno Becker, Marius Valkhoff, and Sape van der Woude (Leiden: E. J. Brill, 1951), pp. 43ff.

7. James MacKinnon, *Calvin and the Reformation* (1936; New York: Russell & Russell, 1962), pp. 116–20; Francois Wendel, *Calvin: The Origins and Development of His Religious Thought*, trans. Philip Mairet (London: Collins, 1963), pp. 90–91.

8. Gilby first wrote about predestination in a commentary on Malachi published in England in 1553. See Dan G. Danner, "Anthony Gilby: Puritan in Exile: A Biographical Approach," *Church History* 40 (December 1971):415–16. See also the stimulating article by O. T. Hargrave, "The Predestinarian Offensive of the Marian Exiles at Geneva," *Historical Magazine of the Protestant Episcopal Church* 42 (June 1973):111–23.

9. *Zürich Letters* (Second Series), ed. Robinson, pp. 35–36.

10. This is the position of Laing in Knox's *Works*, 5:15, contrary to Ridley, *John Knox*, p. 290.

11. Knox, *Works*, 6:14.

12. "Which booke, written in the English tongue, doeth contein aswell the lies and the blasphemies imagined by Sebastian Castalio, and laid to the charge of that moste faithfull servant of God, John Calvine; as also the vane reasons of Pighius, Sadoletus, and Georgius Siculus, pestilent Papistes, and expressed ennemies of God's free mercies." Knox, *Works*, 5:24–25. There is no evidence to suggest the book was aimed at Bôlsec. Neither has a copy of the work refuted by Knox been discovered, despite Knox's copious quotations. Pighius and Georgius were the primary targets of Calvin in his treatise *Concerning the Eternal Predestination of God*. Pighius contended that the wicked deprived themselves of the benefits of election which God universally offered to man. Georgius argued that according to Scripture salvation was offered to believers on the basis of their faith, and that the offer was made to all men. Calvin, *Concerning the Eternal Predestination of God*, trans. with intro. by J. K. S. Reid (London: James Clarke, 1961), pp. 53–56.

13. Percy, *John Knox*, p. 203.

14. McEwen, *Faith of Knox*, pp. 69–70. Cf. Althaus, *Theology of Luther*, pp. 274ff.

15. Knox, *Works*, 5:31.

16. Ibid., 5:25–27.

17. Ibid., 5:35.

18. Calvin, *Concerning Eternal Predestination*, p. 162.

19. Knox, *Works*, 5:35.

20. Ibid., 5:36.

21. Ibid., 5:42.

22. Ibid., 5:65; cf. pp. 62–63, 124ff. There is a similar tendency in Calvin to write primarily of the reprobate being "justly left in death, for in Adam they are dead and condemned." Yet Calvin admits that "Paul taught that God chose and reprobated out of the mass of perdition those whom He willed. . . ." *Concerning Eternal Predestination*, pp. 121, 124–25. Parallel statements are found throughout the treatise.

23. Knox, *Works*, 5:390.

24. Ibid.

25. Ibid., 5:38, 390–391. Cf. Calvin, *Institutes*, III, xxiii, 5–8; McEwen, *Faith of Knox*, p. 77; Henry Kuizenga, "The Relation of God's Grace to His Glory in John Calvin," *Reformation Studies*, ed. Franklin H. Littell (Richmond, VA: John Knox Press, 1962), pp. 95–105.

26. Knox, *Works*, 5:134.

27. Ibid., 5:136.

28. Ibid., 5:142. According to J. S. McEwen, "the nonelect do God's will involuntarily, while the elect obey it voluntarily." *Faith of Knox*, p. 75. Actually, both do God's will voluntarily, according to Knox. The difference is that the elect do God's will knowingly and gladly, whereas the reprobate do it without acknowledgment.

29. Knox, *Works*, 5:359.

30. Ibid., 5:113. Cf. Calvin: "What was done contrary to His will was yet not done without His will, because it would not have been done at all unless He had allowed it. So He permitted it . . . willingly. . . . In sinning, they did what God did not will in order that God through their evil will might do what He willed." *Eternal Predestination*, p. 123; cf. pp. 168ff., 179–82. Calvin is following Augustine.

31. Ibid., 5:364; cf. pp. 140–41, 143.

32. Cf. McEwen, *Faith of Knox*, p. 64. McEwen has pointed out that one should probably not seek logical consistency in Knox's treatise since Knox followed Calvin on this subject, and Calvin himself was inconsistent on this matter.

33. Knox, *Works*, 5:73; cf. pp. 75–76, 147, 156–57, 203, 466–68.

34. Ibid., 5:117, 302.

35. Knox demanded, for example, that Mary Stewart be executed for adultery, but not John Spottiswoode, a former elder and (also) an adulterer. Ridley, *Knox*, pp. 466–67. This might also reflect a double standard for men and women.

36. Knox, *Works*, 5:307.

37. Ibid., 5:113.

38. Calvin, *Concerning Eternal Predestination*, p. 123.

39. Knox, *Works*, 5:114.

40. Ibid., 5:359; cf. p. 364.

41. Calvin, *Concerning Eternal Predestination*, p. 123.

42. Knox, *Works*, 5:71.

43. Ibid., 5:160, 344.

44. Ibid., 5:85; cf. pp. 84, 90–91, 160–61, 387. Calvin treated John 9:3 identically: "Here our nature cries out, when calamity comes before birth itself, as if God with so little mercy thus punished the undeserving. Yet Christ testifies that in this miracle the glory of his Father shines, provided our eyes be pure." *Institutes*, I, xvii, 1.

45. Lorimer, *Knox and the Church of England*, p. 258.

46. Cf. Hooper, *Early Writings*, p. 264, but note Ridley's contrast between the two men in *John Knox*, pp. 128–29. Calvin's treatise *Concerning the Eternal Predestination of God* was published in 1551 or early 1552, and influenced the discussions concerning the formulation of articles for the Church of England. William Cunningham, *The Reformers and the Theology of the Reformation* (Edinburgh: T. and T. Clark, 1862), p. 181. Knox may have been aware of these discussions, and he had certainly read Calvin's polemical treatise; see *Works*, 5:38–39. On the basis of the relatively few statements on predestination in Knox's early works it is impossible to determine whether or not he was influenced by later medieval thought on this subject. For samples of that thought see Oberman, *The Harvest of Medieval Theology*, chap. VII; and *Forerunners of the Reformation*, chap. III. Knox's major treatise on predestination reflects the decided influence of Calvin.

47. Knox, *Works*, 3:122.

48. Ibid., 3:201.

49. Ibid., 3:349.

50. Ibid., 3:367.

51. Ibid., 3:231–36, 239–49.

52. Ibid., 4:135.

53. Ibid., 4:123–24.

54. Ibid., 4:171–72; cf. pp. 208, 213.

55. Ibid., 4:270–71.

56. John Strype, *The Life and Acts of Matthew Parker*, 3 vols. (Oxford: Clarendon Press, 1821), 1:409; Lloyd E. Berry, "Introduction," *The Geneva Bible: A Facsimile of the 1560 Edition* (Madison: University of Wisconsin Press, 1969), p. 8; Brooke F. Westcott, *A General View of the History of the English Bible* (New York: Macmillan Company, 1927), p. 91.

57. Hardin Craig, Jr., "The Geneva Bible as a Political Document," *Pacific Historical Review* 7 (1938):48–49; Bruce M. Metzger, "The Geneva Bible of 1560," *Theology Today* 17 (October 1960):348, 350; Leonard J. Trinterud, ed., *Elizabethan Puritanism* (New York: Oxford University Press, 1971), pp. 202–8. Basil Hall, however, frankly calls the Geneva Bible "an instrument of Puritan propaganda." *The Genevan Version of the English Bible* (London: The Presbyterian Historical Society of England, 1957), p. 9.

58. Berry, "Introduction," *The Geneva Bible*, p. 19. Quotations from the Geneva Bible are from this edition. William Haller hints at a possible psychological motive for the interest of the exiles in election: "If their having fled the fire [in Marian England] left them at all doubtful of their own election,

banishment went a long way towards easing compunction by assuring them that they had been reserved for a purpose which could not fail to be presently achieved and in which they were bound to participate." *Foxe's Book of Martyrs and the Elect Nation* (London: Jonathan Cape, 1963), pp. 84–85.

59. *Knox's History*, 2:259, 260–61, 265, 268, 271–72.

60. Cf. Denney, "John Knox," p. 285.

61. Edward A. Dowey, Jr., *A Commentary on the Confession of 1967 and an Introduction to "The Book of Confessions"* (Philadelphia: Westminster Press, 1968), p. 179.

62. Article x does say that Christ was "ordayned and geuen" to redeem man. *Miscellany of the Wodrow Society*, pp. 13–14.

63. Knox, *Works*, 4:171–72. All these confessions are printed in *Reformed Confessions*, ed. Cochrane.

64. Cited in B. A. Gerrish, "The Confessional Heritage of the Reformed Church," *McCormick Quarterly* 19 (January 1966):131. The whole treatise is in *Zwingli and Bullinger*, trans. with intro. and notes by G. W. Bromiley (Philadelphia: Westminster Press, 1953). For Zwingli's views on election see Gottfried W. Locher, "The Change in the Understanding of Zwingli in Recent Research," trans. Kenneth Hagen, *Church History* 34 (March 1965):10–12.

65. Duncan Shaw, "John Willock," *Reformation and Revolution*, ed. Shaw (Edinburgh: Saint Andrew Press, 1967), p. 60. The non-Calvinist treatment of predestination in the *Confession* is observed by Alex C. Cheyne, "The Scots Confession of 1560," *Theology Today* 17 (October 1960):232, contrary to Lewis Lupton, *A History of the Geneva Bible*, 2 (London: Olive Tree Press, 1969), p. 58.

66. Shaw, "John Willock," pp. 43–60; West, "John Hooper," p. 367; *Original Letters*, ed. Robinson, pp. 234–38, 406–7, 416, 426.

67. McEwen, *Faith of Knox*, p. 78.

INTRODUCTION TO SECTION TWO

1. *Knox's History*, 1:189–90.

2. Knox, *Works*, 5:413.

3. See Katharine R. Firth, *The Apocalyptic Tradition in Reformation Britain, 1530–1645* (Oxford: Oxford University Press, 1979), chap. IV.

CHAPTER THREE

1. David McRoberts, "The Scottish Church and Nationalism in the Fifteenth Century," *Innes Review* 19 (Spring 1968):3–14.

2. *Knox's History*, 2:85, 87, 92.

3. Knox, *Works*, 3:41.

4. Ibid., 3:40–42. Cf. this with the liberality of the *Augsburg Confes-*

sion, pt. I, articles vii and xv, in *The Creeds of Christendom*, ed. Philip Schaff, 3 vols. (New York: Harper, 1877), 3:12, 16.

5. Knox, *Works*, 3:186.

6. Ibid., 3:319; cf. pp. 275, 287, 291, 300, 302, 322, 326.

7. Ibid., 4:262–63.

8. Ibid., 4:263–67.

9. *Knox's History*, 2:265; Knox, *Works*, 6:486–87.

10. *Knox's History*, 2:266–67.

11. Ibid., 2:271–72.

12. Knox, *Works*, 6:489.

13. *Zürich Letters* (First Series), ed. Robinson, p. 168.

14. Burrage, *Early English Dissenters*, 1:86. Horton Davies argues that this church was not Separatist because it was attached to Geneva, and because Robert Browne had not yet advanced his argument for the autonomy of each local congregation. *Worship and Theology in England from Cranmer to Hooker, 1534–1603* (Princeton: Princeton University Press, 1970), p. 344. Yet Fitz looked to the English congregation at Geneva, to Scotland, and to à Lasco and Pullain, whereas his fellow Separatists looked to Knox to support their position. The fact that Browne had not yet written his plea simply indicates that he was not the first Separatist.

15. M. M. Knappen, *Tudor Puritanism* (Chicago: University of Chicago Press, 1939), p. 212; Patrick McGrath, *Papists and Puritans under Elizabeth I* (London: Blandford Press, 1967), p. 98; Trinterud, ed., *Elizabethan Puritanism*, pp. 7–8; Collinson, *Elizabethan Puritan Movement*, p. 91.

16. Knox's letter is printed in Lorimer, *John Knox*, pp. 298–300.

17. Knappen, *Tudor Puritanism*, p. 215. This was also akin to Calvin's position. Gordon Donaldson, *The Making of the Scottish Prayer Book of 1637* (Edinburgh: Edinburgh University Press, 1954), p. 12.

18. Lorimer, *John Knox*, p. 298; Knappen, *Tudor Puritanism*, pp. 215–16; Charles Davis Cremeans, *The Reception of Calvinistic Thought in England* (Urbana: University of Illinois Press, 1949), p. 54; Collinson, *Elizabethan Puritan Movement*, pp. 89–90, 131; Davies, *Worship and Theology*, pp. 343–44. Cf. Donaldson, *Making of the Scottish Prayer Book*, pp. 10–12.

19. Heinrich Bullinger, *The Decades of Henry Bullinger*, ed. Thomas Harding, 3 vols. (Cambridge: Cambridge University Press, 1849–52), 3:49ff.; Calvin, *Institutes*, IV, i, 12–13.

20. *Knox's History*, 2:265; Gordon Rupp, *The Righteousness of God: Luther Studies* (New York: Philosophical Library, 1953), pp. 312–16; Althaus, *Theology of Luther*, pp. 294–313.

21. John T. McNeill, "The Church in Sixteenth-Century Reformed Theology," *Journal of Religion* 22 (July 1942):255.

22. *Miscellany of the Wodrow Society*, p. 16.

23. *Catechisms*, ed. Bonar, p. 24. According to T. F. Torrance, Knox, Peter Martyr, and Calvin, unlike Luther, were influenced by Bucer's emphasis on Ephesians 4 in developing the doctrine of the church. *Kingdom and Church:*

A Study in the Theology of the Reformation (Edinburgh and London: Oliver and Boyd, 1956), p. 73, n. 6.

24. Martin Luther, *D. Martin Luthers Werke*, 50 (Weimar: Herman Böhlaus Nachfolger, 1914), p. 629, 11. 28—35.

25. Calvin, *Institutes*, IV, i, 9; Benjamin Charles Milner, Jr., *Calvin's Doctrine of the Church* (Leiden: E. J. Brill, 1970), chap. IV. Cf. William P. Haugaard's argument that the failure of Calvin to include discipline as the third mark of the church separates him from Bucer "and from much of later 'Calvinism'." "John Calvin and the Catechism of Alexander Nowell," *Archiv für Reformationsgeschichte* 61 (1970):59.

26. *Miscellany of the Wodrow Society*, p. 16.

27. *Reformed Confessions*, ed. Cochrane, p. 125.

28. David Calderwood, *The History of the Kirk of Scotland*, 4 vols. (Edinburgh: Wodrow Society, 1842—43), 1:280.

29. Janet G. MacGregor, *The Scottish Presbyterian Polity* (Edinburgh: Oliver and Boyd, 1926), p. 58. For à Lasco, see Frederick A. Norwood, "The Strangers' 'Model Churches' in Sixteenth-Century England," *Reformation Studies*, ed. Franklin H. Littell (Richmond, VA: John Knox Press, 1962), pp. 187—88.

30. James C. Spalding, "The *Reformatio Legum Ecclesiasticarum* of 1552 and the Furthering of Discipline in England," *Church History* 39 (June 1970):162—71.

31. *Miscellany of the Wodrow Society*, p. 18.

32. John Tonkin, *The Church and the Secular Order in Reformation Thought* (New York: Columbia University Press, 1971), pp. 122—24.

33. Knox, *Works*, 4:172—73.

34. Ibid., 4:267.

35. Bullinger, *Decades*, 3:17—18. It is inaccurate to refer to the doctrine of the church in the *Scots Confession* as "undiluted Calvinism"; Cheyne, "The Scots Confession," p. 334. There is no evidence to support A. R. MacEwen's contention that the three marks of the church are found in Wishart and Calvin. *History*, 2:153, n. 1.

36. Cf. the similar usage in *The Book of Discipline* associated with the name of Walter Travers. The Scottish *Second Book of Discipline* (1578) retained the dual usage of the term.

37. MacGregor, *Scottish Presbyterian Polity*; Gordon Donaldson, "The Polity of the Scottish Church, 1560—1600," *Records of the Scottish Church History Society* 11 (1955):212—26; Donaldson, " 'The Example of Denmark' in the Scottish Reformation," *Scottish Historical Review* 27 (April 1948):57—64. Discipline was also to a limited degree an inheritance from the Catholic church. G. D. Henderson, "Foreign Influences in Scottish Church Worship," *Transactions of the Scottish Ecclesiological Society* 11 (1934):50.

38. Knox, *Works*, 4:42.

39. Ridley, *John Knox*, p. 4.

40. Trinterud, ed., *Elizabethan Puritanism*, p. 134.

41. Walzer, *Revolution of the Saints*, pp. 308—9.

42. Knox, *Works*, 4:240; 5:212ff.; Robert M. Kingdon, "The Control of Morals in Calvin's Geneva," *The Social History of the Reformation*, ed. Lawrence P. Buck and Jonathan W. Zophy (Columbus: Ohio State University Press, 1972), pp. 3–16. For the workings of the Genevan Consistory see Walther Köhler, *Zürcher Ehegericht und Genfer Konsistorium*, 2 vols. (Leipzig: M. Heinsius Nachfolger, 1932, 1942). The kind of discipline to be exercised in the church was one of the issues between Knoxians and Coxians at Frankfurt. Vander Molen, "Anglican against Puritan," pp. 50, 53–54, 57.

43. See McEwen, *Faith of Knox*, pp. 59–60.

44. Donaldson, *Scottish Reformation*, p. 79.

45. *Knox's History*, 2:306.

46. Ridley, *John Knox*, pp. 368–71; Anthony Ross, "Reformation and Repression," *Essays on the Scottish Reformation, 1513–1625*, ed. David McRoberts (Glasgow: Burns, 1962), pp. 390, 394.

47. *Knox's History*, 2:306–8.

48. Knox, *Works*, 6:447–70; George B. Burnet, *The Holy Communion in the Reformed Church of Scotland, 1560–1960* (Edinburgh: Oliver and Boyd, 1960), pp. 35–40.

49. Cf., e.g., MacGregor, *Scottish Presbyterian Polity*, p. 159; Edwin Muir, *John Knox: Portrait of a Calvinist* (London: Jonathan Cape, 1929), p. 225.

50. Cf. Norwood, "The Strangers' 'Model Churches'," p. 192, for à Lasco.

51. Knox, *Works*, 5:518–20.

52. R. Douglas Brackenridge, "The Development of Sabbatarianism in Scotland, 1560–1650," *Journal of Presbyterian History* 42 (September 1964):150–51; David Hay Fleming, *The Reformation in Scotland* (London: Hodder and Stoughton, 1910), pp. 295–96.

53. *Knox's History*, 2:263, 312.

54. Knox, *Works*, 6:145–46; William Law Mathieson, *Politics and Religion: A Study in Scottish History from the Reformation to the Revolution*, 2 vols. (Glasgow: J. Maclehose & Sons, 1902), 1:192.

55. *Catechisms*, ed. Bonar, pp. 41, 43.

56. Calvin, *Institutes*, II, viii, 31; cf. 32.

57. *Knox's History*, 2:190; *Reformed Confessions*, ed. Cochrane, p. 291.

58. *Booke of the Universall Kirk of Scotland*, ed. Alexander Peterkin (Edinburgh: Edinburgh Printing and Publishing Co., 1839), pp. 11, 29.

CHAPTER FOUR

1. Knox, *Works*, 6:433–34.

2. Bannatyne, *Memoriales*, pp. 280–81.

3. Knox, *Works*, 3:289.

4. Bannatyne, *Memoriales*, p. 273.

5. Cf. Knox, *Works*, 6:15–20, 47–51, 527, 530–32.

6. McEwen, *Faith of Knox*, p. 64.

7. Collinson, *Elizabethan Puritan Movement*, p. 435.

8. Muir, *John Knox*, p. 32.

9. Knox, *Works*, 3:348–50.

10. Florence A. MacCunn, *John Knox* (Boston and New York: Houghton Mifflin, 1895), p. 25.

11. Knox, *Works*, 3:350–51, 355–56, 364–65, 366–67, 375 (quoted), 392–94.

12. Ibid., 3:341–42.

13. Ibid., 3:135ff., 318.

14. See Robert Louis Stevenson, "John Knox and His Relations to Women," *Familiar Studies of Men and Books* (New York: Scribner, 1905); Muir, *John Knox*, *passim*; Hugh Trevor-Roper, "John Knox," *The Listener* 80 (December 5, 1968):745–47.

15. Knox, *Works*, 6:514.

16. Ibid., 4:219–22, 225–36; 6:21–27; *Knox's History*, 2:74–76.

17. W. J. Anderson, "John Knox as Registrar," *Innes Review* 7 (Spring 1956):63.

18. *Knox's History*, 1:81–86.

19. Ibid., 1:124; Knox, *Works*, 4:464, 468–69.

20. *Knox's History*, 1:182.

21. Ibid., 1:337.

22. Ibid., 2:269. Repudiation of Catholic ordination was common in the Reformed churches. See Duncan Shaw, "The Inauguration of Ministers in Scotland: 1560–1620," *Records of the Scottish Church History Society* 16 (1967):41–43.

23. Winzet, *Certain Tractates*, 1:21; cf. pp. 18ff.

24. Ibid.

25. Ibid., 1:98–99; Watt, *Knox in Controversy*, pp. 42–43; Ridley, *John Knox*, pp. 408–11; Maurice Taylor, "The Conflicting Doctrines of the Scottish Reformation," *Essays on the Scottish Reformation, 1513–1625*, ed. McRoberts, pp. 268–69.

26. Quintin Kennedy, *Quintin Kennedy (1520–1564): Two Eucharistic Tracts: A Critical Edition*, ed. Cornelius Henricus Kuipers (Nijmegen: Drukkerij Gebr. Janssen N. V., 1964), p. 151.

27. Knox, *Works*, 6:191–92. Calvin also was not reordained.

28. Ibid., 3:25; 4:271–72.

29. Calvin, *Institutes*, IV, ii, 2–3.

30. *Knox's History*, 2:266; Knox, *Works*, 6:497ff.

31. Knox, *Works*, 6:604–6.

32. Shaw, "The Inauguration of Ministers," pp. 38–41.

33. *Knox's History*, 2:283–85; MacGregor, *Scottish Presbyterian Polity*, p. 39; J. M. S. Burleigh, *A Church History of Scotland* (London: Oxford University Press, 1960), p. 168; Calvin, *Institutes*, IV, iii, 15.

34. *Knox's History*, 2:285.

35. Ibid., 2:286–87. Cf. Shaw, "The Inauguration of Ministers," pp. 35–37, 40, 45, 48.

36. Donaldson, *Scottish Reformation*, p. 117.

37. Calvin, *Institutes*, IV, xix, 6.

38. *Reformed Confessions*, ed. Cochrane, p. 271.

39. *Knox's History*, 2:286–87.

40. Ibid., 2:287–88; Knox, *Works*, 3:235; MacGregor, *Scottish Presbyterian Polity*, pp. 47–48.

41. Knox, *Works*, 5:518. Cf. Lorimer, *Knox and the Church of England*, p. 191.

42. *Calendar of State Papers, Scotland*, 1:170.

43. Knox, *Works*, 6:508–9, where his sympathies are, however, more with Henry IV than Gregory VII because of his opposition to the papacy *per se*.

44. Ridley, *John Knox*, pp. 506–8; Donaldson, *Scottish Reformation*, pp. 168–69. But cf. James L. Ainslie, *The Doctrines of Ministerial Order in the Reformed Churches of the 16th and 17th Centuries* (Edinburgh: T. & T. Clark, 1940), pp. 115–19.

45. Knox, *Works*, 3:26; 6:620–21; *Knox's History*, 1:87.

46. Donaldson, *Socttish Reformation*, p. 124.

47. Gordon Donaldson, "The Scottish Episcopate at the Reformation," *English Historical Review* 60 (September 1945):349.

48. *Knox's History*, 2:291–93.

49. See, e.g., MacGregor, *Scottish Presbyterian Polity*, p. 45; Burleigh, *Church History*, p. 170; John T. McNeill, *The History and Character of Calvinism* (New York: Oxford University Press, 1954), p. 300; Alfred Coutts, "Ninian Winzet: Abbot of Ratisbon, 1577–1592," *Records of the Scottish Church History Society* 11 (1951–53):242; Mathieson, *Politics and Religion*, 1:285; W. Stanford Reid, "French Influence on the First Scots Confession and Book of Discipline," *Westminster Theological Journal* 35 (1972–73):11ff.

50. See, e.g., Donaldson, *Scottish Reformation*, p. 114; Donaldson, *Common Errors in Scottish History* (London: The Historical Association), p. 14; G. D. Henderson, *The Burning Bush* (Edinburgh: Saint Andrew Press, 1957), p. 50.

51. *Knox's History*, 2:295.

52. *Register of the Minister Elders and Deacons of the Christian Congregation of St. Andrews . . . 1559–1600, Part First: 1559–1582*, trans. and ed. with notes by David Hay Fleming (Edinburgh: Edinburgh University Press, 1889), p. 75.

53. Cf. Donaldson, *Scottish Reformation*, p. 147.

54. A. R. MacEwen (*History*, 2:166) acknowledges the affinity of the Scottish superintendent with the ideas of Luther and Melanchthon, but contrasts it strongly with Calvinist thought.

55. G. B. Beeman, "The Early History of the Strangers' Church, 1550 to 1561," *Proceedings of the Huguenot Society of London* 15 (1935):271; Norwood, "The Strangers' 'Model Churches'," p. 183; Donaldson, *Scottish Reformation*, p. 115; MacGregor, *Scottish Presbyterian Polity*, pp. 45, 47.

56. Calvin, *Institutes*, IV, v, 11; Yule, "Continental Patterns and the Reformation," p. 314; Donaldson, *Scottish Reformation*, pp. 109–10.

57. Donaldson, " 'The Example of Denmark'," p. 57.

58. *Reformed Confessions*, ed. Cochrane, p. 270; Donaldson, *Scottish Reformation*, p. 109.

59. Knox, *Works*, 6:614.

60. Shaw, "John Willock," p. 61.

61. *Knox's History*, 2:293–95.

62. J. G. MacGregor suggests that the way in which the Scottish congregations elected elders and deacons reflected the practice of Pullain's church. *Scottish Presbyterian Polity*, p. 41.

63. *Knox's History*, 2:309–11.

64. Elders were elected annually, in February, along with all municipal officials. "In most of these elections, however, the voters simply ratified slates of candidates prepared by the outgoing small council." In the case of the elders the small council was required by the ecclesiastical ordinances to consult the city's pastors on the nominations. At the end of each year, the small council determined which elders would be reelected and which replaced. Until 1560 all elders were native-born citizens. Robert M. Kingdon, "The Control of Morals in Calvin's Geneva," *The Social History of the Reformation*, ed. Buck and Zophy, pp. 6–8. Cf. E. William Monter, *Calvin's Geneva* (New York: Wiley, 1967), p. 139.

65. MacEwen, *History*, 2:75–76; *Knox's History*, 1:148; 2:277–78; *Register of the Minister*, ed. Fleming, 1:1; Burleigh, *Church History*, p. 171; MacGregor, *Scottish Presbyterian Polity*, pp. 28–29.

66. R. Stuart Louden, *The True Face of the Kirk* (London: Oxford University Press, 1963), p. 41.

67. Norwood, "The Strangers' 'Model Churches'," pp. 186, 189; MacGregor, *Scottish Presbyterian Polity*, pp. 28–29.

68. *Knox's History*, 2:311–12.

69. MacGregor, *Scottish Presbyterian Polity*, pp. 40–42. This work must be tempered by Donaldson, *Scottish Reformation*, especially pp. 147–48; and Donaldson, " 'The Example of Denmark'," pp. 57–64. Tracing the antecedents of Scottish polity is difficult, but one thing is certain: it is not a mere replica of Genevan polity.

CHAPTER FIVE

1. Ridley, *John Knox*, pp. 229–30.

2. Knox, *Works*, 4:119–28.

3. Ibid., 4:119.

4. Ibid., 4:120.

5. Ibid., 4:121.

6. Cf., e.g., McEwen, *Faith of Knox*, chap. III, especially pp. 46–47.

7. Knox, *Works*, 4:120.

8. Ibid., 4:123.

9. Ibid.

10. Francis Procter and Walter Howard Frere, *A New History of the Book of Common Prayer, with a Rationale of Its Offices* (London: Macmillan and Co., 1919), p. 586.

11. Cited in Knox, *Works*, 4:61.

12. Ridley, *John Knox*, pp. 194–95.

13. Calvin, *Institutes*, IV, xv, 20; Egil Grislis, "Calvin's Doctrine of Baptism," *Church History* 31 (March 1962):49; William D. Maxwell, *John Knox's Genevan Service Book, 1556* (Edinburgh: Oliver and Boyd, 1931), pp. 111–12.

14. Knox, *Works*, 6:76, 95–97.

15. Ibid., 6:96.

16. *Knox's History*, 2:308. Cf. Bullinger's attempt to retain the link between baptism and faith in *Decades*, 3:340 ff.

17. Winzet, *Certain Tractates*, 1:84.

18. *Knox's History*, 2:308.

19. William McMillan, *The Worship of the Scottish Reformed Church, 1550–1638* (London: James Clarke, 1931), p. 248; Lupton, *The Geneva Bible*, 2:101; Knox, *Works*, 4:186–87; Calvin, *Theological Treatises*, trans. with intro. and notes by J. K. S. Reid (London: Westminster Press, 1954), pp. 66, 79; Maxwell, *Genevan Service Book*, pp. 114–15.

20. *Knox's History*, 2:268.

21. Grislis, "Calvin's Doctrine of Baptism," pp. 46–65; Bullinger, *Decades*, vol. 3, sermons 7 and 8; A. Ian Dunlop, "Baptism in Scotland after the Reformation," *Reformation and Revolution*, ed. Shaw, pp. 82–99.

22. *Miscellany of the Wodrow Society*, pp. 18–19.

23. *Knox's History*, 2:238.

24. *Miscellany of the Wodrow Society*, pp. 18–19.

25. Watt, *Knox in Controversy*, pp. 6–7.

26. Lorimer, *Knox and the Church of England*, p. 258.

27. *Booke of the Universall Kirk*, pp. 41–42.

28. *Catechisms*, ed. Bonar, p. 74.

29. Ulrich Zwingli, *Huldreich Zwingli's Werke*, ed. Melchior Schuler and J. Schulthess, 8 vols. (Zürich, 1828–42), 5:73; cf. p. 71.

30. Bullinger, *Decades*, 3:245. Also see Bullinger, *Summa Christenlicher Religion* (Zürich: C. Froschouer, 1556), pp. 137ff.

31. Leonard J. Trinterud, "The Origins of Puritanism," *Church History* 20 (March 1951):41, 45; Jens G. Møller, "The Beginnings of Puritan Covenant Theology," *Journal of Ecclesiastical History* 14 (April 1963):47–50; Richard L. Greaves, "The Origins and Early Development of English Covenant Thought," *The Historian* 31 (November 1968):23–26; Everett H. Emerson, "Calvin and Covenant Theology," *Church History* 25 (June 1956):136–44; Milner, *Calvin's Doctrine of the Church*, pp. 123–25.

32. See William A. Clebsch, *England's Earliest Protestants, 1520–1535* (New Haven: Yale University Press, 1964). Leonard Trinterud de-emphasizes

Tyndale's Lutheranism in "A Reappraisal of William Tyndale's Debt to Martin Luther," *Church History* 31 (March 1962):24—45.

33. William Tyndale, *Doctrinal Treatises and Introductions to Different Portions of the Holy Scriptures*, ed. Henry Walter (Cambridge: Cambridge University Press, 1848), p. 362. See Clebsch, *England's Earliest Protestants*, pp. 161, 172—74, 181—85, 197, 317; Trinterud, "The Origins of Puritanism," p. 39; Møller, "The Beginnings of Puritan Covenant Theology," pp. 50—54; Greaves, "The Origins of Covenant Thought," pp. 26—27; C. H. Williams, *William Tyndale* (London: Thomas Nelson, 1969), p. 132.

34. Clebsch, *England's Earliest Protestants*, p. 193.

35. West, "John Hooper," pp. 356—59; Norwood, "The Strangers' 'Model Churches'," pp. 188—89.

36. See *Knox's History*, 1:11ff; W. Stanford Reid, "Lutheranism in the Scottish Reformation," *Westminster Theological Journal* (1943—45):91—111.

37. *Knox's History*, 1:93.

38. Ibid., 1:26, n. 1; Calderwood, *History*, 1:116; *Miscellany of the Wodrow Society*, 1:159; Watt, *Knox in Controversy*, pp. 6—7. In May 1540 Sir John Borthwick was accused of possessing heretical books by such authors as Oecolampadius, Melanchthon, and Erasmus, but no titles are indicated. *The Acts and Monuments of John Foxe*, ed. Stephen Reed Cattley, 8 vols. (1843—49; New York: AMS Press, 1965), 5:620.

39. For Wishart see *Knox's History*, 1:60—72; John Durkan, "George Wishart: His Early Life," *Scottish Historical Review* 32 (1953):98—99, and "The Cultural Background in Sixteenth-Century Scotland," *Essays on the Scottish Reformation*, ed. McRoberts, pp. 274—331.

40. Cf. Reid, "Lutheranism," p. 107; E. G. Leonard, *A History of Protestantism: 2. The Establishment*, ed. H. H. Rowley and trans. R. M. Bethell (London: Thomas Nelson, 1967), p. 73.

41. Hastings Eells, *Martin Bucer* (New Haven: Yale University Press, 1931), pp. 194—95; James MacKinnon, *Calvin and the Reformation*, p. 194; T. H. L. Parker, "Calvin the Biblical Expositor," *John Calvin*, ed. G. E. Duffield (Grand Rapids: Eerdmans, 1966), p. 179; *Miscellany of the Wodrow Society*, 1:3—4.

42. Cited in W. P. Stephens, *The Holy Spirit in the Theology of Martin Bucer* (Cambridge: Cambridge University Press, 1970), p. 251. Bucer's doctrine of the Lord's Supper is discussed in Stephens, chap. XIII; Johannes Müller, *Martin Bucers Hermeneutik* (Gütersloh: Gütersloher Verlagshaus G. Mohn, 1965), pp. 132—35; Constantin Hopf, *Martin Bucer and the English Reformation* (Oxford: Oxford University Press, 1946), pp. 41—51; Hastings Eells, "The Contributions of Martin Bucer to the Reformation," *Harvard Theological Review* 24 (January 1931):32—33, and "The Genesis of Martin Bucer's Doctrine of the Lord's Supper," *Princeton Theological Review* 24 (1926):225ff.

43. Cited in Hopf, *Martin Bucer*, p. 48.

44. B. A. Gerrish, "John Calvin and the Reformed Doctrine of the Lord's Supper," *McCormick Quarterly* 22 (January 1969):96.

45. Calvin, *Institutes*, IV, xvii, 12, 24, 31, 33, 39, 42. Cf. *Catechisms*, ed. Bonar, pp. 77–88; Gerrish, "John Calvin," pp. 85–98; R. S. Wallace, *Calvin's Doctrine of the Word and Sacrament* (Grand Rapids: Eerdmans, 1957), chap. XVI; Kilian McDonnell, *John Calvin, the Church, and the Eucharist* (Princeton: Princeton University Press, 1967). For a comparison of Calvin and Bucer see J. C. McLelland, *The Visible Words of God: An Exposition of the Sacramental Theology of Peter Martyr Vermigli* (Edinburgh: Oliver & Boyd, 1957), pp. 272–73.

46. Concerning Calvin's debt to Bucer see François Wendel, *Calvin: Sources et Évolution de sa Pensée Religieuse* (Paris: Presses Universitaires de France, 1950), pp. 251–71; McDonnell, *John Calvin*, pp. 77–85; Bard Thompson, "Bucer Study since 1918," *Church History* 25 (March 1956):64–68, 81; and Eells, "Martin Bucer and the Conversion of John Calvin," *Princeton Theological Review* 22 (1924). At Newcastle Knox "substituted common bread for the wafers, thus anticipating the practice adopted in the Prayer Book of 1552 on Bucer's recommendation." F. J. Smithen, *Continental Protestantism and the English Reformation* (London: J. Clarke & Co., 1927), p. 232.

47. *Miscellany of the Wodrow Society*, 1:19–20.

48. Gerrish, "The Lord's Supper in the Reformed Confessions," *Theology Today* 23 (July 1966):232. See Eells, *Martin Bucer*, p. 195.

49. Gerrish, "John Calvin," pp. 96–97; *Reformed Confessions*, ed. Cochrane, p. 284 (italics mine). See Joachim Staedtke, *Die Theologie des jungen Bullinger* (Zürich: Zwingli Verlag, 1962), pp. 234–54. Not even Zwingli taught a bare memorialism. The fact that Christ is spiritually present and active among the believers prevents such an understanding. Zwingli also makes use of an ecclesiological concept in interpreting the phrase "body of Christ." "For when you offer thanks with the cup and the bread, eating and drinking together, you signify thereby that you are one body and one bread, namely, the body which is the Church of Christ. . . ." *Zwingli and Bullinger*, trans. and ed. Bromiley, pp. 183, 237 (quotation). For the ecclesiological aspect, see Jacques Courvoisier, *Zwingli: A Reformed Theologian* (Richmond, VA: John Knox Press, 1963), pp. 74ff.

50. Bullinger, *Decades*, 3:433; *Reformed Confessions*, ed. Cochrane, p. 287.

51. Bullinger, *Decades*, vol. 3, sermon 9.

52. Gerrish, "The Lord's Supper," p. 234; *Zürich Letters* (Second Series), ed. Robinson, p. 364. The *Second Helvetic Confession* is printed in *Reformed Confessions*, ed. Cochrane.

53. Knox, *Works*, 3:73–75.

54. Ibid. À Lasco made the interesting observation that this biblical passage was meant to apply to the entire Lord's Supper, not simply the physical element. See Hermann Dalton, *John à Lasco*, trans. M. J. Evans (London: Hodder and Stoughton, 1886), p. 285.

55. Hooper, *Early Writings*, pp. 536–37.

56. This was the practice of à Lasco's congregation of foreigners in London. An expository edition of its liturgy was subsequently prepared for

publication by à Lasco. Included in it were his arguments against kneeling. Due to Edward's death it was not published until 1555 in Frankfurt, with the title *Forma ac ratio tota Ecclesiastici Ministerii, in peregrinorum Ecclesia*. C. H. Smyth, *Cranmer & the Reformation under Edward VI* (Cambridge: Cambridge University Press, 1926), pp. 262–63; Norwood, "The Strangers' 'Model Churches'," p. 191.

57. Knox subsequently praised Cranmer's treatise against transubstantiation, *A Defence of the True and Catholic Doctrine of the Sacrament* (1550). Knox, *Works*, 3:279. Cranmer's views on the Lord's Supper are the subject of extensive debate; see, e.g., C. W. Dugmore, *The Mass and the English Reformers* (London: Macmillan, 1958), chap. VIII; Smyth, *Cranmer*; P. E. Hughes, *Theology of the English Reformers* (London: Hodder and Stoughton, 1965), chap. VI; G. W. Bromiley, *Thomas Cranmer, Theologian* (New York: Oxford University Press, 1956), chaps. VI, VII; C. C. Richardson, *Zwingli and Cranmer on the Eucharist* (Evanston, IL: Seabury-Western Theological Seminary, 1949); Gregory Dix, *The Shape of the Liturgy* (Westminster: Dacre Press, 1947), chap. XVI; D. C. Timms, "Dixit Cranmer," *Church Quarterly Review* 143 (1947):217–34 and (1948):35–51; P. N. Brooks, *Thomas Cranmer's Doctrine of the Eucharist* (New York: Seabury Press, 1965). For Peter Martyr's views see McLelland, *Visible Words*; Dugmore, *The Mass*, pp. 144–48; Foxe, *Acts and Monuments*, 6:297ff.

58. Contrary to E. C. Ratcliff, "The Liturgical Work of Archbishop Cranmer," *Journal of Ecclesiastical History* 7 (October 1956):200.

59. Smyth, *Cranmer*, pp. 263–65.

60. Ibid., p. 266; Smithen, *Continental Protestantism*, p. 233; Ridley, *Thomas Cranmer*, p. 337.

61. *Tudor Royal Proclamations*, ed. P. L. Hughes and J. F. Larkin, 3 vols. (New Haven: Yale University Press, 1964–1969), 1:538–39.

62. *Acts of the Privy Council of England, A.D. 1552–1554*, ed. J. R. Dasent (London: Her Majesty's Stationery Office, 1892), p. 154.

63. Foxe, *Acts and Monuments*, 6:510.

64. Lorimer, *Knox and the Church of England*, pp. 261–62.

65. McEwen, *Faith of Knox*, pp. 47, 57, 114.

66. Percy, *John Knox*, p. 56.

67. McEwen, *Faith of Knox*, p. 56.

68. Percy, *John Knox*, pp. 189–90.

69. Ridley, *John Knox*, p. 231.

70. Dunlop, "Baptism in Scotland," pp. 85–86.

71. Knox, *Works*, 4:119–20, 124.

72. Kennedy, *Quintin Kennedy*, p. 63. Willock was a disciple of Bullinger and his follower, John ab Ulmis. See *Original Letters*, ed. Robinson, 1:314–16; 2:393; Shaw, "John Willock," pp. 43–60; West, "John Hooper," p. 367.

73. *Knox's History*, 2:268–69.

74. Ibid., 2:269.

75. Ibid., 2:282–83; Burnet, *Holy Communion*, p. 18.

76. Norman Sykes, *The Crisis of the Reformation*, rev. ed. (London: Centenary Press, 1946), pp. 55, 68, 91–92; cf. Calvin, *Institutes*, IV, xvii, 44. Frequency of celebration is, of course, not an accurate test of centrality. The major reformers were agreed on the centrality of the Lord's Supper in worship, as well as on the fundamental preeminence of the Word. My discussion of frequency involves administrative practice, not theology.

77. William McMillan, "The Anglican Book of Common Prayer in the Church of Scotland," *Records of the Scottish Church History Society* 4 (1932):138–49.

78. *Booke of the Universall Kirk*, p. 13; Calderwood, *History*, 2:291.

79. Burnet, *Holy Communion*, pp. 6, 9, 11, 13–14; J. H. Nichols, *Corporate Worship in the Reformed Tradition* (Philadelphia: Westminster Press, 1968), pp. 68–69; Yngve Brilioth, *Eucharistic Faith and Practice*, trans. A. G. Hebert (London: S.P.C.K., 1953), p. 186.

80. Knox, *Works*, 6:14.

81. *Knox's History*, 2:282.

82. Burnet, *Holy Communion*, p. 51; *Statutes of the Scottish Church*, *1225–1559*, ed. David Patrick (Edinburgh: T. and A. Constable, 1907), pp. 188–90.

83. Burnet, *Holy Communion*, pp. 48–49, 53.

84. Maxwell, *Genevan Service Book*; Maxwell, *A History of Worship in the Church of Scotland* (London: Oxford University Press, 1955), chap. III; S. A. Hurlbut, *The Liturgy of the Church of Scotland since the Reformation*, 2 vols. (Washington: St. Albans Press, 1944–45); Brilioth, *Eucharistic Faith*, p. 186; John MacRae, "The Scottish Reformers and Their Order of Public Worship," *Records of the Scottish Church History Society* 3 (1929):22–30; W. S. Dauerty, "The Sources of Reformed Worship," *Journal of the Presbyterian Historical Society* 36 (December 1958):219ff.; G. J. van de Poll, *Martin Bucer's Liturgical Ideas* (Assen: Van Gorcum, 1954).

85. Dugmore, *The Mass and the English Reformers*, pp. 78–80, 160–61.

86. Knox, *Works*, 3:75.

87. *Knox's History*, 2:134 (italics mine).

88. Alexander Alane discussed Eucharistic theory with Bucer in 1540. Durkan, "The Cultural Background," p. 297.

INTRODUCTION TO SECTION THREE

1. G. D. Henderson, *The Claims of the Church of Scotland* (London: Hodder and Stoughton, 1951), pp. 145, 160; William Croft Dickinson, *Andrew Lang, John Knox, and Scottish Presbyterianism* (Edinburgh: Thomas Nelson, 1952), p. 14. Cf. Wilhelm Niesel, *The Theology of Calvin*, trans. Harold Knight (Philadelphia: Westminster Press, 1956), p. 230.

2. J. W. Allen, *A History of Political Thought in the Sixteenth Century*, 2d ed. (London: Methuen & Co., 1941), p. 116.

3. Hans Baron, "Calvinist Republicanism and Its Historical Roots," *Church History* 8 (1939):36–37.

4. See Duncan Shaw, *The General Assemblies of the Church of Scotland, 1560–1600* (Edinburgh: Saint Andrew Press, 1964), pp. 21–22.

5. *Knox's History*, 2:19–20.

6. Knox, *Works* 3:26, compared with 3:526–31.

7. Ibid., 4:325.

8. Ibid., 5:463.

9. Ibid., 4:472–75, 486–87.

10. *Knox's History*, 2:271.

11. Mathieson, *Politics and Religion*, 1:211.

12. Thompson, "Bucer Study," p. 74.

CHAPTER SIX

1. Knox, *Works*, 3:74.

2. Ibid., 3:143.

3. Ibid., 3:190–91, 193, 195.

4. Ridley, *John Knox*, pp. 132, 141–43, 158.

5. Knox, *Works*, 3:192.

6. Ibid., 3:194. J. H. Burns interprets the phrase "Civill Magistrate" to mean only the sovereign, in which case Knox would not yet be thinking of active resistance in any form. "The Political Ideas of the Scottish Reformation," *Aberdeen University Review* 36 (1955–56):254. Yet for Knox to write in 1553–54 that no one but sovereigns had the authority to slay idolaters would incriminate the Castilians, with whom he rebelled at St. Andrews in 1547, who executed Cardinal Beaton.

7. Knox, *Works*, 3:190–95.

8. Ibid., 4:123–25.

9. Ibid., 4:187, 189; Maxwell, *Genevan Service Book*, p. 148.

10. Knox, *Works*, 4:489–90; *Knox's History*, 2:16–17.

11. Knox, *Works*, 4:500–501.

12. Ibid., 4:539–40.

13. *Knox's History*, 2:72.

14. Knox, *Works*, 4:505.

15. Ibid., 4:527, 533–35.

16. *Knox's History*, 2:122. John Ponet discusses the execution of Athaliah, following which "the people made a newe bāde with God to serue him syncerely accordīg to his worde. . . ." *A Shorte Treatise*, p. 115, reprinted in W. S. Hudson, *John Ponet: Advocate of Limited Monarchy* (Chicago: University of Chicago Press, 1942). Cf. Little, "John Knox," pp. 121–26.

17. S. A. Burrell, "The Covenant Idea as a Revolutionary Symbol: Scotland, 1596–1637," *Church History* 27 (December 1958):339–41.

18. *Knox's History*, 1:122.

19. Ibid., 1:136–37; *Register of the Minister*, ed. Fleming, pp. 6–7; David Hay Fleming, *The Story of the Scottish Covenants in Outline* (Edinburgh:

Oliphant, Anderson & Ferrier, 1904), pp. 8–17; John Lumsden, *The Covenants of Scotland* (Paisley: A. Gardner, 1914). Cf. *Calendar of State Papers, Scotland*, 1:115, where Knox is instructed by the congregation to enter into a political league with England.

20. C. S. Meyer, *Elizabeth I and the Religious Settlement of 1559* (St. Louis: Concordia Publishing House, 1960), p. 132.

21. Clebsch, *England's Earliest Protestants*, p. 199.

22. Trinterud, "The Origins of Puritanism," pp. 37, 40. Covenant ideas were present in later medieval theology. Duns Scotus, for example, used the covenant in the context of the sacrament of penance, distinguishing between sinners with an intrinsic quality of attrition who are justified *ex merito* and sinners less attrite who are justified *ex pacto divino*. Biel used the concept of *pactum* in discussing the rewarding of good acts by God, who has freely made an agreement, in eternity, to reward certain actors and acts, namely, every act performed in a state of grace. The contractual element in Biel is pronounced; though God established the rules, he must abide by them. Similarly man must act, but the initial grace enabling him to act is a gift of God. This gift, according to Biel, is not a *pactum*, but is an eternal commitment. Oberman, *The Harvest of Medieval Theology*, pp. 132, 148, 167–74, 190–93; cf. pp. 246–47. While later medieval theologians stressed a contractual covenant, there is a deep gulf between their usage and Knox's, hinging essentially on the conflicting doctrines of justification. The position of Johann von Staupitz on the covenant is actually closer to a Protestant conception, for his covenant is "not the *bilateral* Covenant between God and his partners, the *Covenant of Works* in which the partners have to fulfill the Covenant law—as is the case with [Robert] Holcot and Biel. For Staupitz it is the *unilateral Covenant* which God had made with his elect, a *Covenant of Grace*, because it provides for the works of justification." For Staupitz the chosen sinner is unconditionally elected in eternity, and the covenant is subsequently implemented in time when the soul is divinely called and justified. Once this has happened, good works spontaneously follow. Oberman, *Forerunners of the Reformation*, p. 139; cf. pp. 175–88. The relation of Protestant thought on the covenant to later medieval thought needs to be studied in the light of recent research. The study by Kenneth Hagen, "From Testament to Covenant in the Early Sixteenth Century," *Sixteenth Century Journal* 3 (April 1972):1–24, is weakened by the failure to take into account late medieval views. Luther's emphasis on *testamentum* is discussed without, for example, comparing his view to that of Staupitz. Hagen shows that the development away from the stress on *testamentum* begins with Melanchthon, who writes more in terms of a *pactum*. This contractual emphasis needs to be seen in the light of the contractual emphasis in late medieval covenant thought, though there are obvious difference (e.g. the doctrines of justification involved). I have found no evidence that would link Knox directly to the writings of later medieval theologians on the covenant, except the possibility of such a link through John Major.

23. Tyndale, *Doctrinal Treatises*, p. 403; Tyndale, *Expositions and Notes on Sundry Portions of the Holy Scriptures*, ed. H. Walter (Cambridge: Cam-

bridge University Press, 1849), pp. 87, 95–96, 108; cf. pp. 90, 109–10. For Tyndale's views on the covenant see Clebsch, *England's Earliest Protestants*, pp. 114, 158, 161, 172–74, 181–84, 188, 197, 203, 317; Trinterud, "The Origins of Puritanism," p. 39; Møller, "The Beginnings of Puritan Covenant Theology," pp. 50–54; Greaves, "The Origins of English Covenant Thought," pp. 26–27.

24. Clebsch, *England's Earliest Protestants*, p. 193; J. F. Mozley, *Coverdale and His Bibles* (London: Lutterworth Press, 1953), p. 22.

25. Hooper, *Early Writings*, pp. 255–56. For Hooper's views on the covenant see West, "John Hooper," pp. 356–59; Møller, "The Beginnings of Puritan Covenant Theology," pp. 55–56. For Bullinger's position see Møller, p. 48; Greaves, "The Origins of English Covenant Thought," pp. 24–25.

26. Greaves, "The Origins of English Covenant Thought," p. 24; Trinterud, "The Origins of Puritanism," p. 41. The possibility of Oecolampadius' views influencing Knox must remain tentative unless fresh evidence is discovered.

27. Knox, *Works*, 3:201.

28. Calvin, *Institutes*, III, xvii, 5. Cf. *Calvin: Commentaries*, ed. Joseph Haroutunian and Louise Pettibone Smith (London: SCM Press, 1958), pp. 61–62, 84, 100–101; *Commentaries on the First Book of Moses Called Genesis*, trans. John King, 2 vols. (Grand Rapids: Wm. B. Eerdmans, 1948), 1:450–52.

29. For Calvin's views on the covenant see Trinterud, "The Origins of Puritanism," p. 45; Møller, "The Beginnings of Puritan Covenant Theology," pp. 49–50; Greaves, "The Origins of English Covenant Thought," pp. 25–26; Emerson, "Calvin and Covenant Thology," pp. 136–44; Niesel, *The Theology of Calvin*, chap. VI; McDonnell, *John Calvin*, pp. 286–87.

30. Cf. Calvin, *Institutes*, IV, xx, 32; Allen, *History of Political Thought*, pp. 57–60. Ultimately Knox probably influenced Calvin, for in the aftermath of the Scottish Reformation Calvin adopted a position of active resistance by the people in his commentary on Daniel. *Commentaries on the Prophet Daniel*, trans. T. Myers (Grand Rapids: Eerdmans, 1948), 1:382.

31. Cf., e.g., G. H. Dodge, *The Political Theory of the Huguenots of the Dispersion* (New York: Columbia University Press, 1947), p. 99; F. G. Shirley, *Richard Hooker and Contemporary Political Ideas* (London: S.P.C.K., 1949), pp. 23, 31, 113; R. H. Murray, *The Political Consequences of the Reformation* (1926; New York: Russell & Russell, 1960), p. 105; Christopher Hill, *Intellectual Origins of the English Revolution* (Oxford: Oxford University Press, 1965), pp. 2, 285.

CHAPTER SEVEN

1. James Kirk, "The Influence of Calvinism on the Scottish Reformation," *Records of the Scottish Church History Society* 18 (1974):163. This article

is, despite my criticism on this point, an important contribution to Reformation studies.

2. Reid, *Trumpeter of God*, pp. 150−51.

3. James Gairdner, *The English Church in the Sixteenth Century* (London: Macmillan and Co., 1924), p. 245.

4. Knox, *Works*, 3:26; Lorimer, *Knox and the Church of England*, p. 259.

5. Knox, *Works*, 3:221−25.

6. Ibid., 3:221−26.

7. J. H. Burns appears to misread Bullinger's position. "Knox and Bullinger," *Scottish Historical Review* 34 (1955):91; "John Knox and Revolution, 1558," *History Today* 8 (August 1958):568. Wesley J. Vessey continues the traditional interpretation that Bullinger "*delayed* Knox's conversion to the way of active resistance." "The Sources of the Idea of Active Resistance in the Political Theory of John Knox" (Ph.D. diss., Boston University, 1961), p. 236; cf. pp. 145−51.

8. Burns, "Knox and Bullinger," p. 91. The reply from Bullinger was not responsible for Knox's later reluctance to consult Continental reformers. Calvin's reply might have been a factor, but there was also the matter of Calvin's disapproving view of Knox's *First Blast of the Trumpet*.

9. G. P. Gooch, *English Democratic Ideas in the Seventeenth Century*, 2d ed. (Cambridge: Cambridge University Press, 1954), p. 3.

10. Bullinger, *Decades*, 1:316, 318.

11. Calvin, *Institutes*, IV, xx, 6, 10, 29−31, and note 54 to xx, 31.

12. Ibid., IV, xx, 31−32.

13. Donald R. Kelley, *Francois Hotman: A Revolutionary's Ordeal* (Princeton: Princeton University Press, 1973), p. 110.

14. N. M. Sutherland, "Calvinism and the Conspiracy of Amboise," *History* 47 (June 1962):122, 137.

15. Calvin, *Commentaries on Daniel*, 1:382.

16. Thomas M. Lindsay, *A History of the Reformation*, 2d ed., 2 vols. (Edinburgh: T. & T. Clark, 1907−8), 2:175−76; Allen, *History of Political Thought*, pp. 59−60.

17. Robert D. Linder, "Pierre Viret and the Sixteenth-Century English Protestants," *Archiv für Reformationsgeschichte* 58 (1967):149−71. Hotman as well as Knox visited Viret in Lausanne; Kelley, *Francois Hotman*, pp. 43−44.

18. Linder, "Pierre Viret and the Sixteenth-Century French Protestant Revolutionary Tradition," *Journal of Modern History* 38 (June 1966):130.

19. Ibid., pp. 125−37; Linder, "Viret and the English Protestants," pp. 158, 160−62.

20. Knox, *Works*, 3:166, 184−86, 190−91, 194.

21. Burns, "The Political Ideas of the Scottish Reformation," p. 254; Knox, *Works*, 3:188.

22. Knox, *Works*, 3:231−36.

23. Ibid., 3:239−49.

24. Ibid., 3:293ff., 309, 312, 325–26 (quoted). Viret also approved of Phinehas' action in Numbers 25:1–13, where under special circumstances murder in God's cause is justifiable. Linder, "Viret and the English Protestants," p. 162.

25. Knox, *Works*, 3:295, 308–9.

26. Ibid., 4:500.

27. Ibid., 4:489.

28. Ibid., 4:528, 534.

29. *Knox's History*, 2:122.

30. Knox, *Works*, 4:284–85.

31. Ibid., 4:415–16.

32. Walzer, *Revolution of the Saints*, p. 108, referring to the *Appellation*, but also applicable to *The First Blast*.

33. Knox, *Works*, 4:441–42.

34. *Original Letters*, ed. Robinson, 2:49.

35. Cf. Matthew Parker, *Correspondence of Matthew Parker, D.D., Archbishop of Canterbury*, ed. John Bruce and T. T. Perowne (Cambridge: Cambridge University Press, 1853), p. 61.

36. Knox, *Works*, 4:500–501.

37. Ibid., 4:527, 533–35.

38. Trevor-Roper, "John Knox," p. 747.

39. Knox, *Works*, 4:539–40; cf. pp. 416–17.

40. Ibid., 5:516–19.

41. *Knox's History*, 1:164.

42. Ibid., 1:165, 167, 168–69.

43. Knox, *Works*, 6:36.

44. *Knox's History*, 2:16–17.

45. Ibid., 2:71–72.

46. Ibid., 2:122; cf. pp. 108–34 for the entire debate.

47. Ibid., 2:129–30; Julian H. Franklin, ed., *Constitutionalism and Resistance in the Sixteenth Century* (New York: Pegasus, 1969), pp.32ff. For the context of the *Bekenntnis*, see Oliver K. Olson, "Theology of Revolution: Magdeburg, 1550–1551," *Sixteenth Century Journal* 3 (April 1972):56–79.

48. Vessey, "The Sources," pp. 207–8.

49. Allen, *History of Political Thought*, pp. 103–6.

50. *Knox's History*, 2:131–33.

51. Bannatyne, *Memoriales*, p. 98.

52. Vander Molen states that "the origins of Knox's new political ideas lay in the instability of English and Scottish politics and in Knox's desire to create a Christian theoretical basis for resistance." This is an oversimplification, and it is dubious that Knox set out in 1554 "to develop a new theory," for there were already numerous espousals of the Christian's right to resist. "Anglican against Puritan," p. 54.

53. G. L. Keyes, *Christian Faith and the Interpretation of History* (Lincoln: University of Nebraska Press, 1966), pp. 134–36; Francis Dvornik,

Early Christian and Byzantine Political Philosophy, 2 vols. (Washington: Dumbarton Oaks Center for Byzantine Studies, 1966), 2:841–42.

54. F. Homes Dudden, *The Life and Times of St. Ambrose*, 2 (Oxford: Clarendon Press, 1935), pp. 540–41; Dvornik, *Early Christian and Byzantine Political Philosophy*, 2:679–80.

55. Henderson, "John Knox and the Bible," p. 109. There are differences between the political views of Ambrose and Augusutine, but not on the matter of passive disobedience toward commands contravening divine precepts.

56. Chrysostom, *Homilies on the Epistle to the Hebrews*, ed. Frederic Gardiner, *A Select Library*, 14 vols. (Grand Rapids: Eerdmans, 1956), 14:518–19. Cf. *Homilies on the Epistle to the Romans*, ed. George B. Stevens, *A Select Library*, 11:511–12; *Homilies on the Epistles to Timothy*, ed. Philip Schaff, *A Select Library*, 13:426; Christopher Morris, *Western Political Thought*, 1 (London: Longmans, 1967), p. 204.

57. Tertullian, *Scorpiace*, ed. A. Cleveland Coxe, *The Ante-Nicene Fathers*, 10 vols. (Grand Rapids: Eerdmans, 1951), 3:647–48. Cf. Dvornik, *Early Christian and Byzantine Political Philosophy*, 2:581–82.

58. Dvornik, ibid., 2:601–2; Origen, *Against Celsus*, ed. A. Cleveland Coxe, *The Ante-Nicene Fathers*, 4:397, 561, 649.

59. Ewart Lewis, *Medieval Political Ideas*, 2 vols. (London: Routledge & Paul, 1954), 1:194; R. W. and A. J. Carlyle, *A History of Mediaeval Political Theory in the West*, 6 vols. (New York: Barnes & Noble, 1950), 3:103, 136–37, 164, 166–68. Cf. Otto Gierke, *Political Theories of the Middle Age*, trans. Frederick William Maitland (Cambridge: Cambridge University Press, 1951), p. 35. Cf. the papal bull of 1570 against Elizabeth: "We declare . . . Elizabeth a heretic and an abettor of heretics, and those that cleave to her . . . to have incurred the sentence of anathema. . . . We declare her to be deprived of her pretended right to the aforesaid realm, and from all dominion, dignity and privilege whatsoever. And the nobles, subjects and peoples of the said realm, and all others who have taken an oath of any kind to her we declare to be absolved forever from such oath and from all dues of dominion, fidelity and obedience. . . ." *Documents of the Christian Church*, ed. Henry Bettenson (New York: Oxford University Press, 1947 ed.), p. 341.

60. Carlyle, *History*, 3:142–46; Lewis, *Medieval Political Ideas*, 1:248–49. Francis Oakley observes that "the selection of tyrannicide as a rightful sanction against an evil ruler suggests . . . that such a right of resistance was conceived very much as an individual thing. . . . The person who resisted did so not because he possessed special public powers to do so but because his own conscience told him that, as the ruler was not fulfilling or was exceeding the terms of his office, it was his right and his duty so to resist." *The Political Thought of Pierre d'Ailly* (New Haven: Yale University Press, 1964), p. 156.

61. Lewis, *Medieval Political Ideas*, 1:253; *De regimine principum*, 1:6, cited in Lewis, ibid., 1:286–87.

62. Charles C. Bayley, "Pivotal Concepts in the Political Philosophy of William of Ockham," *Journal of the History of Ideas* 10 (April 1949):199–

218; Carlyle, *History* (1936 ed.), 6:44–51; Michael Wilks, *The Problem of Sovereignty in the Later Middle Ages* (Cambridge: Cambridge University Press, 1963), pp. 187, 207, 223–25. Also see J. B. Morrall, "Ockham's Political Philosophy," *Franciscan Studies* 9 (1949):335–69; Brian Tierney, "Ockham, the Conciliar Theory, and the Canonists," *Journal of the History of Ideas* 15 (January 1954):40–70; E. F. Jacob, *Essays in the Conciliar Epoch*, 2d ed. (Manchester: Manchester University Press, 1953), chap. V.

63. Alan Gewirth, *Marsilius of Padua: The Defender of Peace*, vol. 1: *Marsilius of Padua and Medieval Political Philosophy* (New York: Columbia University Press, 1951), pp. 236–48; cf. vol. 2: *The Defensor pacis* (New York: Columbia University Press, 1956), pp. 37–44, 87–89; Carlyle, *History* (1936 ed.), 6:40–44, 50–51; Wilks, *The Problem of Sovereignty*, pp. 188, 194ff. Wilks stresses that in the *Defensor pacis* it is not the people who control the prince, but the people's *valentior pars*, by which Marsilius meant the magnates.

64. Carlyle, *History* (1936 ed.), 6:51–63; John Stacey, *John Wyclif and Reform* (Philadelphia: Westminster Press, 1964), pp. 62ff. These views are expressed especially in *De officio regis*, yet in the late pages of this treatise Wyclif writes rather paradoxically of opposing a tyrant by actively resisting or killing him. *Tractatus De officio regis*, ed. Alfred W. Pollard and Charles Sayle (Wyclif Society, Trübner & Co., 1887; reprinted New York: Johnson, 1966), pp. 1–9, 16–17, 201.

65. Oakley, *The Political Thought of Pierre d'Ailly*, pp. 161–62; cf. pp. 156ff.

66. Zofia Rueger, "Gerson, the Conciliar Movement and the Right of Resistance (1642–1644)," *Journal of the History of Ideas* 25 (October–December 1964):472–73, 477–78, 486 (quoted); Walter Ullmann, *Principles of Government and Politics in the Middle Ages* (London: Methuen, 1961), pp. 37–38, 50; Lewis, *Medieval Political Ideas*, 1:270.

67. John Major, *A History of Greater Britain as Well England as Scotland*, trans. and ed. Archibald Constable (Edinburgh: T. and A. Constable, 1892), pp. 158, 213ff.

68. Vessey, "The Sources," pp. 99–113; J. H. Burns, "The Conciliarist Tradition in Scotland," *Scottish Historical Review* 42 (October 1963):101–2.

69. Wilks, *The Problem of Sovereignty*, pp. 185–86; Franklin, ed., *Constitutionalism and Resistance*, p. 12.

70. Allen, *History of Political Thought*, pp. 281, 332–36.

71. *Du droit des magistrats*, trans. and ed. Franklin, *Constitutionalism and Resistance*, p. 126.

72. Franklin, ed., *Constitutionalism and Resistance*, pp. 39, 42–43; *Vindiciae contra tyrannos*, trans. and ed. Franklin, ibid., pp. 154, 159–60, 181–82, 188–89, 191, 198. For the use of Roman law in the context of succession, which was a major theme of Hotman's *Francogallia* (1573), see Ralph E. Giesey, "The Juristic Basis of Dynastic Right to the French Throne," *Transactions of the American Philosophical Society*, new series, 51, pt. 5 (September 1961). In 1586 Hotman published his *Observationes in ius civile*. His

251

legal scholarship is examined in Kelley, *Francois Hotman*, pp. 31–32, 88, 145, 183–97, 238–49. Hotman's life and thought is summarized by David Baird Smith, "Francois Hotman," *Scottish Historical Review* 13 (1916):328–65. Roman law was a controversial subject among scholars (including humanists) such as Budaeus, Louis de Caron (Charondas), and Charles Dumoulin in France, Alciatus in France and Italy, and Zasius in Germany, all of whom were especially interested in the relation between princes and magistrates. Myron Piper Gilmore, *Argument from Roman Law in Political Thought, 1200–1600* (Cambridge: Harvard University Press, 1941), chap. II. Cf. Giesey, "When and Why Hotman Wrote the *Francogallia*," *Bibliotheque d'Humanisme et Renaissance* 29 (September 1967):597ff.

73. Knox, *Works*, 4:375–76, 413, 512.

74. *Knox's History*, 2:236; *Miscellany of the Wodrow Society*, pp. 21–22.

75. Tyndale, *Doctrinal Treatises*, pp. 174–77, 194–95, 240; Clebsch, *England's Earliest Protestants*, p. 182; M. M. Knappen, "William Tindale—First English Puritan," *Church History* 5 (1936): 211–12, 214.

76. Ridley, *John Knox*, pp. 146–48; Ridley, *Thomas Cranmer*, pp. 345–46.

77. Knox, *Works*, 3:308–9.

78. Cf. the notes to Exodus 1:19 and Luke 20:45; Craig, "The Geneva Bible," pp. 43–47; Danner, "Anthony Gilby," pp. 418–20, 422.

79. V. Norskov Olsen, *John Foxe and the Elizabethan Church* (Berkeley: University of California Press, 1973), pp. 187–88; Knappen, *Tudor Puritanism*, pp. 173–78.

80. Hudson, *John Ponet*, p. 184; Vessey, "The Sources," pp. 182–88; Allen, *History of Political Thought*, p. 118.

81. Little, "John Knox," pp. 121–22, 124–26.

82. Hudson, *John Ponet*, pp. 171–72, 178.

83. Samuel J. Knox, "Christopher Goodman—A Forgotten Presbyterian," *Journal of the Presbyterian Historical Society* 28 (December 1950):223; Allen, *History of Political Thought*, pp. 116–18; Vessey, "The Sources," pp. 188–97. Goodman and Ponet may have influenced Hotman. See Kelley, *Francois Hotman*, p. 93; Hudson, *John Ponet*, p. 196.

84. Knox refers to this treatise in his polemic on predestination; *Works*, 5:229.

85. Robert M. Kingdon, "The First Expression of Theodore Beza's Political Ideas," *Archiv für Reformationsgeschichte* 46 (1955):88–96. Cf. Vessey, "The Sources," pp. 197–206. See Kingdon, *Geneva and the Consolidation of the French Protestant Movement, 1564–1572* (Madison: University of Wisconsin Press, 1967), pp. 177ff., for examples of Beza's views in practice. See also Paul-F. Geisendorf, *Théodore de Bèze* (Geneva: Labor & Fides, 1949).

86. Shaw, *General Assemblies*, p. 32; Durkan, "The Cultural Background," pp. 312–13; *Knox's History*, 1:250–51. Vessey doubts the influence of Willock on Knox. "The Sources," pp. 138–44, 236.

87. Mathieson, *Politics and Religion*, 1:71; Andrew Lang, *John Knox and the Reformation* (London: Longmans, Green and Co., 1905), p. 109.

88. This is also the judgment of Vessey, "The Sources," p. 224. For a comparison of Knox's views on resistance with those in the marginalia of the Geneva Bible, see Richard L. Greaves, "The Nature and Intellectual Milieu of the Political Principles in the Geneva Bible Marginalia," *Journal of Church and State*, forthcoming in 1980.

89. Cf. especially Calvin's 1561 lecture on Daniel 6:22.

90. Murray, *Political Consequences*, p. 105.

CHAPTER EIGHT

1. *The Works of Sir David Lindsay of the Mount*, ed. Douglas Hamer, 4 vols. (Edinburgh: The Scottish Text Society, 1931–36), 1:295. There are helpful accounts of gynecocracy by James E. Phillips, Jr., "The Background of Spenser's Attitude toward Women Rulers," *Huntington Library Quarterly 5* (October 1941):5–32; and Paula Louise Scalingi, "The Scepter or the Distaff: The Question of Female Sovereignty, 1516–1607," *The Historian* 41 (November 1978):59–75.

2. J. E. Neale, *Queen Elizabeth* (New York: Harcourt, Brace and Company, 1934), p. 66.

3. Knox, *Works*, 3:222–23.

4. Cited in P. Hume Brown, *John Knox: A Biography*, 2 vols. (London: A. and C. Black, 1895), 1:228–29.

5. *The Zürich Letters* (Second Series), pp. 34–36.

6. Agnes M. MacKenzie, *The Scotland of Queen Mary and the Religious Wars, 1513–1638* (Edinburgh: A. Maclehose, 1936), p. 88.

7. *Knox's History*, 1:108.

8. Knox, *Works*, 3:295.

9. John Strype, *Ecclesiastical Memorials* (Oxford: Clarendon Press, 1822), 3, pt. 1, chap. iv, pp. 60–62.

10. Ridley, *John Knox*, p. 267.

11. Knox, *Works*, 4:373.

12. Ibid., 4:366–68, 373–74.

13. Ibid., 4:373–74, 377, 396–400, 415–16, 420, 452. Knox's dislike of Catholic women rulers was also manifested in 1567–68 when he commented on Aventinus' *Annals of Bavaria* as they were read to him by his nephew, Paul Knox.

14. Knox, *Works*, 4:365ff., 376.

15. All of Knox's references to Roman law deal specifically with the legal status of women. Cf. ibid., 4:375–76.

16. Goodman also wrote a commentary on Amos in which he likened Mary Tudor to Proserpine, Queen of Hades.

17. Thomas Becon, *An Humble Supplicacion vnto God* (Strasbourg [i.e. London: H. Singleton], 1554), sig. A7ʳ.

18. Knox, *Works*, 6:19, 45.

19. Ibid., 6:48 – 49.

20. Ibid., 4:75 – 84; *Knox's History*, 1:122 – 23. Cf. Knox, *Works*, 4:457.

21. Knox, *Works*, 4:452 – 53.

22. *Knox's History*, 1:319.

23. Ibid., 2:15.

24. John Strype, *Annals of the Reformation and Establishment of Religion*, new ed. (Oxford: Clarendon Press, 1824), 1, pt. i, pp. 177 – 78, 185.

25. *The Works of John Jewel, Bishop of Salisbury*, ed. John Ayre, 4 vols. (Cambridge: The Parker Society, 1845 – 50), 4:664 – 65.

26. Knox, *Works*, 5:5 – 6.

27. *The Zürich Letters* (Second Series), ed. Robinson, p. 131. Beza also repudiated Knox's attack on female rule in his published *Confession*. See Robert Kingdon's excellent analysis in Beza, *Du droit des magistrats* (Geneva: Droz, 1970), pp. ix – x and Appendix 2.

28. John Aylmer, *An Harborowe for Faithfvll and Trewe Svbiectes* (Strasbourg [i.e. London: John Day], 1559), sig. B2^r.

29. Ibid., sigs. G4^{r}ff., I4^{v}ff., L2^{v}ff.

30. Ibid., sig. M1^{r-v}. Other replies to Knox were written by Richard Bertie, husband of the Duchess of Suffolk, who later exulted at Mary Stewart's downfall, and Henry Howard, Earl of Northampton, whose "A Dutifull Defence of the Lawfull Regiment of Weomen" (1589) was not published. See British Library, Additional Manuscripts 12,453; 12,513; 12,515.

31. John Leslie, *A Defence of the Honour of . . . Marie Quene of Scotlande* (London: Eusebius Dicaeophile, 1569), p. 125.

32. Peter Frarin, *An Oration against the Vnlawfvll Insurrections of the Protestantes of Our Time, vnder Pretence to Refourme Religion* (Antwerp: Ioannis Fouleri, 1566), sigs. F2^v – F3^r. At one point (sig. F2^r) Frarin confuses Knox and Goodman. In a series of woodcuts appended to the volume one has this caption: "No Queene in her kingdome can or ought to syt fast, / If Knokes or Goodmans bookes blowe any true blast." Sig. K6^v.

33. Knox, *Works*, 6:558 – 59.

34. Ibid., 6:594.

CHAPTER NINE

1. Knox, *Works*, 6:235 – 37.

2. Ibid., 3:26.

3. *A Brieff Discours off the Troubles begonne at Frankford in Germany* (1574).

4. John T. McNeill, "The Democratic Element in Calvin's Thought," *Church History* 18 (September 1949):159 – 61.

5. Calvin, *Institutes*, IV, xx, 8.

6. Knox, *Works*, 6:236.

7. Ibid., 3:194.

8. Burns, "The Political Ideas of the Scottish Reformation," p. 254.

9. Knox, *Works,* 3:188.

10. Ibid., 3:247.

11. Ibid., 3:309, 312, 325–26.

12. Ibid., 4:415–16.

13. Ibid., 4:500–501.

14. Ibid., 4:527, 533–35.

15. Helmut G. Koenigsberger, "The Organization of Revolutionary Parties in France and the Netherlands during the Sixteenth Century," *Journal of Modern History* 27 (December 1955):336; cf. pp. 335–51. Cf. J. H. M. Salmon, "The Paris Sixteen, 1584–1594: The Social Analysis of a Revolutionary Movement," *Journal of Modern History* 44 (December 1972):540–76. For the English situation see Leo F. Solt, "Revolutionary Parties in England under Elizabeth I and Charles I," *Church History* 27 (September 1958):234–39.

16. W. Stanford Reid, "The Coming of the Reformation to Edinburgh," *Church History* 42 (March 1973):27–44.

17. Reid, *Trumpeter of God,* pp. 163–64, 176.

18. Ibid., pp. 166–67.

19. Knox, *Works*, 3:194.

20. Ibid., 4:506.

21. The best case for the democratic tendencies in Calvin's resistance theory is made by Winthrop Hudson, "Democratic Freedom and Religious Faith in the Reformed Tradition," *Church History* 15 (1946):177–94.

22. See Chapter Six.

23. Burrell, "The Covenant Idea," pp. 339–41.

24. *Knox's History*, 1:22, 136–37.

25. Hans Baron, "Calvinist Republicanism and Its Historical Roots," *Church History* 8 (1939):30–42.

26. See Chapter Five.

27. Calvin did not respond in writing to queries posed by Knox, but his political views in these years are well known. Bullinger's written replies to Knox are found in Knox's *Works*, 3:221–26. Cf. Burns, "Knox and Bullinger," pp. 90–91.

28. Robert D. Linder, *The Political Ideas of Pierre Viret* (Geneva: Droz, 1964), p. 138; see Chapter Seven. Also cf. Linder, "Viret and the English Protestants," pp. 149–71.

29. Knox, *An Answer to a Great Number of Blasphemous Cauillations*, in *Works*, 5:21–468. Toward the end of this treatise Knox recounts the story of the Anabaptist experiment at Münster, using it as an occasion to condemn

those who claim "libertie that no man should be troubled for his conscience, cloking under that title all blasphemie and diabolicall doctrine" (5:461).

30. Ibid., 5:213.

31. *Knox's History*, 2:309; Knox, *Works*, 4:527.

32. Robert M. Kingdon, "Calvinism and Democracy: Some Political Implications of Debates on French Reformed Church Government, 1562–1572," *American Historical Review* 69 (January 1964):393–401. Calvin opposed Morely, whose congregational proposals were rejected by the national synod at Orleans in 1562. The political implications of polity were recognized in England: cf. the remark of a Royalist pamphleteer: "He that would rightly understand them must read for Presbytery, aristocracy; and democracy, for Indpendency." Cited in Christopher Hill, *The Century of Revolution, 1603–1714* (Edinburgh: Thomas Nelson and Sons, 1961), p. 165.

33. Donaldson, "The Polity of the Scottish Church," pp. 212–26. Donaldson observes that real controversy over episcopacy did not commence until the arrival of Andrew Melville in 1575, three years after Knox's death.

34. *Knox's History*, 2:283–85. Cf. Calvin, *Institutes*, IV, iii, 15.

35. *Knox's History*, 2:293–95.

36. Ibid., 2:309–12.

37. Ibid., 2:271; *Booke of the Universall Kirk*, p. 50; Calderwood, *History*, 2:390, 396–97. In 1560, however, Knox defended Parliament when it defied the Treaty of Edinburgh by enacting laws to institute religious reform.

38. *Knox's History*, 2:115, 117.

39. See Chapter Ten.

INTRODUCTION TO SECTION FOUR

1. Walzer, *The Revolution of the Saints*, p. 103.

2. Knox, *Works*, 3:295.

3. Ibid., 4:471.

4. Harry M. Orlinsky, *Ancient Israel*, 2d ed. (Ithaca: Cornell University Press, 1960), p. 132. Cf. Little, "John Knox," pp. 123–24.

5. Firth, *The Apocalyptic Tradition*, chap. IV.

CHAPTER TEN

1. Reid, *Trumpeter of God*, p. 289.

2. As does Georgia Harkness, *John Calvin: The Man and His Ethics* (New York: Abingdon Press, 1958 ed.), p. 238.

3. See, e.g., Natalie Z. Davis, "Poor Relief, Humanism, and Heresy: The Case of Lyon," *Studies in Medieval and Renaissance History*, ed. William M. Bowsky, 5 (1968):215–75; and Harold J. Grimm, "Luther's Contributions to Sixteenth-Century Organization of Poor Relief," *Archiv für Reformationsgeschichte* 61 (1970):222–34.

4. W. Murison, *Sir David Lyndsay: Poet, and Satirist of the Old Church in Scotland* (Cambridge: Cambridge University Press, 1938), p. 16; J. M. McPherson, *The Kirk's Care of the Poor* (Aberdeen: J. Avery, 1941), pp. 182–83; James MacKinnon, *A History of Modern Liberty*, 3 vols. (London: Longmans, 1906–8), 2:428.

5. The epistle is printed in Lorimer, *Knox and the Church of England*, p. 264.

6. Knox, *Works*, 4:127–28.

7. Ibid., 4:480, 515.

8. *Knox's History*, 2:290–91.

9. Reid, "The Coming of the Reformation to Edinburgh," pp. 41–43; McPherson, *The Kirk's Care*, pp. 27, 38, 113; *Booke of the Universall Kirk*, pp. 18–19, 29.

10. Knox, *Works*, 6:412–14.

11. David Craig, *Scottish Literature and the Scottish People, 1680–1830* (London: Chatto & Windus, 1961), p. 64.

12. Robert M. Kingdon, "Social Welfare in Calvin's Geneva," *American Historical Review* 76 (February 1971):50–69; André Biéler, *La Pensée Économique et Sociale de Calvin* (Geneva: Librairie de l'Université, 1961), pp. 152–56; Monter, *Calvin's Geneva*, p. 139.

13. Knox, *Works*, 5:295–96, 520; *Knox's History*, 2:134.

14. Bannatyne, *Memoriales*, pp. 258, 262; Knox, *Works*, 6:619–20, 630.

15. *Knox's History*, 2:295–302.

16. D. B. Horn, *A Short History of the University of Edinburgh, 1556–1889* (Edinburgh: Edinburgh University Press, 1967), pp. 3–5; Major, *A History of Greater Britain*, p. 29.

17. James Scotland, *The History of Scottish Education*, 2 vols. (London: University of London Press, 1969), 1:28, 30; Horn, *Short History*, pp. 2–3; *Statutes of the Scottish Church*, ed. Patrick, pp. 108–9.

18. Cf. *Statutes of the Scottish Church*, ed. Patrick, p. 109.

19. Durkan, "The Cultural Background," pp. 288–89; James Grant, *History of the Burgh and Parish Schools of Scotland* (London: W. Collins, 1876), pp. 26–28; D. E. Easson, "The Medieval Church in Scotland and Education," *Records of the Scottish Church History Society* 6 (1938):21.

20. As claimed by W. Forbes-Leith, *Pre-Reformation Scholars in Scotland in the XVIth Century* (Glasgow: James Maclehose and Sons, 1915), p. 6.

21. Cf. P. Hume Brown, *George Buchanan, Humanist and Reformer* (Edinburgh: D. Douglas, 1890), pp. 235–36.

22. *Miscellany of the Maitland Club*, 2, pt. i (Edinburgh: Maitland Club, 1840), pp. 5–7; Easson, "The Medieval Church," pp. 23–24; Grant, *History of the Burgh and Parish Schools*, pp. 24–25; Mathieson, *Politics and Religion*, 1:207.

23. *Booke of the Universall Kirk*, p. 16.

24. Ibid., pp. 16, 29, 66–67.

25. Cf. W. J. Gibson, *Education in Scotland* (London: Longmans, 1912), p. 40; Scotland, *History*, 1:44; Reid, "The Coming of the Reformation to Edinburgh," pp. 42–44.

26. Easson, "The Medieval Church," pp. 24–25.

27. For the vexed question of teinds, see Gordon Donaldson's introduction to *Accounts of the Collectors of Thirds of Benefices, 1561–1572* (Edinburgh: T. and A. Constable, 1949); W. Stanford Reid, "Clerical Taxation: The Scottish Alternative to Dissolution of the Monasteries, 1530–1560," *Catholic Historical Review* 35 (July 1948):151–53.

28. G. G. Coulton, *Scottish Abbeys & Social Life* (Cambridge: Cambridge University Press, 1933), p. 104; *A Source Book of Scottish History*, ed. Dickinson, Donaldson, and I. A. Milne, 3 vols. (London: Thomas Nelson, 1953), 2:115; Annie I. Dunlop, introduction to *Acta Facultatis Artium Universitatis Sanctiandree, 1413–1588* (Edinburgh: T. and A. Constable, 1964), pp. lv–lvi; Forbes-Leith, *Pre-Reformation Scholars*, pp. 148–50; Major, *A History of Greater Britain*, p. 28.

29. For an opposing view, see James Craigie, "Knox's 'Book of Discipline'," *Scottish Educational Journal* (October 14, 1960), pp. 720–22.

30. McNeill, *The History and Character of Calvinism*, pp. 192–95; MacKinnon, *Calvin and the Reformation*, pp. 39–40, 172; W. Fred Graham, *The Constructive Revolutionary: John Calvin & His Socio-Economic Impact* (Richmond, VA: John Knox Press, 1971), pp. 145–51.

31. Allan H. Gilbert, "Martin Bucer on Education," *Journal of English and Germanic Philology* 18 (1919):321–45.

32. Clyde L. Manschreck, *Melanchthon: The Quiet Reformer* (New York: Abingdon Press, 1958), chaps. X–XI.

33. John Edgar, *History of Early Scottish Education* (Edinburgh: James Thin, 1893), p. 162.

34. *Luther's Works*, ed. Walther I. Brandt and Helmut T. Lehmann, 45 (Philadelphia: Muhlenberg Press, 1962), pp. 347–78.

35. Reid, *Trumpeter of God*, p. 293.

CHAPTER ELEVEN

1. Stephen Neill, *The Christian Society* (New York: Harper & Brothers, 1952), p. 156.

2. Ibid., p. 311.

3. Knox, *Works*, 4:446, 468.

4. McRoberts, "The Scottish Church," pp. 3–14.

5. J. H. S. Burleigh, "The Scottish Reforming Councils, 1549 to 1559," *Records of the Scottish Church History Society* 9 (1951–53):189–211; W. Stanford Reid, "The Scottish Counter-Reformation before 1560," *Church History* 14 (1945):109ff.; Maurice Taylor, "The Conflicting Doctrines of the Scottish Reformation," *Essays*, ed. McRoberts, pp. 252–55. *Statutes of the Scottish Church*, ed. Patrick, includes the enactments of the councils. For Ham-

ilton's *Catechism* see *The Catechism of John Hamilton, Archbishop of St. Andrews* (1552), ed. T. G. Law (Oxford: Clarendon Press, 1884).

6. W. Stanford Reid, *The Growth of Anti-Papalism in Fifteenth Century Scotland* (Philadelphia: University of Pennsylvania Press, 1944), pp. 3ff.; Burns, "The Conciliarist Tradition," pp. 89–104; Taylor, "The Conflicting Doctrines," pp. 252–55.

7. Bannatyne, *Memoriales*, p. 103.

8. See Stevenson, "John Knox and His Relations to Women."

9. Marjory A. Bald, "The Pioneers of Anglicised Speech in Scotland," *Scottish Historical Review* 24 (April 1927):184.

10. Knox, *Works*, 3:133.

11. Little, "John Knox," p. 124.

12. Lorimer, *Knox and the Church of England*, p. 263.

13. Ibid., pp. 298–300, for Knox's letter.

14. For a synopsis of their views see Trinterud, ed., *Elizabethan Puritanism*, pp. 10ff.

15. Knox's adamancy on the matter of scriptural precedent has led George Yule to credit him with the negative accomplishment of being the fountain of those who, in the late sixteenth and seventeenth centuries, "barricaded themselvs behind the divine walls of a new scholastic legalism based largely on the use of the Bible as a precedent." This development was obviously contrary to an ecumenical outlook. "Continental Patterns," p. 311.

16. *Knox's History*, 2:199–200. The letter is also included in Knox, *Works*, 6:438–40.

17. See W. Stanford Reid, "Knox's Attitude to the English Reformation," *Westminster Theological Journal* 26 (1963):24ff.

18. Neill, *The Christian Society*, p. 263.

19. A. G. Dickens, *The English Reformation* (London: B. T. Batsford, 1964), p. 286.

20. *Knox's History*, 2:190.

21. Knox, *Works*, 6:544, 613.

22. Ibid., 6:75–77, 94–98, 123–24, 133–35, 562–65, 613–15.

23. Ridley, *John Knox*, p. 462.

24. *Miscellany of the Wodrow Society*, pp. 283–84, 287–88.

25. *Knox's History*, 2:134 (italics mine).

26. Cf. his tract on baptism and his 1557 letter to his brethren in Scotland. Knox, *Works*, 4:119–28, 261–75.

27. Ibid., 3:349.

28. Ibid., 3:9. Cf. *Knox's History*, 1:92; and Watt, "Henry Balnaves," pp. 23–29.

29. McEwen, *Faith of Knox*, p. 47. Cf. Percy, *John Knox*, p. 56.

30. Cf. McEwen, *Faith of Knox*, p. 56. Percy disagrees; *John Knox*, pp. 189–90.

31. Eells, *Martin Bucer*, pp. 194–95.

32. *Knox's History*, 1:93.

33. See Chapter Five.

34. Knox, *Works*, 6:124.

35. Ridley, *John Knox*, p. 255.

36. Knox, *Works*, 5:518.

37. Cf. G. S. M. Walker, "Scottish Ministerial Orders," *Scottish Journal of Theology* 8 (1955):238– 54; Reid, "Knox's Attitude to the English Reformation," pp. 5ff.; Donaldson, *Scottish Reformation*, *passim*.

38. Knox, *Works*, 3:191; cf. pp. 190– 93, 195.

39. Ibid., 3:193. See Chapter Six.

40. Ibid., 3:191.

41. Ibid., 3:295, 308– 9; 4:500; *Knox's History*, 2:72.

42. Ibid., 4:489.

43. *Knox's History*, 2:121– 22.

44. Knox, *Works*, 4:505; cf. p. 506.

45. Cf., e.g., the remarks of Archbishop Matthew Parker; *Correspondence*, p. 61. Also see Chapter Seven.

EPILOGUE

1. This position has been advocated in varying degress by such scholars as Wallace Notestein, *The Scot in History* (New Haven: Yale University Press, 1947), p. 119; Horton Davies, *The Worship of the English Puritans* (Westminster: Dacre Press, 1948), p. 26; H. Y. Reyburn, "Calvin and Scotland," *Records of the Scottish Church History Society* 1 (1926):209– 16; Williston Walker, *John Calvin* (New York: G. P. Putnam's Sons, 1906), p. 393; Cremeans, *The Reception of Calvinistic Thought*, p. 49. The dominating influence of Calvin is frequently stressed; cf., e.g., Henderson, "John Knox and the Bible," p. 52; Charles Martin, "De la Genese des Doctrines Religieuses de John Knox," *Bulletin Societie de L'Histoire du Protestantisme Francais* 55 (1906):193– 211; W. Stanford Reid, "The Scot and Canadian Identity," *Lakehead University Review* 4 (1971):7– 8; Reid, "The Middle Class Factor in the Scottish Reformation," *Church History* 16 (1947):137, 150– 52; Reid, "Lutheranism in the Scottish Reformation," pp. 109– 10; Ethelbert D. Warfield, "John Knox, Reformer of a Kingdom," *Princeton Theological Review* 3 (1905):380.

2. Donald MacMillan, *John Knox: A Biography* (London: A. Melrose, 1905); Geddes MacGregor, "John Knox: The Thundering Scot," *Journal of the Presbyterian Historical Society* 38 (March 1960):19; Watt, "Henry Balnaves," pp. 23– 29; Vessey, "The Sources"; McEwen, *Faith of Knox*. Cf. Burns, "The Conciliarist Tradition," pp. 101– 2.

3. Cf. Kingdon, "The First Expression of Beza's Political Ideas," p. 96.

4. E.g., Knox, "Christopher Goodman," pp. 228ff.; Vessey, "The Sources"; Burns, "The Political Ideas of the Scottish Reformation," pp. 261– 62; Henderson, "John Knox and the Bible," pp. 97– 100; Hudson, *John Ponet*, p. 184.

5. MacGregor, *Scottish Presbyterian Polity*; Donaldson, *Socttish Refor-*

mation; "The Scottish Episcopate," pp. 349–64; " 'The Example of Denmark'," pp. 57–64.

6. Kingdon, *Geneva and the Coming of the Wars of Religion*, p. 21; Trinterud, ed., *Elizabethan Puritanism*, p. 79. Knox's description of Geneva as "the maist perfyt schoole of Chryst" (*Works*, 4:240) is often quoted by modern writers. Virtually no one cites his more extensive comments on Geneva in the predestinarian treatise; *Works*, 5:212ff.

7. In addition to the references at the end of Chapter Six, see A. F. Scott Pearson, *Thomas Cartwright and Elizabethan Puritanism* (Cambridge: Cambridge University Press, 1925), pp. 158, 340, 409; William Pierce, *John Penry: His Life and Writings* (London: Hodder and Stoughton, 1923), pp. 258–59; George F. Sensabaugh, *That Grand Whig Milton* (Stanford: Stanford University Press, 1952), pp. 120, 176; Christopher Hill, *Milton and the English Revolution* (Harmondsworth: Penguin Books, 1979), p. 167; Christopher Morris, *Political Thought in England* (London: Oxford University Press, 1953), pp. 170–71; J. H. M. Salmon, *The French Religious Wars in English Political Thought* (Oxford: Clarendon Press, 1959), p. 95. Because of Knox's political views, the University of Oxford burned his books in 1683 along with those of Milton, Buchanan, Hobbes, John Goodwin, John Owen, and others. Hill, p. 230.

Select Bibliography

(Additional sources are cited in the notes to each chapter.)

I. Primary Sources

The Acts of the Parliaments of Scotland, 1424 – 1707. 2d ed. London: Her Majesty's Stationery Office, 1966.

Aylmer, John. *An Harborowe for Faithfvll and Trewe Svbiectes*. Strasbourg [i.e., London: John Day], 1559.

Bannatyne, Richard. *Memoriales of Transactions in Scotland, MDLXIX – MDLXXIII*. Edinburgh: Bannatyne Club, 1836.

Beza, Theodore. *Du droit des magistrats*. Edited by Robert M. Kingdon. Geneva: Droz, 1970.

Booke of the Universall Kirk of Scotland. Edited by Alexander Peterkin. Edinburgh: Edinburgh Printing and Publishing Co., 1839.

Bullinger, Heinrich. *The Decades of Henry Bullinger*. Edited by Thomas Harding. 3 vols. Cambridge: Cambridge University Press, 1849 – 52.

Calderwood, David. *The History of the Kirk of Scotland*. 4 vols. Edinburgh: Wodrow Society, 1842 – 43.

Calendar of State Papers, Domestic Series, of the Reigns of Edward VI, Mary, Elizabeth, 1547 – 1580. Edited by Robert Lemon. London: Longman, Brown, Green, Longmans, & Roberts, 1856.

Calendar of the State Papers, Relating to Scotland. Edited by Markham John Thorpe. 2 vols. London: Longman, Brown, Green, Longmans, & Roberts, 1858.

Calvin, John. *Commentaries on the Book of the Prophet Daniel*. Translated by Thomas Myers. 2 vols. Grand Rapids: Wm. B. Eerdmans, 1948.

————. *Concerning the Eternal Predestination of God*. Translated with introduction by J. K. S. Reid. London: James Clarke, 1961.

————. *Institutes of the Christian Religion*. Edited by John T. McNeill and translated by Ford Lewis Battles. 2 vols. Philadelphia: Westminster Press, 1960.

_____. *Theological Treatises*. Translated with introduction and notes by J. K. S. Reid. London: Westminster Press, 1954.

The Catechism of John Hamilton, Archbishop of St. Andrews, 1552. Edited with introduction by T. G. Law. Oxford: Clarendon Press, 1884.

Catechisms of the Scottish Reformation. Edited by Horatius Bonar. London: Nisbet, 1866.

The Creeds of Christendom. Edited by Philip Schaff. 3 vols. New York: Harper, 1877.

Foxe, John. *The Acts and Monuments of John Foxe*. Edited by Stephen Reed Cattley. 8 vols. 1843–49. Reprint. New York: AMS Press, 1965.

Frarin, Peter. *An Oration against the Vnlawfull Insurrections of the Protestantes of Our Time, vnder Pretence to Refourme Religion*. Antwerp: Ioannis Fouleri, 1566.

The Geneva Bible: A Facsimile of the 1560 Edition. Introduction by Lloyd E. Berry. Madison: University of Wisconsin Press, 1969.

Hooper, John. *Early Writings of John Hooper, D.D.* Edited by Samuel Carr. Cambridge: Cambridge University Press, 1843.

_____. *Later Writings of Bishop Hooper*. Edited by Charles Nevinson. Cambridge: Cambridge University Press, 1852.

Knox, John. *John Knox's History of the Reformation in Scotland*. Edited by William Croft Dickinson. 2 vols. London: Thomas Nelson and Sons, 1950.

_____. *The Works of John Knox*. Edited by David Laing. 6 vols. 1846–64. Reprint. New York: AMS Press, 1966.

Leslie, John. *A Defence of the Honour of . . . Marie Quene of Scotlande*. London: Eusebius Dicaeophile, 1569.

Lyndsay, David. *The Works of Sir David Lindsay of the Mount, 1490–1555*. Edited by Douglas Hamer. Vol. 2. Edinburgh: The Scottish Text Society, 1931.

Major, John. *A History of Greater Britain as Well England as Scotland*. Translated and edited by Archibald Constable. Edinburgh: T. and A. Constable, 1892.

Melanchthon and Bucer. Edited by Wilhelm Pauck. Philadelphia: Westminster Press, 1969.

Melville, James. *The Autobiography and Diary of Mr James Melvill*. Edited by Robert Pitcairn. Edinburgh: Wodrow Society, 1842.

The Miscellany of the Wodrow Society. Edited by David Laing. Vol. 1. Edinburgh: Wodrow Society, 1844.

Original Letters Relative to the English Reformation. Edited by Hastings Robinson. 2 vols. Cambridge: The Parker Society, 1846–47.

Parker, Matthew. *Correspondence of Matthew Parker, D.D. Archbishop of Canterbury*. Edited by John Bruce and T. T. Perowne. Cambridge: Cambridge University Press, 1853.

Quintin Kennedy (1520–1564): Two Eucharistic Tracts: A Critical Edition.

Edited by Cornelius Henricus Kuipers. Nijmegen: Drukkerij Gebr. Janssen N.V., 1964.

Reformed Confessions of the Sixteenth Century. Edited with introduction by Arthur C. Cochrane. Philadelphia: Westminster Press, 1966.

Register of the Minister Elders and Deacons of the Christian Congregation of St. Andrews . . . 1559–1600, Part First: 1559–1582|. Transcribed and edited by David Hay Fleming. Edinburgh: Edinburgh University Press, 1889.

The Register of the Privy Council of Scotland. Edited by John Hill Burton. Vol. 1. Edinburgh: H. M. General Register House, 1877.

Sadler, Ralph. *The State Papers and Letters of Sir Ralph Sadler.* Edited by Arthur Clifford. 2 vols. Edinburgh: A. Constable and Co., 1809.

A Source Book of Scottish History. Edited by William Croft Dickinson, Gordon Donaldson, and Isabel A. Milne. Vol. 2. London: Thomas Nelson, 1953.

Spottiswoode, John. *History of the Church of Scotland.* Vols. 1 and 2. Edinburgh: Spottiswoode Society, 1851.

Statutes of the Scottish Church, 1225–1559. Introduction by David Patrick. Edinburgh: T. and A. Constable, 1907.

Trinterud, Leonard J., ed. *Elizabethan Puritanism.* New York: Oxford University Press, 1971.

Tyndale, William. *Doctrinal Treatises and Introduction to Different Portions of the Holy Scriptures.* Edited by Henry Walter. Cambridge: Cambridge University Press, 1848.

Winzet, Ninian. *Certain Tractates Together with the Book of Four Score Three Questions and a Translation of Vincentius Lirinensis.* Edited with introduction by James King Hewison. 2 vols. Edinburgh: The Scottish Text Society, 1888–90.

The Zürich Letters. Translated and edited by Hastings Robinson. Cambridge: The Parker Society, 1842.

The Zürich Letters (Second Series). Translated and edited by Hastings Robinson. Cambridge: The Parker Society, 1845.

Zwingli and Bullinger. Translated with introduction by G. W. Bromiley. Philadelphia: Westminster Press, 1953.

II. SECONDARY SOURCES

Ainslie, James L. *The Doctrines of Ministerial Order in the Reformed Churches of the 16th and 17th Centuries.* Edinburgh: T. & T. Clark, 1940.

Allen, J. W. *A History of Political Thought in the Sixteenth Century.* 2d ed. London: Methuen & Co., 1941.

Althaus, Paul. *The Theology of Martin Luther.* Translated by Robert C. Schultz. Philadelphia: Westminster Press, 1966.

Anderson, W. J. "John Knox as Registrar." *Innes Review* 7 (Spring 1956):63.

Andrews, Charles M. "The Times of John Knox." *Hartford Seminary Record* 15 (August 1905):233–58.

Baron, Hans. "Calvinist Republicanism and Its Historical Roots." *Church History* 8 (1939):30—42.

Biéler, André. *La Pensée Économique et Sociale de Calvin.* Geneva: Librairie de l'Université, 1961.

Bouvier, André. *Henri Bullinger: Réformateur et Conseiller Oecuménique.* . . . Zürich: Delachaux et Niestlé, 1940.

Brackenridge, R. Douglas. "The Development of Sabbatarianism in Scotland, 1560—1650." *Journal of Presbyterian History* 42 (September 1964):149—65.

Brown, P. Hume. *George Buchanan, Humanist and Reformer: A Biography.* Edinburgh: D. Douglas, 1890.

————. *John Knox: A Biography.* 2 vols. London: A. and C. Black, 1895.

Buck, Lawrence P. and Zophy, Jonathan W., eds. *The Social History of the Reformation.* Columbus: Ohio State University Press, 1972.

Burleigh, J. H. S. *A Church History of Scotland.* London: Oxford University Press, 1960.

————. "The Scottish Reforming Councils, 1549 to 1559." *Records of the Scottish Church History Society* 9 (1951—53):189—211.

Burnet, George B. *The Holy Communion in the Reformed Church of Scotland, 1560—1960.* Edinburgh: Oliver and Boyd, 1960.

Burns, J. H. "Catholicism in Defeat: Ninian Winzet, 1519—1592." *History Today* 16 (November 1966):788—95.

————. "The Conciliarist Tradition in Scotland." *Scottish Historical Review* 42 (October 1963):89—104.

————. "John Knox and Revolution, 1558." *History Today* 8 (August 1958):565—73.

————. "Knox and Bullinger." *Scottish Historical Review* 34 (1955):90—91.

————. "New-Light on John Major." *Innes Review* 1:5—20; 5:83—97.

————. "The Political Ideas of the Scottish Reformation." *Aberdeen University Review* 36 (1955—56):251—68.

Burrell, Sidney A. "The Covenant Idea as a Revolutionary Symbol: Scotland, 1596—1637." *Church History* 27 (December 1958):338—50.

Cameron, Alexander, ed. *Patrick Hamilton: First Scottish Martyr of the Reformation.* Edinburgh: Scottish Reformation Society, 1929.

Carlyle, R. W. and A. J. *A History of Mediaeval Political Theory in the West.* 6 vols. New York: Barnes & Noble, 1950.

Cheyne, Alex C. "The Scots Confession of 1560." *Theology Today* 17 (October 1960):323—38.

Clark, Francis. *Eucharistic Sacrifice and the Reformation.* Westminster, MD: Newman Press, 1960.

Clebsch, William A. *England's Earliest Protestants, 1520—1535.* New Haven: Yale University Press, 1964.

Collinson, Patrick. "The Authorship of *A Brieff Discours off the Troubles Begonne at Franckford.*" *Journal of Ecclesiastical History* 9 (October 1958):188—208.

——————. *The Elizabethan Puritan Movement*. Berkeley and Los Angeles: University of California Press, 1967.

——————. "The Role of Women in the English Reformation Illustrated by the Life and Friendships of Anne Locke." *Studies in Church History* 2 (1965):258–72.

Coutts, Alfred. "Ninian Winzet: Abbot of Ratisbon, 1577–1592." *Records of the Scottish Church History Society* 11 (1951–53):240–53.

Cowell, Henry J. "English Protestant Refugees in Strasbourg, 1553–1558." *Proceedings of the Huguenot Society of London* 15 (1934):69–120.

——————. "The Sixteenth-Century English-Speaking Refugee Churches at Geneva and Frankfurt." *Proceedings of the Huguenot Society of London* 16 (1937–41):209–30.

——————. "The Sixteenth-Century English-Speaking Refugee Churches at Strasbourg, Basle, Zurich, Aarau, Wesel and Emden." *Proceedings of the Huguenot Society of London* 15 (1937):612–55.

——————. "The Sixteenth-Century French-Speaking and English-Speaking Refugee Churches at Frankfort." *Proceedings of the Huguenot Society of London* 14 (1929–33):62–95.

Craig, Hardin, Jr. "The Geneva Bible as a Political Document." *Pacific Historical Review* 7 (1938):40–49.

Cremeans, Charles Davis. *The Reception of Calvinistic Thought in England*. Urbana: University of Illinois Press, 1949.

Dalton, Hermann. *John à Lasco: His Earlier Life and Labours*. Translated by Maurice J. Evans. London: Hodder and Stoughton, 1886.

Danner, Dan G. "The Marian Exiles and the English Protestant Tradition." *Social Groups and Religious Ideas in the Sixteenth Century*. Edited by Miriam Usher Chrisman and Otto Gründler. Kalamazoo: Medieval Institute, 1978.

D'Assonville, V. E. *John Knox and the Institutes of Calvin*. Durban: Drakensberg Press, 1969.

Dauerty, W. Shackelford. "The Sources of Reformed Worship." *Journal of the Presbyterian Historical Society* 36 (December 1958):217–53.

Davidson, Donald. "Influence of the English Printers on the Scottish Reformation." *Records of the Scottish Church History Society* 1 (1926):75–87.

Davies, Horton. *Worship and Theology in England from Cranmer to Hooker, 1534–1603*. Princeton: Princeton University Press, 1970.

Denney, James. "John Knox: His Religious Life and Theological Position." *The Hartford Seminary Record* 15 (August 1905):282–96.

Dickens, A. G. *The English Reformation*. London: B. T. Batsford, 1964.

Dickinson, William Croft. *Andrew Lang, John Knox, and Scottish Presbyterianism*. Edinburgh: Thomas Nelson, 1952.

——————. *Scotland from the Earliest Times to 1603*. London: Thomas Nelson and Sons, 1961.

——————. *The Scottish Reformation and Its Influence upon Scottish Life and Character*. Edinburgh: Saint Andrew Press, 1960.

Donaldson, Gordon. " 'The Example of Denmark' in the Scottish Reformation." *Scottish Historical Review* 27 (April 1948):57—64.

_____. " 'Flitting Friday', the Beggars' Summons and Knox's Sermon at Perth." *Scottish Historical Review* 39 (October 1960):175—76.

_____. *The Making of the Scottish Prayer Book of 1637*. Edinburgh: Edinburgh University Press, 1954.

_____. "The Polity of the Scottish Church, 1560—1600." *Records of the Scottish Church History Society* 11 (1955):212—26.

_____. "The Scottish Episcopate at the Reformation." *English Historical Review* 60 (September 1945):349—64.

_____. *The Scottish Reformation*. Cambridge: Cambridge University Press, 1960.

Dugmore, C. W. *The Mass and the English Reformers*. London: Macmillan, 1958.

Durkan, John. "George Wishart: His Early Life." *Scottish Historical Review* 32 (1953):98—99.

_____. "John Major: After 400 Years." *Innes Review* 1 (1950):131—39.

Eells, Hastings. "The Contributions of Martin Bucer to the Reformation." *Harvard Theological Review* 24 (January 1931):29—42.

_____. *Martin Bucer*. New Haven: Yale University Press, 1931.

Emerson, Everett H. "Calvin and Covenant Theology." *Church History* 25 (June 1956):136—44.

Finlayson, C. P. "A Volume Associated with John Knox,." *Scottish Historical Review* 38 (October 1959):170—72.

Firth, Katharine R. *The Apocalyptic Tradition in Reformation Britain, 1530—1645*. Oxford: Oxford University Press, 1979.

Fleming, David Hay. "The Influence of Knox." *Scottish Historical Review* 2 (January 1905):131—35.

_____. *The Reformation in Scotland*. London: Hodder and Stoughton, 1910.

_____. *The Story of the Scottish Covenants in Outline*. Edinburgh: Oliphant, Anderson & Ferrier, 1904.

Forstman, H. Jackson. *Word and Spirit: Calvin's Doctrine of Biblical Authority*. Stanford: Stanford University Press, 1962.

Franklin, Julian H., trans. and ed. *Constitutionalism and Resistance in the Sixteenth Century*. New York: Pegasus, 1969.

Fraser, Antonia. *Mary Queen of Scots*. London: Weidenfeld & Nicolson, 1969.

Garrett, Christina Hallowell. *The Marian Exiles*. Cambridge: Cambridge University Press, 1938.

Geer, Curtis M. "The Life of John Knox." *Hartford Seminary Record* 15 (August 1905):259—68.

Gerrish, B. A. "The Confessional Heritage of the Reformed Church." *McCormick Quarterly* 19 (January 1966):120—34.

_____. "John Calvin and the Reformed Doctrine of the Lord's Supper." *McCormick Quarterly* 22 (January 1969):85—98.

————. "The Lord's Supper in the Reformed Confessions." *Theology Today* 23 (July 1966):224–43.

Gilmore, Myron Piper. *Argument from Roman Law in Political Thought, 1200–1600*. Cambridge: Harvard University Press, 1941.

Glasse, John. *John Knox: A Criticism and an Appreciation*. London: Adam and Charles Black, 1905.

Graham, W. Fred. *The Constructive Revolutionary: John Calvin & His Socio-Economic Impact*. Richmond, VA: John Knox Press, 1971.

Gray, John R. "The Political Theory of John Knox." *Church History* 8 (June 1939):132–47.

Greaves, Richard L. "The Nature and Intellectual Milieu of the Political Principles in the Geneva Bible Marginalia." *Journal of Church and State*, forthcoming.

————. "The Origins and Early Development of English Covenant Thought." *The Historian* 31 (November 1968):21–35.

Grislis, Egil. "Calvin's Doctrine of Baptism." *Church History* 31 (March 1962):46–65.

Hart, Albert Bushnell. "John Knox as a Man of the World." *American Historical Review* 13 (January 1908):259–80.

Henderson, G. D. *The Burning Bush: Studies in Scottish Church History*. Edinburgh: Saint Andrew Press, 1957.

————. *Church and Ministry: A Study in Scottish Experience*. London: Hodder and Stoughton, 1951.

————. *The Claims of the Church of Scotland*. London: Hodder and Stoughton, 1951.

————. "Foreign Influences in Scottish Church Worship." *Transactions of the Scottish Ecclesiological Society* 11 (1934):48–60.

————. "John Knox and the Bible." *Records of the Scottish Church History Society* 9 (1946):97–110.

Hewat, Kirkwood. *Makers of the Scottish Church at the Reformation*. Edinburgh: Macniven & Wallace, 1920.

Hopf, Constantin. *Martin Bucer and the English Reformation*. Oxford: Oxford University Press, 1946.

Hudson, Winthrop S. *John Ponet (1516?–1556): Advocate of Limited Monarchy*. Chicago: University of Chicago Press, 1942.

Hughes, Philip Edgcumbe. *Theology of the English Reformers*. London: Hodder and Stoughton, 1965.

Hunt, George L. and McNeill, John T., eds. *Calvinism and the Political Order*. Philadelphia: Westminster Press, 1965.

Hurlbut, Stephen A. *The Liturgy of the Church of Scotland since the Reformation*. 2 vols. Washington: St. Albans Press, 1944–45.

Hutchinson, F. E. *Cranmer and the English Reformation*. London: English Universities Press, 1951.

Innes, A. Taylor. *John Knox*. Edinburgh: Oliphant, Anderson & Ferrier, 1905.

Janton, Pierre. *John Knox (ca. 1513–1572): L'homme et l'oeuvre*. Paris: Didier, 1967.

Johnston, George. "Scripture in the Scottish Reformation: I. Historical Statement." *Canadian Journal of Theology* 8 (1962):249–57.

_____. "Scripture in the Scottish Reformation: II. Scripture in the Public and Private Life of Church and Nation." *Canadian Journal of Theology* 9 (1963):40–49.

Kelley, Donald R. *Francois Hotman: A Revolutionary's Ordeal*. Princeton: Princeton University Press, 1973.

Kenneth, Brother. "Sir David Lyndsay, Reformer." *Innes Review* 1 (1950):79–91.

Kerr, Hugh Thomson. "The Story of the Book of Common Worship." *Journal of the Presbyterian Historical Society* 29 (December 1951):195–211.

Kerr, T. Angus. "The Early Ministry of John Craig at St. Giles', 1562–1566." *Records of the Scottish Church History Society* 14:1–17.

_____. "The Later Ministry of John Craig at St. Giles', 1567–1572." *Records of the Scottish Church History Society* 14:81–99.

Kingdon, Robert M. "The First Expression of Theodore Beza's Political Ideas." *Archiv für Reformationsgeschichte* 46 (1955):88–100.

_____. *Geneva and the Coming of the Wars of Religion in France, 1555–1563*. Geneva: E. Droz, 1956.

_____. *Geneva and the Consolidation of the French Protestant Movement, 1564–1572*. Madison: University of Wisconsin Press, 1967.

_____. "The Political Resistance of the Calvinists in France and the Low Countries." *Church History* 27 (September 1958):220–33.

Knappen, M. M. *Tudor Puritanism*. Chicago: University of Chicago Press, 1939.

Knox, Samuel J. "Christopher Goodman—A Forgotten Presbyterian." *Journal of the Presbyterian Historical Society* 28 (December 1950):221–32.

Lang, Andrew. *John Knox and the Reformation*. London: Longmans, Green and Co., 1905.

_____. "Knox as Historian." *Scottish Historical Review* 2 (January 1905):113–30.

Lee, Maurice, Jr. "John Knox and His *History*." *Scottish Historical Review* 45 (April 1966):79–88.

_____. "The Scottish Reformation after 400 Years." *Scottish Historical Review* 44 (October 1965):135–47.

Lewis, Ewart. *Medieval Political Ideas*. 2 vols. London: Routledge & Paul, 1954.

Linder, Robert D. "Pierre Viret and the Sixteenth-Century English Protestants." *Archiv für Reformationsgeschichte* 58 (1967):149–71.

_____. "Pierre Viret and the Sixteenth-Century French Protestant Revolutionary Tradition." *Journal of Modern History* 38 (June 1966):125–37.

_____. *The Political Ideas of Pierre Viret*. Geneva: Droz, 1964.

Littell, Franklin H., ed. *Reformation Studies*. Richmond, VA: John Knox Press, 1962.

Little, Paul M. "John Knox and English Social Prophecy." *Journal of the Presbyterian Historical Society of England* 14 (May 1970):117–27.

Lorimer, Peter. *John Knox and the Church of England*. London: H. S. King & Co., 1875.

——. *Precursors of Knox: 1. Patrick Hamilton*. Edinburgh: T. Constable, 1857.

Louden, R. Stuart. *The True Face of the Kirk: An Examination of the Ethos and Traditions of the Church of Scotland*. London: Oxford University Press, 1963.

Lumsden, John. *The Covenants of Scotland*. Paisley: A. Gardner, 1914.

McCrie, Thomas. *Life of John Knox*. Philadelphia: Presbyterian Board of Publication, 1898.

MacCunn, Florence A. *John Knox*. Boston and New York: Houghton Mifflin, 1895.

MacDonald, Colin M. "John Major and Humanism." *Scottish Historical Review* 13 (1916):149–58.

McDonnell, Kilian. *John Calvin, the Church, and the Eucharist*. Princeton: Princeton University Press, 1967.

MacEwen, Alexander R. *A History of the Church in Scotland*. 2d ed. 2 vols. London: Hodder and Stoughton, 1915–18.

McEwen, James S. *The Faith of John Knox*. Richmond, VA: John Knox Press, 1961.

McFarland, H. S.N. "The Book of Discipline." *Aberdeen University Review* 38:246–48.

MacGregor, Geddes. "John Knox, the Thundering Scot." *Journal of the Presbyterian Historical Society* 38 (March 1960):13–25.

——. *The Thundering Scot: A Portrait of John Knox*. Philadelphia: Westminster Press, 1957.

MacGregor, Janet G. *The Scottish Presbyterian Polity*. Edinburgh: Oliver and Boyd, 1926.

McHardy, Joseph. "The Priesthood of Knox." *Innes Review* 7 (Spring 1956):62–63.

Mackenzie, Agnes Mure. *The Scotland of Queen Mary and the Religious Wars, 1513–1638*. Edinburgh: A. Maclehose & Co., 1936.

Mackie, J. D. *John Knox*. 2d ed. rev. London: Historical Association, 1968.

MacKinnon, James. *A History of Modern Liberty*. Vol. 2. London: Longmans, 1906.

——. *Calvin and the Reformation*. 1936. Reprint. New York: Russell & Russell, 1962.

——. *Luther and the Reformation*. Vol. 4. 1930. Reprint. New York: Russell & Russell, 1962.

McLelland, Joseph C. *The Visible Words of God: An Exposition of the Sacramental Theology of Peter Martyr Vermigli*. Edinburgh: Oliver & Boyd, 1957.

MacMillan, Donald. *John Knox: A Biography*. London: A. Melrose, 1905.

McMillan, William. "The Anglican Book of Common Prayer in the Church of Scotland." *Records of the Scottish Church History Society* 4 (1932):138–49.

—————. *The Worship of the Scottish Reformed Church, 1550–1638*. London: James Clarke, 1931.

McNeill, John T. "The Church in Sixteenth-Century Reformed Theology." *Journal of Religion* 22 (July 1942):251–69.

—————. "The Democratic Element in Calvin's Thought." *Church History* 18 (September 1949):153–71.

—————. *The History and Character of Calvinism*. New York: Oxford University Press, 1954.

McPherson, J. M. *The Kirk's Care of the Poor*. Aberdeen: J. Avery, 1941.

MacRae, John. "The Scottish Reformers and Their Order of Public Worship." *Records of the Scottish Church History Society* 3 (1929):22–30.

McRoberts, David, ed. *Essays on the Scottish Reformation, 1513–1625*. Glasgow: Burns, 1962.

—————. "The Scottish Church and Nationalism in the Fifteenth Century." *Innes Review* 19 (Spring 1968):3–14.

Martin, Charles. "De la Genèse des Doctrines Religieuses de John Knox." *Bulletin Societe de L'Histoire du Protestantisme Francais* 55 (1906):193–211.

—————. *Les Protestants Anglais Réfugiés à Genève aut temps de Calvin, 1555–1560*. Geneva: A. Jullien, 1915.

Mathieson, William Law. *Politics and Religion: A Study in Scottish History from the Reformation to the Revolution*. Vol. 1. Glasgow: James Maclehose & Sons, 1902.

Maxwell, William D. *A History of Worship in the Church of Scotland*. London: Oxford University Press, 1955.

—————. *John Knox's Genevan Service Book, 1556*. Edinburgh: Oliver and Boyd, 1931.

Metzger, Bruce M. "The Geneva Bible of 1560." *Theology Today* 17 (October 1960):339–52.

Milner, Benjamin Charles, Jr. *Calvin's Doctrine of the Church*. Leiden: E. J. Brill, 1970.

Møller, Jens G. "The Beginnings of Puritan Covenant Theology." *Journal of Ecclesiastical History* 14 (April 1963):46–67.

Monter, E. William. *Calvin's Geneva*. New York: Wiley, 1967.

Morris, Christopher. *Political Thought in England: Tyndale to Hooker*. London: Oxford University Press, 1953.

Muir, Edwin. *John Knox: Portrait of a Calvinist*. London: Jonathan Cape, 1929.

Murison, W. *Sir David Lyndsay: Poet, and Satirist of the Old Church in Scotland*. Cambridge: Cambridge University Press, 1938.

Murray, R. H. *The Political Consequences of the Reformation*. 1926. Reprint. New York: Russell & Russell, 1960.

Nichols, James Hastings. *Corporate Worship in the Reformed Tradition*. Philadelphia: Westminster Press, 1968.

Niesel, Wilhelm. *The Theology of Calvin*. Translated by Harold Knight. Philadelphia: Westminster Press, 1956.

Norwood, Frederick A. "The Marian Exiles: Denizens or Sojourners?" *Church History* 13 (1944):100 – 10.

————. "The Strangers' 'Model Churches' in Sixteenth-Century England." *Reformation Studies*, ed. Franklin H. Littell. Richmond, VA: John Knox Press, 1962.

Oberman, Heiko A. *Forerunners of the Reformation*. New York: Holt, Rinehart and Winston, 1966.

————. *The Harvest of Medieval Theology*. 2d rev. ed. Grand Rapids: Wm. B. Eerdmans, 1967.

Parker, T. H. L. "Calvin the Biblical Expositor." *John Calvin*, ed. G. E. Duffield. Grand Rapids: Wm. B. Eerdmans, 1966.

Percy, Eustace. *John Knox*. Richmond, VA: John Knox Press, 1965.

Phillips, James E., Jr. "The Background of Spenser's Attitude toward Women Rulers." *Huntington Library Quarterly* 5 (October 1941):5 – 32.

Rait, Robert S. "John Knox and the Scottish Reformation." *Quarterly Review* 205 (July 1906):169 – 95.

————. "Scotland and John Knox." *Fortnightly Review* 78 (July 1905):95 – 108.

Reid, J. M. *Kirk and Nation: The Story of the Reformed Church of Scotland*. London: Skeffington, 1960.

Reid, W. Stanford. "The Coming of the Reformation to Edinburgh." *Church History* 42 (March 1973):27 – 44.

————. "French Influence on the First Scots Confession and Book of Discipline." *Westminster Theological Journal* 35 (1972 – 73):1 – 14.

————. *The Growth of Anti-Papalism in Fifteenth Century Scotland*. Philadelphia: University of Pennsylvania Press, 1944.

————. "John Knox and His Interpreters." *Renaissance and Reformation* 10 (1974):14 – 24.

————. "Knox's Attitude to the English Reformation." *Westminster Theological Journal* 26 (1963):1 – 32.

————. "Lutheranism in the Scottish Reformation." *Westminster Theological Journal* (1943 – 45):91 – 111.

————. "The Middle Class Factor in the Scottish Reformation." *Church History* 16 (1947):137 – 53.

————. "The Scottish Counter-Reformation before 1560." *Church History* 14 (1945):104 – 25.

————. *Trumpeter of God: A Biography of John Knox*. New York: Charles Scribner's Sons, 1974.

Reyburn, H. Y. "Calvin and Scotland." *Records of the Scottish Church History Society* 1 (1926):209 – 16.

Ridley, Jasper. *John Knox*. New York: Oxford University Press, 1968.

————. *Thomas Cranmer*. Oxford: Clarendon Press, 1962.

Rupp, Gordon. "Patterns of Salvation in the First Age of the Reformation." *Archiv für Reformationsgeschichte* 57 (1966):52–66.

Scalingi, Paula Louise. "The Scepter or the Distaff: The Question of Female Sovereignty, 1516–1607." *The Historian* 41 (November 1978):59–75.

Shaw, Duncan. *The General Assemblies of the Church of Scotland, 1560–1600*. Edinburgh: Saint Andrew Press, 1964.

_____. "The Inauguration of Ministers in Scotland: 1560–1620." *Records of the Scottish Church History Society* 16 (1967):35–62.

_____, ed. *Reformation and Revolution*. Edinburgh: Saint Andrew Press, 1967.

Simpson, Samuel. "John Knox's Contribution to America." *Hartford Seminary Record* 15 (August 1905):269–81.

Smithen, Frederick J. *Continental Protestantism and the English Reformation*. London: James Clarke, 1927.

Smyth, C. H. *Cranmer & the Reformation under Edward VI*. Cambridge: Cambridge University Press, 1926.

Southgate, W. M. "The Marian Exiles and the Influence of John Calvin." *History* 27 (September 1942):148–52.

Stevenson, Robert Louis. "John Knox and His Relations to Women." *Familiar Studies of Men and Books*. New York: Scribner, 1905.

Straukamp, James E. "Knox, Calvin, and English Diplomacy." *Heythrop Journal* 4 (January 1963):61–63.

Strype, John. *Annals of the Reformation and Establishment of Religion*. New ed. Vol. 1, pts. 1–2. Oxford: Clarendon Press, 1824.

_____. *Ecclesiastical Memorials, Relating Chiefly to Religion*. Oxford: Clarendon Press, 1822.

Tonkin, John. *The Church and the Secular Order in Reformation Thought*. New York: Columbia University Press, 1971.

Torrance, Thomas F. *Kingdom and Church: A Study in the Theology of the Reformation*. Edinburgh and London: Oliver and Boyd, 1956.

Trevor-Roper, Hugh. "John Knox." *The Listener* 80 (December 5, 1968):745–47.

Trinterud, Leonard J. "The Origins of Puritanism." *Church History* 20 (March 1951):37–57.

Vander Molen, Ronald J. "Anglican against Puritan: Ideological Origins during the Marian Exile." *Church History* 42 (March 1973):45–57.

Vessey, Wesley James. "The Sources of the Idea of Active Resistance in the Political Theory of John Knox." Ph.D. dissertation, Boston University, 1961.

Walker, G. S. M. "Scottish Ministerial Orders." *Scottish Journal of Theology* 8 (1955):238–54.

Wallace, Ronald S. *Calvin's Doctrine of the Word and Sacrament*. Grand Rapids: Wm. B. Eerdmans, 1957.

Walzer, Michael. *The Revolution of the Saints*. Cambridge: Harvard University Press, 1965.

Warfield, Ethelbert D. "John Knox, Reformer of a Kingdom." *Princeton Theological Review* 3 (1905):376–98.

Watt, Hugh. "Henry Balnaves and the Scottish Reformation." *Records of the Scottish Church History Society* 5 (1935):23–29.

Watt, Hugh. *John Knox in Controversy*. London: Thomas Nelson and Sons, 1950.

Wendel, François. *Calvin: The Origins and Development of His Religious Thought*. Translated by Philip Mairet. London: Collins, 1963.

West, W. Morris S. "John Hooper and the Origins of Puritanism." *Baptist Quarterly* 15 (October 1954):346–68.

Yule, George. "Continental Patterns and the Reformation in England and Scotland." *Scottish Journal of Theology* 22 (September 1969):305–23.

INDEX OF NAMES